Russian Bombers

Russian Bombers

David Baker

TEMPEST
BOOKS

Published in Great Britain by Tempest Books
an imprint of Mortons Books Ltd.
Media Centre
Morton Way
Horncastle LN9 6JR
www.mortonsbooks.co.uk

ISBN 978-1-911704-13-3

The right of David Baker to be identified as the author of this work has been asserted in accordance with the Copyright, Designs and Patents Act 1988.

Typeset by: Druck Media Pvt. Ltd.

CONTENTS

CHAPTER 1

CLUTCHING AT STRAWS

The Second World War was fought by the Soviet Union in response to Operation Barbarossa, beginning on 22 June 1941, when Nazi Germany launched the largest land invasion in history against the USSR. For Russians, it was a defensive war that lasted four years. During that time Soviet forces reversed the early successes of the Wehrmacht and pursued German troops across Eastern Europe all the way from the outskirts of Moscow to the Reichstag in Berlin, a distance of 1,600km (1,000 miles).

German tanks roll across the Soviet frontier with the largest invasion force in history on 22 June 1941 during Operation Barbarossa. (Author's collection)

This incredible fightback had been accomplished largely without the use of long-range bombers able to deliver strategic retribution. Unlike most European powers with large air forces, Russia had not been successful in developing heavy bombers.

It was not for lack of trying though. Attempts had been made to develop a strategic bombing capability from the days of the Imperial Russian Air Service, before the Bolshevik revolution of 1917, right up to the war itself. The revolution had triggered a reconsolidation of former Tsarist air units to deal with the threat posed by White Russian air elements fighting to overthrow the Soviets.

As part of a general move to expand the industrialisation of Russia, aircraft production was expanded and output increased significantly during the 1930s. But that stalled when the successful commander of Soviet air forces, General Yakov Alksnis, was imprisoned during the Stalinist purges. The Commissariat for the Aviation Industry had responsibility for organising the expansion of aeronautical engineering and aircraft production but in 1940 its leader, M. M. Kaganovich, shot himself because of the purges. His place was taken by A. I. Shakurin, who held the position for the duration of the war.

By the end of the war, despite the political purges, the mass industrialisation of the USSR had enabled the aviation industry to expand immensely – with production rising to 40,000 aircraft annually. Of these, more than 80% were single-engine types and all had piston engines. This dearth of multi-engine types reflected an emphasis on defensive fighters and ground attack aircraft to support the army across its broad war-fighting front line which, at its fullest extent, stretched from the Baltic to the Black Sea.

Soviet air power played a seminal role in tactical operations, destroying German tanks, ground equipment, artillery positions, munitions and supply dumps on or close to the front line – but efforts to produce long-range bombers for strikes deep within enemy territory were never fully extinguished. Before the war, Stalin looked to long-range aviation as a useful propaganda tool – just as Hitler would do

Considered superior to the Heinkel He 111 as a medium bomber by many, the Ilyushin DB-3 entered service several years prior to the German attack and became the first Russian bomber to hit Berlin. (Author's collection)

with aircraft such as the Focke-Wulf Fw 200 – and this opened funds which would otherwise have been blocked for the development of such machines.

This resulted in the Ilyushin DB-3 (TsKB-26) and 3A in 1936, used to great effect in showcasing Soviet capabilities. Developing aircraft for publicity and propaganda was not the surest route to creating a successful combat aircraft but the Ilyushin was nevertheless a moderately useful bomber capable of carrying a 1,000kg (2,200lb) bomb load a distance of 4,000km (2,485 miles) or 2,495kg (5,500lb) over shorter distances.

It could even be regarded as superior to the Luftwaffe's Heinkel He 111; the DB-3B had a greater range and more effective defensive armament. It was this type which became the first Soviet aircraft to attack Berlin, in a raid on the night of 7-8 August 1941. This was but the first in an extended series of Soviet bombing raids on the German capital, following the first raid by the French in June 1940 and then the British from August 1940. Over the course of several weeks during the second half of 1941, Soviet bombers based on islands in the Baltic and in Estonia dropped 36,000kg (79,000lb) of bombs on Berlin.

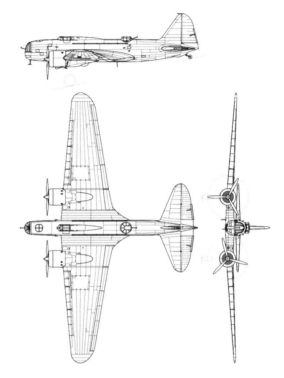

The defensive armament of the Ilyushin DB-3 was provided in nose and dorsal positions but the type of weapon carried varied between 62mm machine guns and 20mm cannon, according to operating units. (Kaboldy)

Developed as the DB-3F, the Ilyushin Il-4 was employed to great effect on short-range strikes carrying a maximum bomb load of up to 2,720kg (6,000lb). (Author's collection)

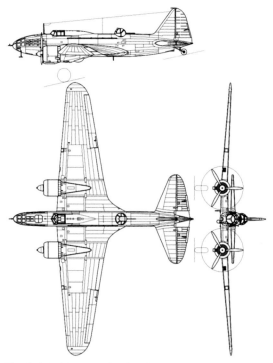

The Il-4 had improved defensive armament but used the same engines as the DB-3 with no overall performance improvement. (Kaboldy)

Ilyushin made around 6,700 DB-3 types and a developed version, the Il-4, but as German troops swept east – overrunning airfields – the opportunity to attack Germany receded and the Soviet Union began using medium and long-range bombers for close support operations instead. But Ilyushin was not alone in seeking to provide the USSR with long-range bombers.

Graduating from the Taganrog Technical School, Vladimir Mikhailovich Petlyakov joined the Tsentral'nyy Aerogidrodinamicheskiy Institut, or TsAGI, the Central State Aerodynamic and Hydrodynamic Institute in 1920. After the customary imprisonment under the universal purges of the 1930s, Petlyakov was set to work on Project 100, which would become the Petlyakov Pe-2. This was one of the most famous Russian aircraft of the war; a long-range, twin-engine fighter pressed into a ground-attack and close-support combat role.

His design bureau, Petlyakov OKB, also worked on a four-engine long-range bomber design, initially designated TB-7, which would become the Pe-8. Petlyakov's incarceration, along with Andrey Tupolev, compromised the Pe-8's development but it made its first flight in July 1938. Plagued by Soviet bureaucracy and persistent technical problems with successive engine types, the giant aircraft entered slow production in 1940 but only one squadron was equipped with the type when the Germans attacked in June 1941 they were not combat-ready.

Vladimir Petlyakov emerged from the gulag with the Pe-2, or Project 100, which was utilised in close-support operations, gaining experience for Petlyakov which informed development of the Pe-8. (Author's collection)

Essentially a mid-wing monoplane of all-metal, stressed-skin construction, the Pe-8 bristled with defensive firepower including a 20mm (0.79in) ShVAK cannon in the nose, a dorsal gun position with a 7.62mm (0.30in) ShKAS machine gun and another of the same type in a ventral turret. A tail gunner had a ShVAK cannon in a powered turret and a manually operated UBT machine gun was housed in each inboard engine nacelle, accessed through the wing. The Pe-8 had an internal bomb load of 4,000kg (8,800lb) with two 500kg (1,100lb) bombs, one under each wing.

With a crew of 11, the Pe-8 had a range of 3,700km (2,300 miles) but a top speed of only 443km/h (275mph). Although kept in operational use throughout the war, fewer than 100 were produced and the type was increasingly assigned to tactical support operations and bombing raids against German depots in occupied territory. Nevertheless, some raids were conducted against Finland and Estonia as well as against German forces occupying beleaguered Russian cities. It was Russia's only four-engine bomber in active service during the Second World War.

Compromised by the incarceration of Petlyakov, the only four-engine, long-range bomber available to the Russians during the 1941-45 war was the Pe-8, this example bringing foreign minister Vyacheslav Molotov to RAF Tealing, Scotland, on 20 May 1942 for the signing of the Anglo-Russian Treaty six days later. (World War Photos)

Fabricated primarily from duralumin, the Pe-8 saw only limited use and fewer than 100 were built, the type being involved in experimental engine trials after the war. (Author's collection)

The Soviets' desire for a strategic bomber increased considerably, however, when it became clear how successful the four-engine bomber fleets operated by the RAF and USAAF had been in striking at strategic targets within Germany. A new development programme for a long-range, four-engine bomber with high altitude and high speed capabilities was launched in 1943. Three design bureaus, led by Vladimir M. Myasishchev, Andrey Tupolev and Iosif F. Nezval were tasked with producing designs. By this time the Russians had also been made aware of the Boeing B-29 Superfortress through the ill-advised boasting of Edward V. Rickenbacker during a special mission to the USSR. On 19 July 1943, General Belyaev, chief of the military mission to the US, requested that this type be included in the Lend-Lease programme, which was already providing American aircraft to Russia.

The request was refused only to be reiterated on 28 May 1945, three weeks after the end of the war in Europe, on the pretext that they would be needed in forthcoming raids against Japan. The Russians wanted at least 120 B-29s, but the Americans again refused. This only encouraged the Soviet government to press ahead determinedly with plans for an equivalent Russian-made design. Meanwhile, Tupolev was well

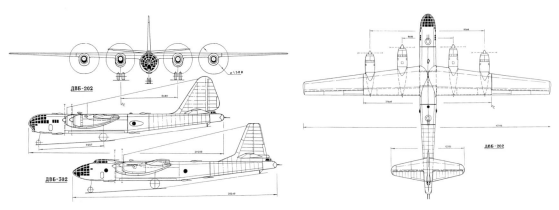

Design work on the Myasishchev DVB-202 long-range bomber began in 1944 but further work in 1945 focused on the DVB-203, which was similarly unsuccessful. (via Tony Buttler)

along with the development programme begun in 1943. Competing concepts from Myasishchev, such as the DVB-202, and Nezval were also under way but they were unsuccessful, as was the Il-14 from Ilyushin.

With Dimitry Markov in charge of design, the Tupolev design bureau (Opytnoe Konstrutorskoe Byuro – OKB for short) had begun work on what was designated Aircraft 64 in September 1943, shortly after the rejection of Russia's request for B-29s. The intention was to produce a fully pressurised, high altitude bomber with a bombload of 18,000kg (39,683lb), a speed of 500km/h (311mph) and a range of up to 6,000km (3,729 miles). The Russians had never produced anything approaching this capability and were highly motivated by the impending operational debut of the B-29. The initial design that emerged had a length of 29.975m (98.3ft),

a wingspan of 42m (137.75ft), a maximum speed of 600km/h (373mph), a cruising speed of 400km/h (249mph) and a ceiling of 12,000m (39,370ft).

The monocoque structure employed conventional manufacturing techniques with stressed skins and high-lift devices on the wings, each of which incorporated two spars. At this stage the tail consisted of two vertical stabilisers. There were four different engine options, including three liquid-cooled types and a radial, the Shvetsov ASh-83FN. The bombload was to be carried in two bays separated by the carry-through wing centre-section with comprehensive defensive armament provided by four turrets equipped with 23mm (0.9in) cannon.

After several months of initial design studies, overall weight was becoming a problem so in mid-1944 the overall concept was reduced in size. This

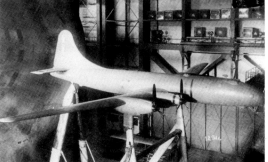

The Tupolev Aircraft 64 concept had several design iterations including single or twin-fin tail assemblies as seen here during wind tunnel testing in 1944 and 1945. (Russian Aviation Research Trust via Tony Buttler)

resulted in a lower maximum ceiling of 11,000m (36,089ft). In August 1944 a further compromise was necessary when the requirement was amended to include photo-reconnaissance capability. Worse still, a derivative was now required that could carry 72 fully-equipped troops or a mixed load of military vehicles potentially including a T-60 light tank.

In the subsequent redesign the armament was reconfigured to four twin-gun turrets with cannon and a tail turret with optional guns. A full-scale mock-up was inspected in September 1944 but there were clear shortcomings including the absence of a bomb-aiming radar, which was now specified. Crew complement increased to 10 with the addition of a radar-operator for the new bomb-aiming system and final approval for construction was granted on 27 April 1945. The engines were to be Mikulin AM-43s or AM-46s, with TK-300 turbo-superchargers. In this iteration, maximum range was predicted to be 5,000km (11,023 miles) with an 18,000kg (39,683lb) bomb load.

By this time, the Soviet aircraft industry had become a vast machine dedicated to supplying wartime production needs. Projects that would not become operational for at least two years necessarily had to take a back seat when it came to the allocation of manpower and resources – including Aircraft 64.

There was also a lack of development in new materials, emergent technologies, sophisticated electrical systems and new integrated bomb-aiming and navigation equipment. The Aircraft 64 project consequently became bogged down by technical obstacles, resulting in spiralling delays.

Meanwhile, three B-29s (serial numbers 42-6256 'Ramp Tramp', 42-6365 'General H. H. Arnold Special' and 42-6358 'Ding Hao') had been impounded after force-landing on Russian territory following raids on Japanese cities in July, August and November 1944. The wreckage of a fourth – 42-93829 'Cait Paomat II' – was also recovered for study.

At the time Russia was not at war with Japan and this was the excuse made for not returning them.

Cancellation of the Aircraft 64 project followed a decision to reverse-engineer the Boeing B-29, here represented by 42-24612 built by Boeing-Wichita and delivered to the USAAF on 31 July 1944, several of which type were impounded in the USSR. (USAAF)

The Tu-4, seen here at Russia's Monino aviation museum outside Moscow, provided Russia with a stimulus to the development of long-range bombers. (Author's collection)

The Chinese National Air Museum outside Beijing has the only KJ-1 (c/n 2805601) ever built. (Ronidong)

One of the aircraft was left untouched as a model, another was used for flight testing and the third was carefully disassembled so that its components could be measured and copied.

In May 1945 the decision was made to all but cease work on Aircraft 64 and to begin the large-scale reverse engineering of the B-29 instead, with a view to developing a bomber suitable for mass production.

This enabled the Soviets to sidestep all the years of development work undertaken by Boeing and begin churning out an aircraft that was far more advanced than anything on their own drawing boards.

With fully pressurised crew compartments, remotely controlled gun turrets and capable of high-altitude bombing using advanced navigation and bombing equipment, the B-29 was state-of-the-art in every way. For the US, it had been the most

expensive military programme of the war, including the Manhattan atomic bomb project, and now the Soviets were getting it, arguably, for free.

The detailed story of the energy and effort that went into creating what became the Tupolev Tu-4 has been told elsewhere, suffice to say here that given the enormous engineering challenges posed by the reverse-engineering process, the results were outstanding. Not only had the Russians converted imperial measurements into metric, developed appropriate metals and materials for the purpose and retrofitted some radio equipment from the B-25s they had acquired through Lend-Lease, they had also created the Shvetsov ASh-73 engine – a development from the Wright R-1820 but with TK19 superchargers directly copied from the B-29's Wright R-3350-23A engine, itself a development

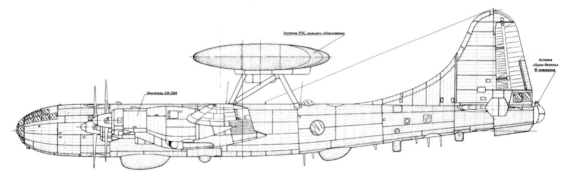

China built the KJ-1, an AEWC derivative of the Tu-4 powered by four AI-20M turboprop engines, in the early 1970s. It had increased horizontal tail area and a large radome but was a failure and no more were produced. (Author's collection)

China received 10 Tu-4s from Russia on 28 February 1953 with two more seven years later. Eleven were retrofitted with AI-20K turboprop engines as seen here on the sole survivor (c/n 2205008). (Author's collection)

of the R-1820. Armament consisted of ten 23mm (0.91in) Nudelman NS-23 cannon – two in each of the four turrets and another two in the tail barbette – and it could carry up to six 1,000kg (2,200lb) bombs.

The State Defence Committee authorised the project on 6 June 1945, followed by a production order two weeks later for what was then designated the B-4, assigned to Plant 22 in Kazan. Some 900 industrial organisations were involved in manufacturing the bomber and a number were set up specifically to support the process. Initially, 20 pre-production aircraft were approved, following an inspection of the full-scale mock-up in mid-1946. Test pilot Nikolai Rybko took the first Tu-4 into the air on 19 May 1947 from the Kazan-Borisoglebskoye airfield.

The Tu-4 was displayed publicly for the first time during the Tushino aviation parade on 3 August 1947 when three aircraft flew over the heads of invited guests and dignitaries including defence attaches. When a fourth appeared it proved that, as some already suspected, the Russians had successfully adapted the Boeing bomber for Soviet production. In fact, that fourth aircraft was reportedly a prototype Tu-70 commercial airliner which had made its first flight on 27 November 1946 some six months before the Tu-4 but which never entered production.

The intense effort applied to reverse engineering of the B-29 into the Tu-4 was a seminal moment in Soviet aircraft design and engineering; it encouraged innovation and resulted in new manufacturing techniques being developed as well as a broad range of new materials including alloys and synthetics.

This sudden and incredible leap forward in technology supercharged the Soviet aviation industry and led to a whole generation of new long-range bombers that would appear less than a decade after the Tu-4's first flight – including the Myasishchev M-4/3M and the Tupolev range, predominantly the Tu-16 and the Tu-95.

Production of the Tu-4 ended in 1952 and the type served into the early 1960s. Today it appears as little more than a footnote in the history of Soviet aviation but at the time it caused great alarm in the West. Out of the blue, the Russians suddenly had a strategic bomber theoretically capable of flying across the North Pole and into North American airspace to drop its bombs and return with impunity. What should have been a decisive weapon for the US, ensuring American airborne supremacy, had instead been turned on its creator and now posed a very real threat to Canada and the US, not to mention all of Western Europe.

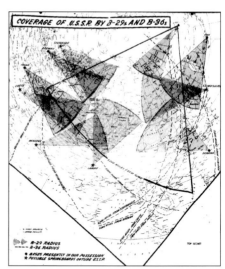

A US map charting the industrial zones for materials and war production which would form the basis for an attack by penetrating bombers in the event of war with the Soviet Union. (Author's collection)

US attack strategies targeted centres of major Soviet manufacturing and political control with range capabilities of the B-29 and the B-36 indicated. (Author's collection)

The very existence of the Tu-4 transformed the defence strategy of America and its allies, playing no small part in the formation of NATO in April 1949, followed four months later by the detonation of Russia's first atomic bomb. Development of the Soviet bomb coincided with a further development of the Tu-4 to improve performance, identified in the Aircraft 80 (Tu-80) programme. This would see some drag-inducing design features on the engine nacelles removed and the forward gun turret made retractable. Two others were recessed down into the fuselage line.

Improvements too were made to the shape of the chin radome and the bomb bays were lengthened.

An order dated 12 June 1948 authorised the development of a Tu-80 prototype and assembly was already underway by the end of the year. By July 1949 the aircraft was ready for trials, albeit devoid of non-essential equipment for its first flight on 1 December. However, it was now overtaken by another more extreme development of the Tu-4 on which work had begun in mid-1948 as Project 485. A wider mandate freed up the design options and alternative concepts

While Russian physicists were developing and testing Russia's first atom bomb, in 1949 Tupolev designed and built the Tu-80 as a longer-range successor to the Tu-4, the sole example of which made its first flight on 1 December 1949. (Author's collection)

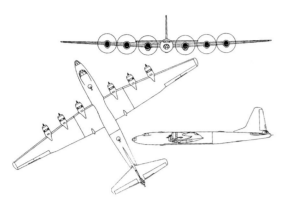

In a flurry of design iterations on the project line from the Tu-4, the 1948 Tu-485 shown here would have had six engines serving the requirement for an aircraft to drop atom bombs on the United States. (via Tony Buttler)

with four or six engines, a potential maximum range of 6,000km (3,729 miles) and with a crew of up to 12 were studied. It was designed from the outset for a range of cutting edge new weapons, including cruise missiles and guided bombs.

The design soon progressed into Project 489 which included concepts with six or eight engines – alternatives featuring a variety of reciprocating, turboprop or jet engine types, or combinations of any two. It was apparent that the project had been influenced to some extent by Convair's B-36 and its six piston engines which, from March 1949, ushered in the definitive configuration for the US Air Force by adding four jet engines, transforming it into a truly intercontinental bomber.

With the designation Tu-85, authorisation was given to progress with the new development on 16 September 1949, specifying a range of up to 13,000km (8,080 miles), which would give it the capacity to strike North America from western Russia and return without landing. This was a step-change from the capabilities of the Tu-4 or Tu-80 and a direct response to both the operational deployment of the B-36 and the impending arrival of the B-47 in Western Europe. Russia was also aware of the competition for a successor to the B-36, which would

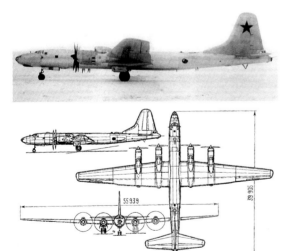

Tupolev was flight testing the Tu-85 by 1951. It was heavier and with twice the range of the Tu-4 from which it had evolved. It is regarded in aero-engineering circles as possessing the finest unswept wing ever designed. Only two were built. (Author's collection)

The Tu-85 had Dobrynin VD-4K 24-cylinder turbo-compound engines. (Author's collection)

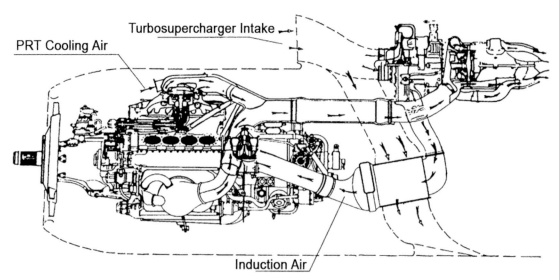

Mounted high and to the rear of the main engine, the turbo-supercharger added weight and complexity without providing the advantages of a turboprop configuration. (Author's collection)

arrive as the B-52 having already gone through the piston-engine/turboprop/jet evolution by 1948.

Driving all this fast-paced development was Joseph Stalin.

In retrospect, there is no justification for believing that Stalin was intent upon a pre-emptive attack on the USA or on fighting a war against America. He was very well aware of the industrial muscle and the financial heft of the United States and that knowledge, together with a lingering fear of over-exposing Russia to erosion of its defensive capabilities during any potential offensive operations, led him to firmly back the development of a long-range bomber fleet.

Standing high above the aft section of the engine nacelle, the turbo-supercharger on the VD-4K engines is clearly visible on this Tu-85. (Yefim Gordon via Tony Buttler)

He wanted a strategic strike capability with which he could threaten North America – allowing the Soviet Union to create a true balance of power on the world stage and forcing the West to treat him with caution and respect. For its part, the West feared that Stalin was indeed building up his forces for a potential invasion, or at least to grab more land in Europe. Even today many people in the West, particularly from those who served in the military during the Cold War, believe that Stalin would have attacked had the opportunity presented itself.

The Tu-85 made its first flight on 9 January 1951 with four Dobrynin 24-cylinder VD-4K turbo-compound engines. From 12-13 September 1951, the first prototype demonstrated a flight of 12,018km (7,469 miles) but by now the Korean War was already proving disastrous for America's aging B-29s. They were easy targets for jet-powered, and Russian-made, MiG-15s. The second Tu-85, with reduced wing area, took to the air on 28 June 1951 but the writing was on the wall. The Korean War had brought an end to the era of piston-powered bombers and plans for production of the Tu-85 at three facilities were abandoned in a directive of July 1951. The work was not wasted however; lessons had been learned which would prove immensely valuable

Seen here removed from a MiG-15bis, the Klimov VK-1 was developed from the Rolls-Royce Nene engine, 40 of which had been delivered to Russia by the British Attlee government in 1946 as a 'goodwill' gesture. (J. J. Messerly)

to the new Aircraft 95 programme – of which more later. The Tu-85 does, however, stand as a landmark in aeronautical history, being the ultimate development of the B-29 family. It was 50% heavier than the original and had nearly double its range.

In a bid to save the Tu-85, engineers examined the plausibility of greatly improving overall performance by swapping its piston engines for Kuznetsov TV-2F turboprop engines. This did promise a further range extension to 16,000km (9,944 miles) and a top speed of 740km/h (460mph) and a further proposal envisaged installing two Klimov VK-1 jet engines, a development of the reverse-engineered British Nene engine, in addition to the four turbo-compound engines.

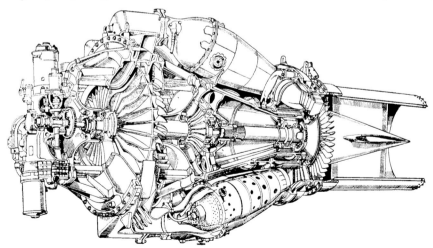

A cutaway diagram of the Klimov VK-1. This engine also powered the MiG-17 and the Il-28 bomber. In China it was designated WP-5. (Author's collection)

Turboprop Transformation

The TV-2F turboprop engine was also proposed for the Aircraft 95 study. It had a fascinating origin and would play an important part of the development story of Russian turboprop bombers, all the way down the decades to the present. Its story began very shortly after the end of the war with work conducted by German engineers and technicians at Experimental Plant No. 2 at Upravlencheskiy on the Volga River, 30km (19 miles) from Kuybyshev. The facility where they were working had been part of the Kuybyshev Hydroelectric plant and had been developed with houses and research laboratories, playing host to the Kirov 145th machine-building plant which had been evacuated from the Moscow district during the war. It had been added to and improved, providing mechanical workshops and test stations in construction work that continued through 1949.

As the Red Army swept through eastern Germany in 1945 it overran numerous advanced production facilities – resulting in large quantities of specialist equipment being captured. Much of this was initial kept in situ before eventually being stripped out and transported back to the Soviet Union by rail. The 14 hectare (35 acre) Experimental Plant No. 2 was where much of this booty ended up – its workers receiving more than 1,000 rail trucks full of it from Dessau, Halle and other German industrial areas by 1947. At that point there were 2,500 staff on site of whom 662 were Germans, many of them formerly employees of various BMW works. Several were leading engine designers and technical specialists who had been renowned in their home country for their expertise. Like their rocket scientist counterparts, some aero-engineers had volunteered to work with the Russians, while others had been less than willing to depart from their native country. One of the latter was Austrian

A sectioned training model of the BMW 003, an axial flow turbojet engine developed in Germany during the war and proposed for the Messerschmitt Me 262 but never used in production variants of that fighter. (Author's collection)

In service faster than the BMW 003, the Junkers Jumo 004 powered the Me 262 and the Arado Ar 234 but both engines were important in giving the Russians a quick start in jet and turbojet propulsion. (USAF)

engineer Ferdinand Brandner from the Junkers works, who had initially believed he would gain his freedom to return to Vienna by surrendering all the documentation and research results in his possession. He also volunteered everything he knew about the Jumo 004 turbojet engine which powered the Me 262 fighter and the Ar 234 reconnaissance/bomber and his information was instrumental to the development of a Russian equivalent.

Instead of being freed to rejoin his family in Austria however, in 1946 Brandner was sent to a concentration camp near Moscow. Then, when the Ministry of Internal Affairs urgently sought skilled technicians, he was sent to Aircraft Plant No 26 in Ufa. There, he worked directly under Vladimir Yakovlevich Klimov,

who had made a reputation for making aero-engines derived from Renault designs through the OKB bearing his name. Brandner was sent to Experimental Plant No. 2 when Klimov was made chief designer at the Leningrad facility in 1946, a factory where mostly Junkers engine specialists were working. The Soviets put German scientists and engineers to work in their original fields of expertise and Brandner had worked on turbojet development – particularly the Jumo 012, a scaled up version of the 004.

At the time Brandner was redeployed a new directive was issued by M. M. Lukin, the deputy minister of the Aviation Industry and sent to N. M. Olekhnovich, the head of Plant No. 2, on 6 December 1946.

Founder of one of the most important engine development companies in Russia, Vladimir Yakovlevich Klimov in his later years. (Author's collection)

by 2,000-2,500km (1,243-1,553 miles), an increase of 80-100% over bombers powered by piston or turbojet engines.

Lukin recommended development of turboprop engines delivering 2,983-3,355kW (4,000-4,500hp) with optimum performance at an altitude of 8,000m (26,248ft) and a cruising speed of 800km/h (497mph).

Engineers Alfred Scheibe, chief designer at OKB-1 and Karl Prestel (OKB-2) were put in charge of initial attempts at adapting the Jumo 012 and the BMW 018 engines for turboprop propulsion and to have those available in 1947. The German engineers reached slightly different conclusions to the specification outlined by the directive and on 11 March 1947 a modified instruction separated work tasks between the two men: Scheibe would build a 3,728kW (5,000hp) turboprop engine designated 022 and a 19,615N (4,410lb) thrust 032 turbojet; Prestel was to design a 5,070kW (6,800hp) turboprop known as the 028 and a 10,297N (2,315lb) thrust turbojet designated 003 C.

In it, turboprop engines were defined as being applicable to aircraft in the 600-900km/h (373-559mph) speed range. The directive also noted that they could extend the range of bombers operating in the speed band of 750-800km/h (466-497mph)

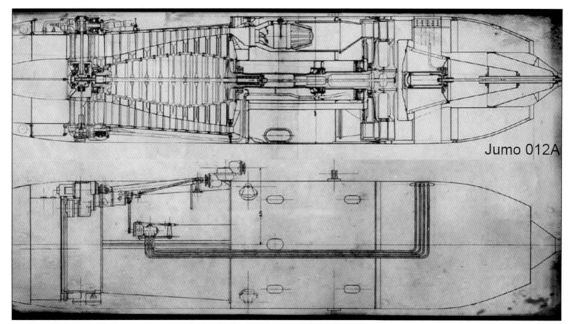

The Jumo 012 was developed for the Russians by German engineers in a competitive race to find the optimum solution via turbojet and turboprop design concepts. (Author's collection)

A Jumo 004 manufactured in the Czech Republic as the Avia M-04, the spoils of war being as exploited just as much by Russian-controlled East European states as they were by the allies in Western Europe. (Author's collection)

The work came with deadlines. The 003 C was to be ready for tests by August 1947, the other three engines by mid-1948. Activities associated with the Jumo 004 were to be moved to Plant No. 26. Prestel gathered together former BMW engineers but they lacked the materials needed to make the turbine blades necessary, having to work with Russian EI-403 alloys rather than the superior German Tinidur material. This led to serious malfunctions, cutting operating time for the 003 C to 25% of the duration of engines made using the German alloy.

The low thrust specified for the 003 C made this an engine of only academic interest and it was transferred to Plant No. 16 in Kazan where development of the BMW 003 (RD-10) was based. Work on the 032 turbojet and its auxiliary compressor was halted in 1947 when it became apparent in calculations that the design promised very little improvement over existing engines of this type.

Development of the turboprop based on the Jumo 012 progressed however. More resources were made available to the project and by the end of 1946 two working examples had been assembled in Dessau and completed, with some improvements, in Russia. These included a new combustion chamber converging the annular chambers of the BMW design and the individual chambers of the Jumo engine. The compression level was decreased from 6.0 to 4.5 and considerable effort was required to solve a turbine blade pitch angle alignment issue, which caused vibrations and turbulent flow in tests. A lot of the challenges came from a lack of instrumentation to measure flow characteristics and nozzle stratification as well as oscillations.

By the end of 1947 initial tests were finished and early production lots were in assembly, with five engines designated 012 B ready by mid-1948. But there was a telling description from a ministry report: "In June No. 5 underwent an endurance test run without takeoff. A compressor rear bearing broke down in the 28th hour. After the bearing and other parts were replaced, the engine ran another 25 hours in July. During this test, cracks were found in turbine blades and compressor stator blades. In the latter half of July, this engine underwent a test in the takeoff mode but, due to defects found, it was removed from the bench."

A static test projected to last 100 hours was conducted late in the year; total success compromised only by a fractured turbine blade at 94 hours. But the days of the 012 B were numbered. By acquiring the British Nene turbojet in 1948 and placing it in production as the RD-45 the Russians obtained the same thrust as the 012 B but with much less weight and that alone sealed the fate of the Jumo derivative. By this time work had progressed on both the 022 and 028 turboprops and working drawings were being released by late 1947 before the decision was made the following year to combine the two OKBs working these separate projects and focus all resources on the 022.

A significant reason for combining the two OKB was in the innate competitiveness between German engineers recruited from BMW and those from Jumo. A lack of shared knowledge fuelled a determination for each to 'race' the other, rather than sharing knowledge and research results. The

Russians had not anticipated this and had believed that by resourcing two different engines the knowledge gained on each would be shared with the other.

Scheibe was appointed chief engineer for the converged teams and J. Vogts was to head the preliminary design group which reported directly to Brandner with Prestel in charge of testing. The Germans got on well with their Russian colleagues but were reportedly frustrated by 'political' interventions, although there was praise for the industrious commitment of young engineers sent directly from graduation to work with the Germans.

Created out of the Jumo 012 turbojet, the 022 had been on the drawing board in Germany during 1944 but had never been fully developed because priority was given to existing engines at that critical stage of the war. Now, with time and resources for a development cycle, the original concept was given a three-stage turbine and a 14-stage compressor before the engineers turned their attention to the design and integration of the propeller, a reduction gear and a governor. The starter would consist of a gas turbine with a shaft power of 44.7kw (60hp), designated TS-1.

Great attention was paid to engine efficiency, requiring tight tolerances on compressor blade tip clearance and careful design of the intake diffuser. To prevent surging, bypass valves had to be added beyond the fifth compressor stage and a lot of development work followed by testing was necessary on the control system for the propeller throttle. A new testbed was built at the plant and by the end of 1948 three prototypes were being built for evaluation. Progress increased when Kuznetsov was appointed director of Plant No. 2.

Kuznetsov liked the Germans. Two years earlier he had visited Germany and made himself aware of their practices, culture and ways of working, all of which made him sympathetic to their requests. Working with Klimov and Brandner, he had introduced production at the Ufa factory and had

played some part in getting an agreement that when the engine tests had been completed the Germans could return home. Not all were allowed to do so, however, due to pressure for an even more powerful turboprop engine. Nevertheless, they had made a major contribution to raising the knowledge level in Russia using new materials and practices, playing no small part in training a new generation of engineers and technicians in the exigencies of jet engine and turboprop design.

What had been the 022 received the official designation TV-2 in 1950 and the following year began the customary 100-hour test required of all new engine designs. In a highly successful series of tests, it demonstrated a shaft power of 3,728kW (5,000hp) with a thrust of 45,734N (10,282lb). The Russians were very pleased and, after a successful conclusion with tests to engine number 14, gave the Germans a cash bonus for their work. Two TV-2 engines were fitted to a Tu-4 in the outer-wing engine positions and 27 flights were made in this configuration, accumulating 70 flying hours.

Further improvements were made and upgrades designed in at the Solov'yev OKB, with contra-rotating propellers replacing the conventional ones. Designated TV-2M, these engines powered the initial models of the An-8 and the Tu-91 transport aircraft before forming the basis for a further development, the TV-2VM helicopter engine for the Mi-6, which made its first flight in 1957. We shall return to the story of the Russian turboprop engine development in the next chapter.

Non-Starters

In the period between the end of the Second World War in 1945 and the end of the Korean War in 1953, a wide range of proposals for medium tactical and heavy strategic bombers were fielded by the Soviet bureaus. Among these were several aircraft designed as successors to existing bombers or as new and innovative concepts, few of which had any realistic chance of success. Established in

January 1933, the Ilyushin OKB rapidly built a worthy reputation through the outstanding success of its Il-2 Sturmovik ground-attack aircraft and the Il-4, an evolution of the DB-3 of 1935. Further concepts such as the Il-6, a long-range successor to the Il-4, had problems. The engines it needed were unavailable and the requirement changed, demanding greater endurance.

A further design initiative for Ilyushin, the Il-14, began on the drawings boards in early 1944. It was another Il-4 replacement concept but faster, with a top speed of 700km/h (435mph). The initial concept had four Mikulin AM-43 liquid propellant V12 engines in tandem pairs placed in pusher and tractor positions at the ends of the mid-wing sections. With a moderately high aspect-ratio, the wing trailing edge was straight while the leading edge had a modest sweep. The chord of the leading edge on the wing centre sections inboard of the tandem engines was considerably forward of the outer panels. Engine coolant and oil radiators were in the wing centre sections between the engines and the fuselage.

It was equipped with tricycle landing gear and a rear fuselage wheel to prevent the pusher propellers striking the ground on rotation. With an emphasis on speed, no defensive armament was proposed for the Il-14 but when the design was inspected in July 1944 there was widespread disagreement with this approach. Ilyushin was told to incorporate both offensive and defensive armament, including a fixed nose cannon operated by the pilot, a dorsal turret in the mid-fuselage and a ventral turret with gunners for each position. The maximum bomb load was 2,500kg (5,510lb), or 2,000kg (4,410lb) for a range of 2,500km (1,553 miles).

Construction of the first prototype began in early 1945 and with an estimated top speed of 600km/h (373mph) and a ceiling of 12,500m (41,010ft); on paper at least the aircraft held great promise. But it came too late to survive the immediate post-war redirection towards long-range strategic bombing

capability and, so as not to waste research and company resources, Ilyushin repurposed the Il-14 project as a heavy long-range fighter intended to intercept B-29s and B-50s.

Unfortunately the Il-14 wasn't needed as a heavy fighter either, because more emphasis was by now being placed on surface-to-air missile (SAM) batteries for air defence rather than piloted aircraft. They were cheaper, easier to maintain and could be quickly positioned to cover the Soviet Union's very lengthy borders. Thus began an increasing dependence on SAMs for perimeter defence of territory and large cities. Piloted fighter aircraft would instead be required to engage incoming threats before they reached Soviet borders – necessitating increased range. It was a philosophy would propel Russian air defence technology ahead of that in the West for several decades.

In response to a general requirement for a strategic bomber issued in 1947, Ilyushin came up with a range of proposals under the general designation Il-26.

Special consideration was given to the type of engines available and appropriate for the mission. These included the 3,355kw (4,500hp) Shvetsov Ash-2TK piston engine, the 4,474kw (6,000hp) Yakovlev M-501 diesel engine and the 3,728kw (5,000hp) Klimov VK-2 turboprop. At this date jet fighters were being introduced and it was agreed that while reciprocating or turboprop engines could provide the necessary range they could never hope to provide enough speed for a quick getaway. Therefore heavy defensive armament was needed. The specification for the Il-26 included a bomb load of 5,000kg (11,025lb) with a range of 11,560km (7,185 miles) and a maximum bomb load of 12,000kg (26,460lb) over a shorter range, defensive armament comprising ten 23mm cannon. Four or six engine layouts were considered with gun positions in nose, tail, dorsal and ventral positions. With a nod to the evolving atom bomb design, a single bomb of 10,000lb

(22,050lb) could be carried or four 3,000kg (6,610lb) bombs. Various configurations were evaluated with various different engine types but the VK-2 turboprop came out best of all, offering a potential range of 11,560km (7,185 miles). The Il-26 was eventually dropped because Ilyushin was already heavily committed to producing the Il-28 jet-powered medium bomber. The jet age had arrived – but the turboprop's hour had not yet come.

The VK-1 gave Russia a robust medium bomber in the Il-28, development resources for which foreclosed work on the Il-26 long-range strategic bomber. More than 6,000 were built for more than 20 export customers, this Il-28U trainer being operated by Egypt. (USAF)

CHAPTER 2

THE CHALLENGE OF THE JET ENGINE

The Soviets had started work on the development of their first jet engine in 1937, the initial draft design having been drawn up by A. M. Lyulka. Most of the initial work took place at the Kharkov Aviation Institute in the Ukraine but it was put on hold following the June 1941 invasion by Germany. As the threat of total national collapse evaporated, in February 1942 some limited work resumed but not at a pace equal to that in Germany, Britain and America. As the war progressed, several engine design teams worked up concepts for a wide range of reaction engines including jet, turbojet, ramjet and rocket propulsion.

A surviving example of the MiG-9, seen here at Russia's Monino museum. This was the first Russian indigenously designed and built jet fighter, powered by two RD-20 engines – re-engineered BMW 003s. (Author's collection)

The Yak-15 made its first flight on 24 April 1946 on the same day as that of the MiG-9, but second to its competitor reputedly on the toss of a coin! (Author's collection)

In February 1944 the GKO (Gosudarstvennoye Kratkosrochnoye Obyazatyelstvo) established the NII-1 scientific research institute to assemble together all these different studies with Lyulka in charge of turbojet design.

As already noted, immediately after the war the Russians leaned heavily on captured German engine designs to power their first jet fighters, the Jumo 004 becoming the Klimov RD-10 in the Yak-15 and the BMW 003 being developed into the eight-stage RD-20 axial-flow turbojet.

However, by early 1945 the domestically-produced S-18 jet engine was seemingly ready for use. It had been in development under Lyulka since May 1944 and promised a rated thrust of 12,720N (2,860lb) prior to the start of static tests on 9 August 1946.

Therefore, in early 1945, Tupolev, Chetvyerikov, Ilyushin, Sukhoi and Myasishchev were ordered to produce concepts for a jet-propelled bomber. At the same time it was decided that progress in jet engine development should be accelerated, with Klimov and Mikulin abandoning some promising piston engines and switching their attention to jet and turbojet designs.

Mikulin came up with the TKRD-1, its first turbojet, which was bench tested in 1947 and earmarked for some of the new jet designs but the results were disappointing and demonstrated just how far behind the Russians were.

The Russians had been aware of British and US jet developments for some time and had made some fruitless efforts to develop their own jet engines. It would be much more straightforward if either of the Soviet Union's two still-friendly wartime allies could be induced to hand over their jet engine technology instead.

It proved very hard to obtain information about America's jet engine projects, largely due to the veil of secrecy placed around this work by the Army Air Force but when Vladimir Klimov visited the UK in 1946 he encountered little difficulty in obtaining approval from its newly installed socialist government

The Rolls-Royce Derwent was sold to Russia in 1947 and adapted by Klimov into the RD-500, seen here as a cutaway training aid preserved at the Kosice Aviation Museum, Slovakia. (Author's collection)

to buy ten each of Rolls-Royce's Nene and Derwent engines on the basis that they must not be used for military purposes.

Stalin was astounded that the British should do this and initially suspected that there was some insidious plot to infiltrate Soviet industry for espionage, until, but still incredulous, he accepted the reality that the socialist government in the UK had simply given no consideration to the military implications of the deal and had made it purely on a commercial basis.

The Yakovlev Yak-23UTI was powered by the RD-500 when it made its first flight on 8 July 1947. (Vitaly V. Kuzmin)

A beneficiary of the VK-1 was Russia's first jet flying boat, the Beriev R-1, the sole example of which made its first flight on 30 May 1952. (Author's collection)

The Derwent was reverse-engineered and designated RD-500 with full, 100-hour static tests completed with great success in 1948. As noted in the previous chapter, the Nene too was swiftly reverse-engineered, rebadged as the RD-45 and used to develop the more powerful Klimov VK-1, which powered the outstanding MiG-15 fighter during the Korean War – mauling American bombers and proving more than a match, in the right hands, for the US Air Force's F-86.

The Russians were able to achieve a more satisfactory match between the basic design of the VK-1 and compatibility with Soviet engineering practices, materials and operating principles. From the basis of that unit, Klimov would produce jet engines for the Ilyushin Il-28 jet bomber, the MiG-15bis, the MiG-17 and the experimental Beriev R-1 jet flying boat. Unfortunately, due to its high fuel consumption, it wasn't an engine that was particularly well suited to long-range bombers.

Meanwhile, the bomber requirement given to the five design bureaus in 1945 had produced some potentially exciting, but usually quite bizarre, proposals.

The Myasishchev bureau, led by Vladimir Myasishchev, had worked on a fast bomber designated R-1 and later RB-17 which incorporated a reconnaissance role. Initially, Myasishchev wanted to re-engine the Pe-2 light bomber with turbojets

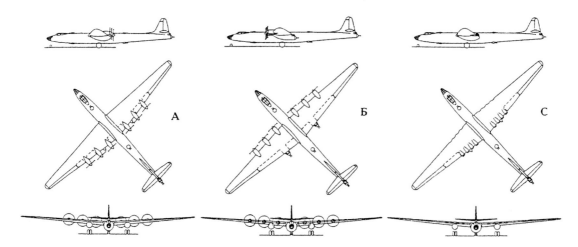

As early as 1946 Myasishchev drew optional plans for a long-range bomber, powered by pusher or tractor reciprocating engines or jet engines. (Russian Aviation Research Trust via Tony Buttler)

but recognising that this would require a complete redesign, focused its full attention on the RB-17.

Selecting the Jumo 004, Myasishchev paired two engines, one above the other, in underwing pods. The initial concept was presented on 28 November 1945 and despite some opposition on technical grounds, a mock-up was prepared and, with TsAGI helping alongside, the OKB received preliminary approval. As designed, it would have had a range of 3,000km (1,865 miles) carrying a 1,000kg (2,205lb) bomb load at a cruising speed of 680km/h (423mph).

Defensive armament would have consisted of a tail turret managed by the wireless operator and a single cannon in the nose.

Myasishchev indicated that more powerful but unspecified engines were to eventually replace the paired turbojets as single units, one under each wing. Various navigation aids were to have been incorporated, giving the pilot an added task and reducing the crew complement. But the overall design of the RB-17 was more advanced than other projects for a jet-powered bomber.

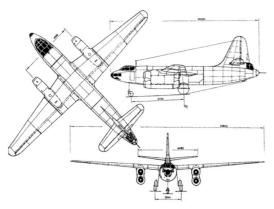

Paired engines under each wing formed the design base for the Myasishchev RB-17 in late 1945, a potential contender for a medium range jet reconnaissance aircraft. (Yefim Gordon via Tony Buttler)

The RB-17 had nose and tail armament and potential for adaptation into a medium bomber. (George Cox via Tony Buttler)

A model of the Myasishchev DSB-17 contender for medium jet bomber, one of three variants of the concept which also included a proposed interceptor. (George Cox via Tony Buttler)

The Ilyushin Il-22 made its first flight on 24 July 1947. It was the first Russian jet bomber to fly and appeared at the Tushino air display less than ten days later. (Yefim Gordon via Tony Buttler)

In early 1946 political intervention brought about the dismantling of Myasishchev's bureau and his work force was dispersed. A difference of opinion over the effectiveness of swept-wing design

had brought him into direct confrontation with Andrey Tupolev, who had considerable influence in the Kremlin and with the various defence establishments.

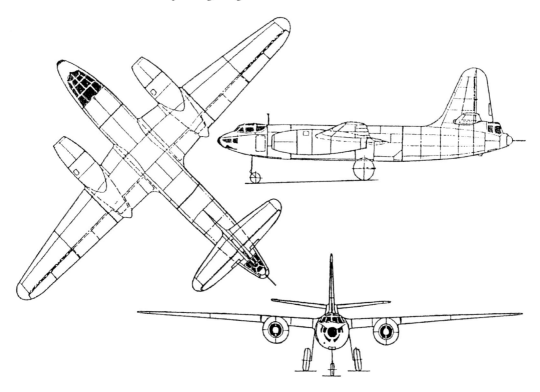

A modified design for the DSB-17 which replaced the paired engines with a single jet motor under each wing. (Yefim Gordon via Tony Buttler)

With four TR-1 engines and straight wings, the Il-22's tail section bears some resemblance to the later Il-28. (Yefim Gordon via Tony Buttler)

Myasishchev went to the Moscow Aviation Institute to run the design faculty but he fell out with the political minders there too and was demoted to head of fixed-wing aircraft. It was here that he developed a working relationship with Georgiy I. Nazarov, in whom he would find a sympathetic ally.

Despite the official abandonment of the RB-17, some further analysis was undertaken and three separate versions were set out: the DSB-17 long-range bomber,

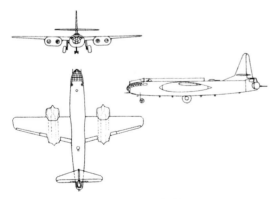

The Il-24 had its proposed AM-TKRD-01 turbojet engines replaced with four RD-45 (Nene) engines in paired nacelles under each wing. It was cancelled before completion. (Yefim Gordon via Tony Buttler)

the RB-17 reconnaissance aircraft and the IDD-17 air defence fighter. None of these were developed further and for a period of two or three years, Myasishchev was disregarded by senior politicians and decision-makers. Work conducted to date was assimilated by other bureaus and the benefit of Myasishchev's designs was distributed to other manufacturers and research institutes.

Ilyushin was one of the beneficiaries of the research data from Myasishchev and fed it into the Il-22, which was designed to carry four TR-1 engines in individual nacelles slung beneath and forward of the wing leading edge. With insufficient room in the nacelles for landing gear the main legs for the tricycle undercarriage were contained in the lower fuselage. But the design was crude in several key aspects of concern to pilots: the cockpit glazing was poor and caused visual distortions; the frames were bulky and produced blind spots; the engines were underpowered and the aircraft's general performance was judged inadequate after the first flight on 24 July 1947.

The Il-22 did fly at the Tushino Aviation Day display on 3 August where it was given the erroneous designation T-10 by the US Air Force. While the aircraft itself never went into production, the basic design was reworked into the new Il-24 which was equipped with two, more powerful Mikulin AM-TKRD-01 jets delivering 32,300N (7,275lb) of thrust. Work on the Il-24 was initially slowed by continued preparation of the Il-22 but after the cancellation of the latter development accelerated and a directive authorising a prototype was signed on 11 March 1947. It was passed for construction on 16 May.

Performance predictions for the Il-24 included a range of 3,000km (1,864 miles) with a 2,000kg (4,409lb) bomb load, a climb-to-height of 5.6 minutes to 5,000m (16,404ft) which was three minutes quicker than the Il-22, and a service ceiling of 14,600m (47,900ft). Political intervention skewed the Il-24 when it was decided that the AM-TKRD-01 engines should be allocated to another bureau, OKB-1, where chief designer Semyon Alekseyev was overseeing German aircraft designers working on a project known as EF 140. Instead, the

Il-24 would get the RD-45, four of which would be carried in twin underwing nacelles.

Those four engines provided less total thrust than the two Mikulin engines, increased weight and slashed performance, which gave the aircraft a very long take-off run which exceeded most airfields. At this date, few Soviet airfields had concrete runways and the Il-24 was almost impossible to operate from grass strips. Because of these imposed burdens, the type was cancelled in a directive issued on 21 June 1948, despite the prototype being two-thirds complete. By now, however, Ilyushin was well underway with the Il-28 powered by two Nene engines.

A Deluge of Designs

The late 1940s saw a veritable plethora of bomber designs emerging from Soviet design bureaus and a considerable overlap of concepts – but they all suffered

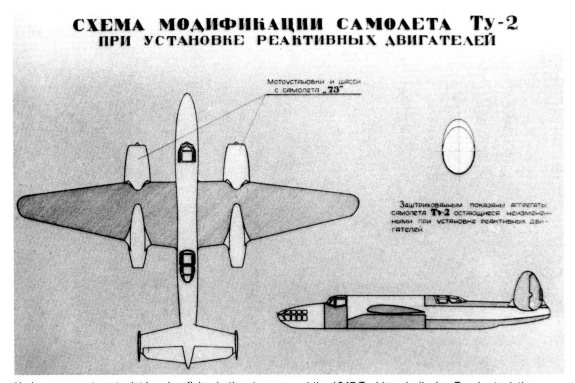

Under pressure to get a jet bomber flying in time to appear at the 1947 Tushino air display, Tupolev took the highly successful Tupolev Tu-2 of wartime medium-bomber fame and re-engined it as the Tu-12 with two turbojets. (Yefim Gordon via Tony Buttler)

Only six Tu-12 development aircraft were built but the type served as a valuable experimental precursor to the first generation of operational Russian jet bombers. (Yefim Gordon via Tony Buttler)

from the same problem: the poor state of Soviet jet engine development. Had it not been for the captured German research archives and test data, the expertise of German engineers and scientists, and the availability of British engines for tear-down, inspection and reverse-engineering, the limited production that did ensue could never have happened. Tupolev's jet bomber efforts had initially involved swapping the piston-engines of its existing wartime Tu-2, the equivalent of Germany's Junkers Ju 88, for imported Rolls-Royce Nene turbojets. Successful and fast, the original Tu-2 had a commendable bomb load of 1,500kg (3,300lb) in its internal bay and 2,270kg (5,000lb) on external racks. The Russians had produced more than 2,200

and it had more than acquitted itself with honour in the Great Patriotic War.

The jet-engined Tu-2 was worked on as Aircraft 77 before being redesignated Tu-10 and then Tu-12. A mock-up was completed in May 1947 with an official evaluation conducted by the end of the month.

Agreement was reached for completion of the first prototype, construction of which began immediately, along with a production plan for reconfiguring Tu-2s as Tu-12s.

Flight tests got underway on 26 July and the aircraft duly appeared at Tushino that August. Several modifications were required but the aircraft proved faster than expected. It did, however, have very high

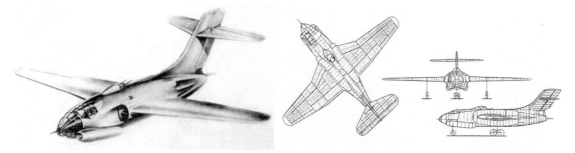

A classic example of rapidly changing design iterations was the Sukhoi Su-10, seen here in its initial configuration with two different wing planforms, two engines mounted to the forward fuselage and four in the fuselage sides. (Yefim Gordon via Tony Buttler)

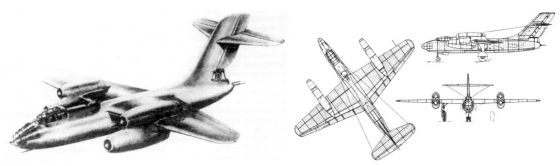

In a modified layout for the Su-10, the engines were arranged on the wings. (Yefim Gordon via Tony Buttler)

fuel consumption. It also lacked pressurisation and it was found that when flying at high speed it became impossible to aim the defensive guns due to the air pressure.

Some mock combat simulations were conducted with MiG-9 and Yak-23 fighters and it became brutally apparent that any reconfigured version of the Tu-2 would be unacceptable. A few Tu-12s were built, flown and tested with domestically-built RD-45 engines. These would continue to fly into the early 1950s, giving flight crews experience with the new type of engine and serving as testbeds for new equipment. One was even used for trialling a ramjet.

Even before the first Tu-12 had flown it had been decided, based particularly on the thirsty nature of early turbojets, that the Soviet Union's first jet bombers should be medium, rather than long-range, aircraft. Sukhoi, Ilyushin and Tupolev were ordered to submit proposals along these lines.

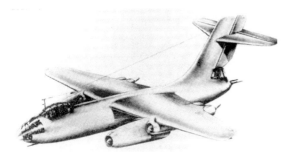

The final Su-10 layout staggered the configuration of the wing-mounted engines and changed the arrangement of defensive armament. (Yefim Gordon via Tony Buttler)

Sukhoi responded to a directive dated 26 February 1946 for a bomber powered by four RD-10 engines. The bureau had not sought this work and was busy on the Su-9 jet fighter but a further order on 27 March directed the company to build the bomber it had proposed, as the Su-10. This was to have a range of 1,500km (932 miles), a bomb load of 1,500kg (2,205lb), a maximum speed of 800km/h (497mph) and a maximum take-off weight no greater than 14,000kg (30,864lb). With external racks, the maximum bomb load was to be 2,000kg (4,410lb).

Pressure was exerted on Sukhoi to have the first prototype flying by the end of January 1947 and the bureau officially began work on the project on 24 April 1946. Sukhoi found it necessary to incorporate six engines in the Su-10, the wings having Fowler flaps and outboard ailerons with a two-wheel undercarriage retracting inwards. Four RD-10s were in vertical pairs within single nacelles either side of the wing with two in the forward fuselage beneath the flight deck.

When the final design was completed on 19 June, weight was considerably greater than desired although a range of 2,000km (1,243 miles) was claimed with a 2,000kg (4,410lb) bomb load. The mock-up inspection on 7 October cleared the way for assembly of the first prototype but several design options remained, providing flexibility for a range of different engines and in various combinations. On 4 December the six-engine arrangement was reduced to four TR-1s and approval for a prototype was granted on 7 January 1947.

Further consolidation of the design followed but Sukhoi sought permission to adopt four RD-500 Derwent derivative engines with take-off assisted by four solid propellant JATO boosters, a configuration agreed on 11 March. At this date the plan was to replace the TR-1 axial-flow turbojet engines with four TR-2 types, initial prototypes of which had demonstrated a thrust of 18,481N (4,155lb), about 25% greater than the TR1 and 20% more than the TR-1A.

In June 1948, however, budget cuts brought about the cancellation of all projects that had not so far made it into the air – including the Su-10. The sole airframe was delivered to the Moscow Aviation Institute for use as an instructional airframe.

Few could gainsay the belief that too many manufacturers were working on too many jet bomber projects, a counter-intuitive conclusion given the strict totalitarian system of control from the Kremlin down. Paradoxically, Western governments working

within the capitalist system where requirements were set down for private industry to pick up on, had tighter constraints over multiple development projects. The Soviet system relied on intense competition between design bureaus using government funds to stimulate the inventive process. The result was duplication of effort and resources wasted on competing proposals that had no application. These themes would be prevalent all the way through the Soviet aerospace bureaucracy up to the collapse of the USSR in 1991.

Back in 1947-48, the changes brought about by reducing the number of bureaus working to a single requirement did improve the situation and allow a credible range of designs to emerge, giving Russia its first jet bombers while continuing development work of longer-range turboprop-powered types. But inventiveness was not the exclusive preserve of Russian design bureaus and one of the failed would-be bomber projects originated in Germany during the last year of the war.

The German Card

Junkers put forward its EF 116 design in response to a jet bomber requirement issued by the German government on July 30, 1943. This called for an aircraft that could be used both during the day and at night and which could fly 2,200km (1,367 miles) at an altitude of 10km (32,788ft) with a 2,000kg (4,409lb) bomb load. It would have a crew of just two seated next to one another in a pressure cabin but staggered, so that the pilot was more to the front and the radio/bomber aimer/defensive gunner was more to the rear.

The engines were to be four Jumo 004s or HeS 011s and it had to be possible to replace the four engines with two of the equivalent or greater power when they became available. Variants with and without defensive armament were to be designed and top speed had to be 950km/h (590mph), with a cruising speed of 780km/h (484mph).

EF 116 consisted of various different jet bomber configurations – some with swept back wings, others with swept forward wings. In November 1943, the

Su-10 static airframe under test. (Yefim Gordon via Tony Buttler)

Powered by four Jumo 004 turbojet engines, the Ju 287 would inspire post-war development of the EF 131. (Author's collection)

swept forward layout was chosen and the project was taken forward under the designation EF 122. This design defeated competitors from Heinkel and Blohm & Voss in early 1944 and received the official designation Ju 287.

While the cockpit, wing and fuselage designs had largely been finalised, Junkers was unable to decide on the best number and arrangement of engines. Eventually it was decided that six Jumo 004s would be best, in two nacelles of three, one under each wing, but in order to test the radical forward swept wing it was necessary to build a flying mock-up. Consequently two prototypes were made using the fuselages of Heinkel He 177s, the tail assemblies of Ju 188s, the landing gear of Ju 352s and nosewheel assemblies made from bits of captured B-24 Liberators.

The first of these flew on August 8, 1944, but the project was soon cancelled – only to be revived again in February 1945.

When the Americans overran Junkers' Dessau facility where it had been built they seized technical documentation and test engines before withdrawing to allow the Russians to occupy the area under an agreement on borders and occupied territories. The Russians found that they had been left very little documentation – what the Americans hadn't taken had been burned – but they were able to round up

key personnel who had been involved in designing and building the Ju 287 and compelled them to replicate their earlier work.

On 17 April 1946 a directive was issued for the development of a Ju 287 type aircraft, in Germany at first and then in Russia. Vital to the project in Russia was Junkers team leader Brunolf W. Baade.

Baade was a mid-level engineer and because he had been a member of the Nazi Party he was held by the Americans for interrogation before being released in June, a few weeks before the area was vacated for the Russians. Baade had a charismatic personality, got on well with people and was a clear leader, although his technical skills were limited. Under the Russians,

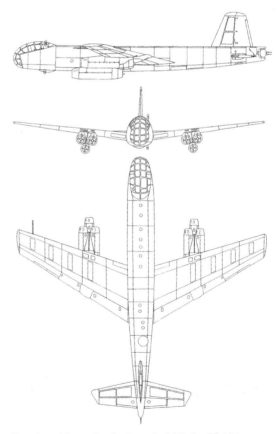

Developed from the Junkers Ju 287, the EF 131 was assembled at Dessau and taken to Moscow, each of two prototypes powered by six RD-10 engines. It was never more than a hedge against failures with Russian designs. (Author's collection)

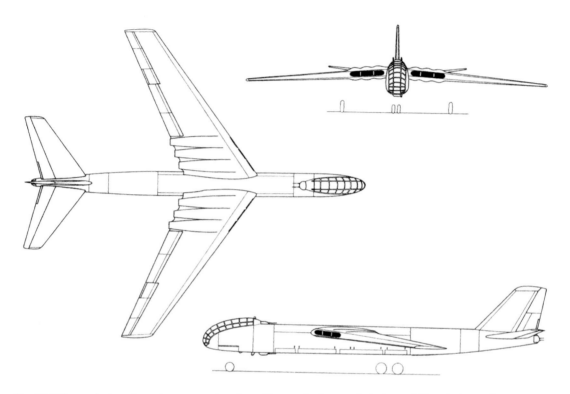

The EF 132 was designed as a long-range bomber with swept wings and six Jumo 012 turbojet engines. (Author's collection)

technicians transported to Russia had a subsistence existence, Baade enjoyed his responsibility rebuilding the Junkers works at Dessau and then construction of similar facilities in the USSR.

The first prototype of what was designated the EF 131 bomber was put together in Germany, where it began, disassembled and taken to Russia where it was reassembled at GOZ-1 (Gosudarstvenny Optniy Zavod) – State Experimental Plant No. 1. It had been hoped that the EF 131 could appear at the 1947 Tushino display but technical problems and structural issues delayed the first flight. TsAGI got involved in static testing and decisions about its suitability for taking to the air. The airframe had to be strengthened and the first flight occurred on 23 May 1947 with German pilot Paul Julge at the controls.

Powered by six Jumo 004 B engines, the flight was made from the Gramov Flight Research Institute

(GFRI) in Zhukovsky but it was only a partial success due to a failure in an undercarriage leg, which resulted in one of the engines scraping the runway. The location, 40km (25 miles) outside Moscow would later be known as the Ramenskoye Air Base. The programme was further compromised in October 1947 by an order banning non-Russian workers from participating in secret research and development activity. The team and the aircraft were returned to Plant No. 1. Slowly, completion of a second prototype progressed but on 21 June 1948 all work was brought to a halt, although some sources claim that 15 test flights took place at the GFRI with Russian pilots.

Little more than two months later, on 23 August an order was issued for a development of a high-speed, long-range bomber, the EF 132. This was a continuation of work at Dessau from late 1945 on a variant of the EF 131 powered by six Jumo 012 engines, each of which had a thrust of 29,423N (6,000lb). The work was moved to the BOZ Mo. 1 plant where it was tagged as an advanced development project powered by six Mikulin AM-TKRD-01 turbojets each rated at a thrust of 32,381N (7,280lb). But it was a completely different design configuration, with the six engines buried in the wing roots and a modest sweep rather than the 19.8-degree forward sweep of the EF 131.

It had a theoretical range of 4,000km (2,486 miles) with a 4,000kg (8,820lb) bomb load; increasing the bomb load was possible at the expense of reduced range. It was a relatively unsophisticated design, with electric autopilot, IFF systems and an instrument landing system as well as provision for cameras and dorsal, ventral and tail turrets, all of which were standard for Russian aircraft of this period. A full-scale

mock-up was ready by late 1947 and further proposals were made for it to have more powerful turbojet engines. Under a directive dated 12 June 1948 all work ceased as attention turned to another concept, a twin-engine variant of the EF 131 with the designation 140.

This took the basic design of the EF 131 and replaced the six Jumo 004 engines with two Mikulin AM-TKRD-01 axial flow turbojet engines. Several variants were proposed, chiefly reconnaissance and reconnaissance/bomber types with a maximum bomb load of 4,500kg (9,922lb). As with so many Soviet concepts, a wide range of defensive armament was considered along with several options for different engines, including two Klimov VK-1 turbojets. Flight tests began on 30 September 1948 but the project failed to survive a directive issued on 18 June 1950

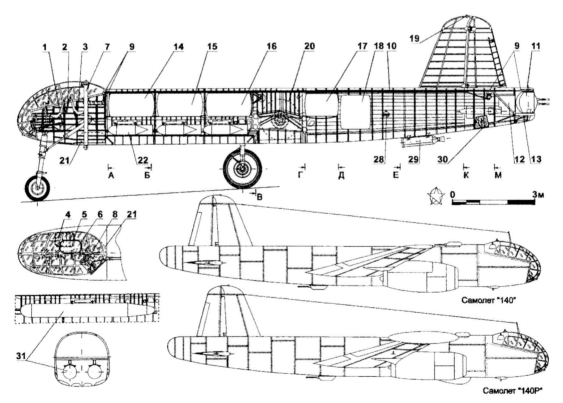

Reverting to the forward swept-wing configuration of the EF 131, the Baade 140 was built as a candidate bomber and reconnaissance aircraft. It had structural problems and the fact that it had been designed by German engineers all but ensured its cancellation. (Author's collection)

A further evolution for the German engineers at OKB-1, Type 150 was a swept-wing jet bomber developed from 1948 and first flown on 5 September 1952. (Yefim Gordon via Tony Buttler)

Plagued with numerous problems including a serious weight issue, the Type 150 was never going to become the jet bomber it was designed to be. (Yefim Gordon via Tony Buttler)

bringing the EF 140 to an end after only four flights, all successful.

This was not the last of Baade's designs. OKB-1 worked up a medium jet bomber concept in 1948 designated RB-2 but the German design team called it the Riese, or Giant, probably after the Riesenflugzeuge of the First World War. The specification originated at the Long-Range Aviation (LRA) group in the Russian air ministry on 22 May just as Semyon M. Alekseyev was put in charge of OKB-1 and GOZ No. 1 got a new boss, Semyon A. Lavochkin from OKB-21, where he had been the chief designer. TsAGI was closely involved with the RB-2 and the design details together with the concept proposal were sent to Minister of Defence Nikolay A. Bulganin on 17 August.

The RB-2 featured wings with a leading edge sweep of 38.5-degrees at quarter-chord with swept tail surfaces and two TKRD-02 turbojets, one under each wing on forward-sloping pylons. An interesting feature of the RB-2 was the tandem main landing gear legs retracting into wells fore and aft of the high-placed wing and with outrigger legs for stability, precisely the arrangement of the Boeing B-47, about which more shortly. But the aircraft incorporated a full suite of avionics and boasted a bomb load of 6,000kg (13,230lb) with optional configurations across a wide range of bomb types. Defensive gun positions included a fixed, forward-firing cannon and

paired NS-23 cannon in dorsal and tail turrets.

Design options allowed for the use of two Lyulka TR-3 engines giving the RB-2 a top speed of 1,000km/h (621mph) on full combat boost but it had airbrakes to limit landing speed to 179km/h (111mph). With a full fuel load and at cruising speed it had a range of 2,000km (1,240 miles), or 2,700km (1,675mph) at optimum low-fuel management, higher for lower bomb loads and optimum cruise altitude. All of this came together at a series of presentations on 24 August 1948, with ministry approval for further development expected. But that did not happen.

TsAGI had looked over the RB-2 design and expressed concern about the general layout internally and with the design of the wing and tail assemblies. Initial drawings were delivered on 20 December and on 19 February 1949 a further set of changes to the landing gear were requested. Blueprints were available by 20 February and the mock-up was ready for inspection on 20 March, at which date it had been given the internal designation Project 150. By now, Baade wanted to incorporate TR-3 engines but he was instructed to use Mikulin AMRD-04 turbojets instead.

Throughout, innovative methods of design and construction had the fuselage broken down into three separate sections, with the forward element being fully pressurised where three crewmembers were stationed including the operator for the remotely-controlled dorsal turret. The centre fuselage section contained the spacious bay for a maximum bomb load of 6,000kg (13,230lb) and optional long-range fuel tanks. The aft fuselage was also pressurised and had the fifth crewmember operating the tail turret. The engine pylons had a forward sweep of 79.5-degrees projecting them ahead of the leading edge to minimise aerodynamic interference and drag, a compromise essential for maintaining optimum performance from the wing, where the engines also served as anti-flutter weights.

The TR-3 was reinstated on 14 June 1949, and around 1,800 detailed engineering drawings were produced over the following three months. But this work was stopped in early September when development of the 140 (EF 131) reconnaissance bomber project was given priority. As noted earlier, that would itself grind to a halt in 1950, after which work returned to the Project 150 bomber. Following a frustrating sequence of indecision and delay, not at all uncommon within Soviet bureaucracy, the EF 150 made the first of 17 test flights on 5 September 1952. The last, on 9 May 1953 ended in a crash landing and the aircraft was never repaired.

By the end of 1953 the fate of the 150 had been sealed as much by a larger political decision as any technical shortfall, of which there were several but none unsurmountable. OKB-1 was to be dismantled and the Germans returned home while their assets and resources were distributed among exclusively Russian design teams. Baade convinced the Russian authorities that on return to Germany he could organise a nascent aircraft industry in his now divided country and that this could work for the benefit of the Soviet state. Russia wanted to revitalise the East German economy and make it less reliant on financial support from Moscow – and Baade had already gained a reputation for organisation and administration. He therefore returned home with grand plans and ambitions.

Baade wanted to use the legacy of the EF 131 and EF 150 to produce a commercial airliner out of the latter, designated Model 152. In his own accounts, Baade made much of his own role in this but the Soviet authorities worked closely with the Ulbricht regime in East Germany – the German Democratic Republic (GDR) – to open a new industrial base for economic autonomy. Projects such as Model 152 were a convenient application of research already

Type 150 had a tandem landing gear and wingtip wheel assemblies much like the B-52 but on a smaller scale; power was provided by two Lyulka TR-3A turbojet engines. (Yefim Gordon via Tony Buttler)

Baade's team designed the 152 as a candidate commercial airliner, favoured more for its export potential by his Russian masters. It fell victim to the building of the Berlin Wall and the closure of all aircraft design offices in East Germany. (Airbus-Group)

conducted in the USSR for exploitation in the GDR. Civilian but not military aircraft manufacturing was now allowed.

The story of the 152 jet airliner begins at the end of 1953 when Baade took up a post with the newly formed VEB Industriewerke, later VEB Flugzeugwerke Dresden. Facilities were set up at the former Luftwaffe base at Klotzsche on the outskirts of the city, with a new seven-storey building erected for engineering offices and adjacent test rigs and wind tunnels in addition to an assembly plant embracing airframes, engines, electronics and ancillary equipment.

Baade joined the East German Central Committee and then, after the obligatory wait of three years, the communist party. The 500 German engineers repatriated from Russia formed the core of a major influx of talent from East German universities and technical institutions. Of all those leaving Russia, only 20 opted to take up employment in the West – testament to their support for a system very different to that in which they had been educated and for whom they had worked. The story of the 152 has been told elsewhere but suffice to say that it bore a very strong resemblance to its bomber ancestry, with four Pirna 014 turbojet engines, each delivering a thrust of 30,900N (6,900lb). Designed by Ferdinand Brandner, the engine was a single-shaft turbojet with a 12-stage compressor and a two-stage turbine. It borrowed much from the Jumo 004 and Jumo 012 engines but incorporated many improvements and design changes to ensure reliability and low operating cost.

Known historically as the Baade 152, the airliner was beset by schedule delays, technical issues and an uncertain market in which it was set against the Sud-Est Caravelle for marketing to Western Europe. It did not fly until 4 December 1958 and the first of three prototypes crashed on 4 March 1959, killing the crew and all personnel on board, including test engineers. It had been practising for an appearance at a fly-past near Leipzig later that day where Nikita Khrushchev was waiting to see this product from the GDR. The loss became a national tragedy and when

the funeral was held in one of the large assembly halls, several thousand Dresden citizens turned out and the local symphony orchestra cancelled a planned trip to China to play for the mourners.

It was hoped that Deutsche Lufthansa would order the type but it never did and the aircraft programme was scrapped in 1961 along with all hope of a domestic civil aircraft industry for the GDR, a sad footnote to the story of Russian bombers and contributions by German engineers from the wartime industries. On 28 February 1961 the East German

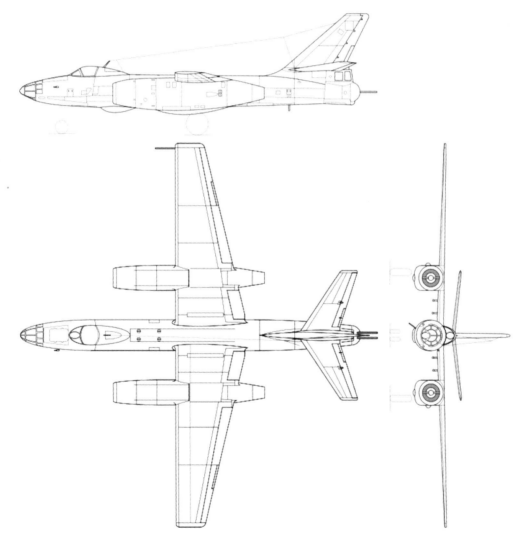

A three-view diagram of the Ilyushin Il-28. (Kaboldy)

With the NATO code name 'Beagle', the Il-28 was successful because its mission was simplified and it was the product of conservative engineering – giving it great export potential. (Author's collection)

Central Committee closed down all aircraft work and several tens of thousands of employees were dispersed to other industries. A number of aircraft workers slipped away to the West before East German leader Erich Honecker closed the border and built a wall.

Survival of the Fittest

As noted earlier, by 1948 Ilyushin was well underway with the Il-28, a project that began on 31 October when Bulganin received a proposal to utilise all the previous work on the Il-22 and leapfrog both that and the Il-24 by minimising the number of crew and the defensive armament. The new Il-28 would have a crew of three, including the pilot, navigator/bomb-aimer and a radio-operator/tail gunner. Ilyushin wanted to achieve success through down-sizing both the mission and the operational turnaround time, so that his aircraft would fly a sortie lasting no more than four hours and be readily available for a second sortie that day.

Incorporating the minimalist armament – a single defensive tail turret – proved one of the most difficult tasks to accomplish. The initial design was far too difficult to operate and slow in azimuth and elevation. Ilyushin selected instead an advanced electro-hydraulically operated Il-K6 with a Nudelman/Richter NR-23 cannon of 23mm calibre capable of traversing at ±70 degrees or elevating from +60 degrees to -40 degrees at a rate of up to 30 degrees per second. Moreover, the turret was relatively light and a considerable improvement on the DK-3 turrets used on the Tu-4. Electrically controlled, it had a computing gunsight capable of adjusting for the motion of the target, its velocity and that of the cannon shell, with accuracy far exceeding the minimum required.

The determination to cut weight and improve performance extended to the reduced wing area compared with the Il-22 and a shorter fuselage (due to the minimal crew and single turret) but a pair of fixed, forward-firing cannon could be operated by the pilot and that arrangement too saved weight. All this allowed the use of two Klimov RD-45 engines which by this year were considerably more reliable than earlier Soviet developments of the Nene, which had been somewhat below the standard of the British-built engines of this type. It had increased power output and a specific fuel consumption up to 30% lower than the TR-1.

The large diameter of the RD-45, however, required each to be contained in a nacelle tight up against the underside of the wing with the intakes as far above ground as possible to minimise foreign object damage. Because centre-of-gravity requirements called for the engines be located well forward in the nacelles, the main landing gear of the tricycle undercarriage could retract into the rear of the nacelle housings providing a wide track for stability on rough landing and take-off strips. On retraction, the main wheels would rotate through 90 degrees, allowing them to lie flat underneath the jet exhaust pipe and behind the combustion chambers. Further advantage was gained by extending the length of the main gear struts, which had not been possible on the Il-22, allowing greater ground clearance for easy access to the bomb bay.

The Il-28's wing had been designed by Yakov M. Serebriyskiy and Maria V. Ryzhova and had the same 12% thickness/chord ratio. Using the TsAGI SR-5S profile, it allowed for a top speed of Mach 0.82 at 8,000m (26,246ft) and moved toward the transonic without any shock wave disturbance or lack of stability. With trailing edge flaps it had good low-speed handling but at high speed a swept tail was called for, which had a sweep of 41 degrees at quarter-chord and that prevented buffeting at speeds far in excess of its maximum. This design also reduced the required tail area by increasing the rudder and elevator arm and that saved weight too.

Following criticism of the Il-22's cockpit glazing, Ilyushin designed the Il-28's cockpit more like that of a fighter, the pilot getting a much better view and only the navigator/bomb-aimer having any form of glazing, which was a significant improvement on the Il-22. There were two pressurised compartments, one for the pilot and the navigator/bomb-aimer and another for the radio-operator/gunner, fed by engine bleed above 1,700m (5,580ft). There were two upward-firing ejection seats and the unfortunate gunner was required to get out through the crew access hatch – though the forward door afforded some protection from the slipstream.

The aircraft was well equipped with the sophisticated avionics and communications of the day, an ILS system for use in bad weather, range beacons, marker beacons, radios and HF and VHF radio direction finders for landing in poor visibility. The standard bomb load was 1,000kg (2,205lb) with a maximum capacity of up to 3,000kg (6,615lb) in a wide variety of types and configurations. The OPB-5S optical bombsight allowed the operator to aim automatically on moving or stationary targets, and an electric release system had a gyro-stabilised sight connected to the autopilot.

At OKB-240 Sergey V. Ilyushin personally signed off on the design on 12 January 1948 and it was included in the Soviet air ministry's aircraft construction plan of 12 June 1948. Ilyushin had managed to procure two imported British-built Nene engines and with those ground tests began on 29 May. Without any official number or even a national insignia, the prototype was then dismantled and taken to Gromov Flight Research Institute in Zhukovsky. It was first flown on 8 July 1948 by company chief test pilot Vladimir K. Kokkinaki. It handled well, appeared stable and when trimmed appropriately could fly straight and level without hands on the controls. There was no tendency to stall and even one-engine-out performance was quite satisfactory. The take-off run was 560m (1,837ft) with two JATO rockets each delivering 14,688N (3,527lb) of thrust. It had excellent performance off dirt strips and pilots claimed to prefer that to save tyres on a concrete runway!

In further tests, the Il-28 established a rated top speed of 833km/h (517mph) at 5,000m (16,404ft) and pilots claimed that it could easily go faster if certain adjustments were made. Speed had already pushed Ilyushin to take extreme care over the manufacturing and assembly of the various structural elements, giving the exterior as smooth a finish as possible and planning for the installation of more powerful engines. But the looming spectre of its competitor was now already in flight test, the Tupolev Tu-73 and the Tu-78 having already taken to the air.

CHAPTER 3

THE LONG-RANGE JET BOMBER

Between 1947 and 1950 great strides were taken by British and American manufacturers supporting the national resolve to fund long-range bombers able to carry an atomic bomb, either as a deterrent or as an instrument of retribution. For some time, neither the West nor the Soviet Union had long-range strategic jet bombers – only tactical or medium jet bombers – but that would soon change.

The US Air Force had the North American B-45 Tornado in the air in March 1947 followed within two years by the British with the English Electric Canberra, jet-powered medium bombers in the same category as the Ilyushin Il-28. More worrying for the Russians was the flight of the Boeing B-47 in December 1947 with a combat range in excess of 3,000km (1,864 miles) carrying a 9,072kg (20,000lb) bomb load. With a top speed of 977km/h (607mph) and a cruising speed of 896km/h (557mph), the B-47 was a formidable threat, especially so when deployed to forward bases.

The formation of the North Atlantic Treaty Organisation (NATO) in April 1949 consolidated a hitherto relatively loose and fragmented transatlantic alliance which saw the return of US forces to Western Europe. The Berlin airlift of 1948-49 cemented concern regarding Soviet ambitions and this catalysed a Western response. The perceived threat from the Soviet Union through its permanent occupation of East European countries pushed that military coalition to which the Russians would respond with the establishment of the Warsaw Pact in May 1955, eight countries being signatories including Russia.

Long before the establishment of the Warsaw Pact, however, the deployment of long-range strategic bombers by the US and Britain had become the underpinning incentive for Russia to speed up development of its own fast, jet-powered bomber force. Flown for the first time in 1951 and 1952, the British V-bombers (Valiant, Victor and Vulcan) were known by the Russians to be in full-scale development by the end of the 1940s while the Americans were in the process of transitioning to an all-jet strategic bomber force. The Boeing B-52 made its first flight in 1952, signalling a significant increase in strike capacity and, with long range, capable of hitting any target in the Soviet Union.

The detonation of the first Soviet atom bomb in August 1949 was followed by the first British A-bomb detonated at Monte Bello in October 1952. That was followed a month later by the first thermonuclear

The three aircraft that worried Russia the most during the early years of the Cold War: the USAF's B-45; the British Canberra, this example bought by the Americans for adaptation as the B-57; and the Boeing B-47 swept-wing bomber. (USAF)

'hydrogen' bomb, detonated by the United States in a ground test. After several years of hybrid fission/fusion development and testing, the Russians had their own H-bomb in November 1955, dropped from a Tu-95. In the ten years since the end of the Second World War, the potential threat to global stability had been upended by the convergence of atomic physics and nuclear engineering.

All these factors, both threats and technological developments, were well known to the Russians in the latter years of the 1940s and fervent efforts were made to provide the long-range air force with jet bombers suitable for strategic operations. A wide-ranging programme of aeronautical research began at TsAGI, particularly on swept-wing designs which were considered crucial to the performance of long-range aircraft. Many questions remained unanswered however – particularly where engines were concerned. The legacy first-generation powerplants obtained from the British had been a useful starting point

Britain's V-bomber force, the Avro Mk. 2 Vulcan shown here, was perceived by Russia as a strategic threat which it sought to match in increasingly hostile times. (RAF)

but, combined with existing Russian work on new jet engines, progress was being made toward a new generation which called for extensive testing.

It was clear that good practical results had been achieved

from swept-wing fighter design such as the MiG-15 and -17 fighters and Tupolev in particular was keen to see whether those similar positive results could be achieved with larger aircraft. In particular, Tupolev was intrigued by the double sweep on the wing leading edge, graduating from 45 degrees at quarter-chord to 42 degrees outboard. On the MiG-17 this allowed for a stiffer wing which maintained wing loadings and symmetry at high stress levels and during manoeuvres.

Working alongside TsAGI, Tupolev began to shortlist wing designs through a range of planform options – resulting in a design with a sweptback leading edge of 35 degrees and aspect ratios between 6 and 11. But there were problems for the stress engineers in the structural strength of the root. It

appeared that in the familiar two-spar design the forward spar would be longer than the other and carry the greater load. Load-carrying and stress factors were of great concern and much time and effort was expended on studying the stress flow in the centre section box structure.

The MiG-17's thin wing with double-sweep angle on the leading edge intrigued Tupolev, who saw aerodynamic efficiency and stiffer wings as crucial for success with long-range bomber concepts. (Author's collection)

The aircraft emerging from this work was the Tu-82, or Aircraft 82, from which would proceed a range of evolutionary concept designs – none of which flew. But the Tu-82 was powered by two RD-45F or VK-1 turbojet engines with a projected top speed close to Mach 0.95. It was in fact a completely revised configuration from Aircraft 73 which had been the progenitor of the Tu-14, a tactical bomber which

With straight wings and two Klimov VK-1 turbojet engines, the Tu-14 was an evolution of Aircraft 73, as described in the preceding chapter. (Edwin Borremans)

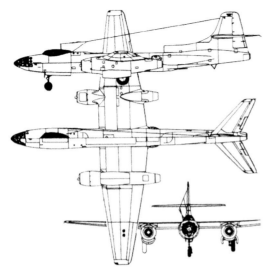

The Tu-73 had three jet engines, a single Nene under each wing and a Derwent V in the rear fuselage with an intake ahead of the tail. (Yefim Gordon via Tony Buttler)

The Tu-14 bore a superficial resemblance to the Il-28 but with the same minimal defensive armament of one tail gun. (Edwin Borremans)

The tri-engine Tu-73 made its first flight on 20 December 1947 and a derivative, Tu-78 photo-reconnaissance version was built but neither was adopted. (Yefim Gordon via Tony Buttler)

First flown on 13 October 1949, the Tu-14 had limited success and only 150 were built before it was retired ten years later. (Yefim Gordon via Tony Buttler)

Adapted from the Tu-14, Aircraft 82 (also designated Tu-82 in some literature) was temporarily numbered Tu-22 and made its first flight on 24 March 1949. (Yefim Gordon via Tony Buttler)

made its first flight on 13 October 1949 and which was the serious competitor to the Il-28, as noted in the previous chapter.

The Tu-14 had straight wings but the pressure to get a bomber with swept wings and a better performance pushed Tupolev to use this airframe as the basis for the new design. The Aircraft 73 concept began as a proposal with three engines: a single Nene engine under each wing and a Derwent V in the tail but the availability of the more powerful Klimov VK-1

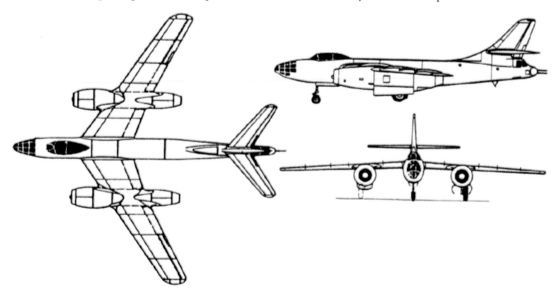

This general arrangement view shows the swept-back design of the Tu-82 developed as a simpler and more efficient twin-engine version of the tri-engined Aircraft 73 concept. (Yefim Gordon via Tony Buttler)

The Tu-82 was a start-point for Aircraft 86, which was larger and designed to be more efficient but which was never taken up. (Yefim Gordon via Tony Buttler)

Aiming to produce a transonic successor to the Il-28, the Il-30 was designed to carry a 2,000kg (4,410lb) bomb load but failed to compete against the equally unsuccessful Tupolev Tu-82. (Yefim Gordon via Tony Buttler)

removed the need for the Derwent. This switched designations to Aircraft 81 which formed the basis for the Tu-14. Around 150 were produced and it found a home with the Russian navy but it was eclipsed in both bomber and reconnaissance roles by the Il-28.

The Tu-82 was a great improvement on the Tu-14, with a reduced crew of three and on 12 June 1948 it was approved by the Council of Ministers and given the official designation Tu-22 (not to be confused with the later Tu-22 Blinder). Piloted by A. D. Perelyot, Aircraft 82 made its first flight on 24 March 1949 but a planned appearance at that year's Tushino display was abandoned after an incident of 'recurrent turbulence' during low level flying tore one of the engines from its nacelle. An emergency landing at Gromov saved the aircraft but emphasised the experimental nature of the programme. Nevertheless, the incident provided Tupolev with invaluable experience of swept-wing aircraft in flight.

Tupolev was not alone in developing an experimental prototype for swept-wing designs on larger aircraft;

Ilyushin achieved the same result with its Il-30. With lessons-learned from Aircraft 82, Aircraft 83 was designed to be a fully operational bomber with a longer fuselage, radar and defensive armament but it was cancelled in 1949. By this time, Tupolev was working on a new generation of designs for more powerful and larger aircraft in the form of Project 486, denoting the sixth project of 1948, followed by Project 491 in 1949. All these were spun off from Aircraft 73 but with engines delivering higher thrust.

The baseline Aircraft 86 was projected as a long-range bomber with two AM-02 gas turbine engines providing 46,881N (10,540lb) of thrust and a maximum bomb load of 6,000kg (13,230lb) with a crew of six. A continuous series of modifications were made and features were redesigned but ultimately it was rejected and attention turned to Aircraft 88, the true progenitor of the Tu-16. This was a derivative evolution of the Project 86 concept but with a wing sweep angle of 35 degrees and an aspect ratio of 7.9:1. Much of the wing design was copied from the

Aircraft 86 gave Tupolev a further derivation of Aircraft 73 but quickly left that behind in its search for a general design concept for high-speed, long range and medium jet bombers. (Yefim Gordon via Tony Buttler)

With swept wings and two turbojet engines, Aircraft 86 morphed from its original, straight-wing design into Aircraft 88, forerunner of the 491 concept. (Yefim Gordon via Tony Buttler)

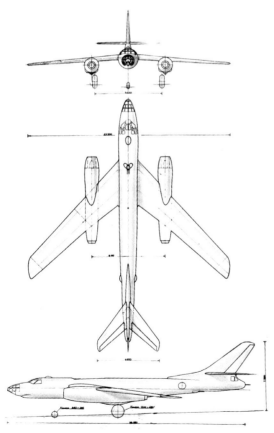

Work began in April 1949 to find a Tu-4 replacement capable of high speed and long range, Tupolev's Aircraft 491 concept having 45-degree swept wings. (Yefim Gordon via Tony Buttler)

EF 132 described earlier. It was intended to have a maximum speed of 1,000km/h (621mph) and a range of 7,500km (4,660 miles) carrying a 6,000kg (13,230lb) bomb load. Alternatively, it could carry a 12,000kg (26,460lb) bomb load over a much shorter range. The selected engine was Lyulka's TR-3A with a thrust of 49,039N (11,025lb) but provision was made for installing Mikulin's under-development AMRD-03 with a potential thrust of 80,424N (18,080lb).

Development of the AMRD-03 had begun in 1949 at Mikulin's OKB-300 and it emerged successfully through a series of tests before production got under way in 1952. It represented the first major engine development in post-war Russia, built only marginally on previous experience with the British and German engines. It would eventually become the mainstay for Soviet combat aircraft and for an expanding range of civilian types. The design was based around an eight-stage compressor and a two-stage turbine with an annular combustion chamber and a fixed-area nozzle. It had a self-starter and a built-in de-icing capability with a heat exchanger for oil cooling which tapped off the main fuel supply bleed.

Aircraft 88 was now subjected to further development and further evolution through a number of concepts, eventually resulting in Aircraft 494 which had a 35-degree wing sweepback and was the responsibility of a team led by B. M. Kondorski. It got the very special attention of Andrey Tupolev himself and with the assistance of engineers Babin, Cheryomukhin and Sterlin, the concept had been fully worked through by June 1950. Three engine arrangements were now considered: two AMRD-03s, four TR-3As or four TR-5s. There were two options for the AMRD-03 version. The first (494/1) had the engines in nacelles a third of the way along each wing, and with space available to accommodate the retracted main landing gear in those nacelles. The second (494/2) had podded engines on pylons, the landing gear retracting into wing fairings protruding from the trailing edge positioned further out from the pods. Wing area was calculated to be variable in the final design in the range 160-200m² (1,722-2,152ft²).

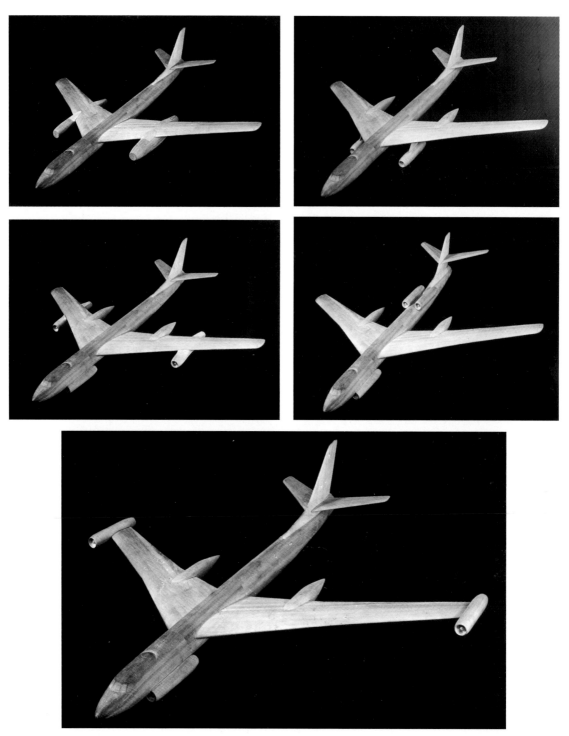

Tupolev's Aircraft 494 project included a wide range of configurations and engine locations, shown here in a selection of wind tunnel models. (Yefim Gordon via Tony Buttler)

There were three options for the TR-3A and TR-5 versions. One had the same wing area as the 494/1 and 494/2, which would place two of the four engines in the forward fuselage and two on the wings between the inboard flaps and the ailerons, the main landing gear being retracted into separate wing fairings. The second option was for a wing area greater than the 494/1 and 494/2 versions. This had a range of alternative engine positions: all four on the sides of the aft fuselage, or two on the fuselage and two on the wingtips, or all four mounted on wing pylons. In each case the landing gear would retract into dedicated fairings.

The third option envisaged a wing area of 200m² (2,152ft²) with the four engines mounted one above the other in pairs either side of the fuselage in wing fairings with the main legs retracting forward into them. Weight increased incrementally across all three options and could be selected along with the engine types depending on availability.

After analysis of all these options, Tupolev opted to recommend a version with two inboard wing fairings, each containing two TR-3As mounted side by side.

But that was far from the end of the story and there were further iterations to come. Project 495 had just two TR-3As, one buried in each inboard wing section and faired over, the wing having an area of 140m² (1,507ft²). Wind tunnel tests showed very positive results. But there was a difference of opinion over the position of the engines; Tupolev preferred pylons with the landing gear retracting into wing fairings while TsAGI doubted the structural value of that configuration.

Strangely, despite their widespread adoption for a range of military and commercial aircraft in the United States, underwing pylons were treated with reticence in Russia. TsAGI had agreed to Baade's 150 project with its podded engines only with reluctance. And it remained unclear which engine type should be adopted.

From all of these studied permutations, three primary requirements emerged: weight needed to remain within the 60,000-100,000kg (132,300-220,500lb) range. Wing area needed to be 150-250m² (1,614-2,691ft²) and the thrust available from whichever combination of engines was chosen needed to be more than 117,694-137,310N (26,460-30,870lb).

These criteria would shape the final configuration and layout and even at this stage the Tupolev designs appeared to be on a more secure course than any of the competing concepts from other bureaus.

On 14 June 1950 the Soviet Council of Ministers issued a directive for Tupolev to deliver a long-range jet bomber powered by two TR-3F engines, which had previously been designated TR-3A, based on Tupolev's original Aircraft 88 design. All the later iterations including Projects 494 and 495 were dropped. The TR-3F engine would subsequently be redesignated once again as the AL-5, with a thrust of 49,039N (11,025lb). There were to be two prototypes and the council wanted the acceptance trials to be held no later than December 1951. Work on Aircraft 88 proceeded slowly however and the schedule was thrown into doubt, a three month extension being granted. As work progressed and the detailed design intensified it became apparent that the selected engines would not be sufficiently powerful and a switch was made to the AMRD-03, known as the AM-3 in production.

In February 1951, Tupolev decided to gamble that this engine would be available, although the commitment would not be finalised until the first engine of that type had been tested. With government pressure to get the AM-3 into production, the air ministry issued an order on 30 August that Aircraft 88 was indeed to be powered by this engine, which promised a thrust of 85,328N (19,180lb). To help speed development, a Tu-4 was assigned as an in-flight testbed for the AM-3 in November 1941.

Before the Soviet directive of June 1950 authorising prototype production, the Council of Ministers issued a formal requirement to match the Aircraft 88 proposal, updated on 11 September to formalise use of the AM-3. A series of evaluations ensued and after design work had been completed on 20 April

1951 the Aviation Technical Committee confirmed its satisfaction with the type on 29 May. Work on the mock-up was already well underway by this date and it was completed by 20 April 1951 but a protracted series of contested changes held the programme back for some time. The Aircraft 88 configuration that finally emerged was considerably different from that of previous iterations.

Area-Rule

Much about the design of Aircraft 88 was the product of extensive research and development at TsAGI and Tupolev where emphasis was placed on aerodynamic performance and on the latest wind tunnel and flight results from tests close to the transonic region. The result was a more extensive range of technical features than had been seen on previous projects. The inclusion of these new and advanced design innovations resulted in delays caused by uncertainties and disagreement over their use.

The prime shift in design philosophy was the application of transonic area-rule. Outside Russia its originator is said to have been American Richard T. Whitcomb in 1952, but the principle had been set down and even patented by Junkers wind tunnel engineer Otto Frenzl in 1943. Frenzl noted that the same wave drag is maintained through a range of different cross-sectional changes quite independent of the total included area, such that a transitional narrowing of the fuselage at the wing juncture ensures minimal added drag.

The area-rule concept had been used by Junkers with location of the engines on the Ju 287 so that the overall cross-section would benefit from this principle.

Other experimental engineers such as Dietrich Küchemann were also working along similar lines. The results of their work were liberated by the Americans shortly after the war. Tupolev applied only a moderate touch of area-rule, principally with the dynamic arrangement of the engine fairings and with the integration of the interface between the wings and the fuselage and between the air intakes, the engines

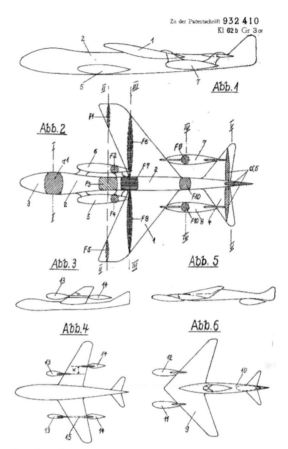

Russian aircraft manufacturers applied the area-rule concept to the design of fast jets, a formula first identified by German engineer Otto Frenzl in a patent (shown here) at the Junkers works in 1943 and taken by the Americans to the USA in 1945 where it was refined by Wallace Hayes two years later. (Author's collection)

and the fairings for the landing gear. Aircraft 88 shifted the focus of Soviet aircraft design towards a new aerodynamic rulebook and Tupolev is rarely given credit for introducing these revolutionary concepts, albeit with significant assistance from TsAGI.

Everything about the Aircraft 88 design was built for high subsonic speed, range and aerodynamic performance. The latter aspect is visibly apparent from the blending of the engine fairing over the inboard wing sections and the recognisable 'coke-bottle' shape

The seminal exponent of area-rule in the US was Richard Whitcomb, posing here beside a wind tunnel model of a 'coke-bottle' fuselage. Details of his work were meticulously documented and sent to the USSR by Russian spies. (NASA)

in planform. The single air intake for each engine was bifurcated, channelling air both through the wing torsion box and below it.

Engineers working on the design emphasised the priority given to the arrangement of the wing/fuselage juncture and the engines so that the jet efflux sucked away air flowing around that part of the airframe, smoothing out the flow over and below the interface. The rear fillet between the wings and the fuselage was a critical part of achieving that. This was one other reason why the engines were buried deep within the wing and close to the root.

So successful was the process of smoothing and integrating aerodynamic flow patterns that TsAGI

was hard pressed to understand how the drag had been reduced so substantially compared to previous designs. Everything was done to prioritise speed, including giving the vertical tail a greater sweepback so that shock-stall occurred later there than it did for the wing. With an aspect ratio of 7:1 in the final wing design, the basic torsion box was formed by webs from the two spars and the upper and lower wing panels – a significant departure from conventional practice in the West.

Boeing led the field on large, swept-wing aircraft for military and commercial markets, followed by Douglas, Convair and Lockheed. But there, wing design was very different. Wings were made flexible to dampen out vertical gusts through substantial deformation, incurring high stress and fatigue levels in the process which would present consistent problems operationally and in service life. It was a practice that became embedded in aircraft designed for high subsonic speeds for the next 50 years and more. The Tupolev wing, in stark contrast, was designed to a more rigid specification and would endure greater stress without the repeated fatigue and repair problems encountered with American aircraft.

Flexible wings require more exotic and expensive materials whereas stiff wings require greater strength, which brings a weight penalty. Of all the American manufacturers, Lockheed alone produced stiff wings and that in itself came with a penalty in the form of cracked spars due largely to insufficient strength. Before the use of composite materials, structural stiffness came at a cost and the ride was noticeably different. Flexible wings smoothed turbulence as energy was absorbed and dissipated through vertical motion, and sometimes axial rotation, of the wing. There was a distinct decrease in that smoothness with stiff wings.

The tricycle landing gear of Aircraft 88 allowed designers to provide a large bomb bay behind the rear spar which could accommodated a wide range of bomb options. Located close to the centre of gravity, the bay was outside the main load-bearing structure and the rigidity of the fuselage was ensured through strong longitudinal beams. Overall, the design of the fuselage ensured a tough and forgiving structure, typical of many Russian aircraft of the period. By comparison, American and to some extent British post-war aircraft designs opted for a balanced approach, shaping both materials and engineering around a mixed concept.

Two pressurised sections accommodated the crew, with two rear gunners now included in the aft compartment to share the tail-gun responsibilities. Aircraft 88 incorporated three remote-control turrets each with two cannon, and a fixed, forward-firing cannon on the starboard side of the nose. The arrangement of the defensive armament was superior

to other aircraft of the period, with optional Topaz or Argon ranging radar.

The landing gear arrangement now included twin wheels on the forward strut to reduce vibration, shimmying and lateral oscillations, making this the first Russian aircraft to incorporate such a feature. Reminiscent of the Vickers Valiant B.2 but developed without reference to that British bomber, the main gear still retracted backwards and the tail incorporated a braking parachute.

In the interests of achieving early operational deployment and availability as the first true nuclear-capable Russian bomber, the overall design philosophy required the use of existing and proven materials and processes. The schedule moved quickly, a full set of blueprints following construction of the prototype between February 1951 and January 1952 with a plan to move it to the flight test centre at the Gromov airfield near Zhukovsky, where it arrived on 25 January 1952. Meanwhile, a static test article was prepared and delivered to TsAGI. Most of that year was then spent determining the structural strength of the aircraft.

Taxi tests began on 24 April 1952 with the first flight taking place three days later, N. S. Rybko flying the prototype for 12 minutes. In all, 46 flights had been made by 29 October accumulating 72 hours and

A successful combination of aerodynamically efficient swept wing and credible performance, the Tu-16 was Russia's first jet-powered strategic bomber with conventional or nuclear capability. (Author's collection)

12 minutes, during which the prototype demonstrated a maximum speed of 1,020km/h (634mph) – higher than the specified requirement. But even without all the necessary in-service equipment fitted the aircraft was heavier than planned, coming in with a take-off weight of 77,350kg (170,556lb) versus the projected 64,000kg (141,120lb).

The extra weight was due to additional margins of safety that had been built in – structures being made stronger and heavier than they really needed to be. At this time, Stalin was returning to an excessive paranoia over malpractice, deception against the state and a suspicion that managers and bosses were siphoning of government funds for personal gain.

Failure – for example, the failure of a major defence project such as a jet bomber prototype – was likely to result in severe consequences. An overcautious approach to risk mitigation therefore prevailed.

Notes and calculations from test engineers had indicated that the overweight first prototype would at least fly and do it sufficiently well to allay any fear of retribution via the ideological watchdogs reporting

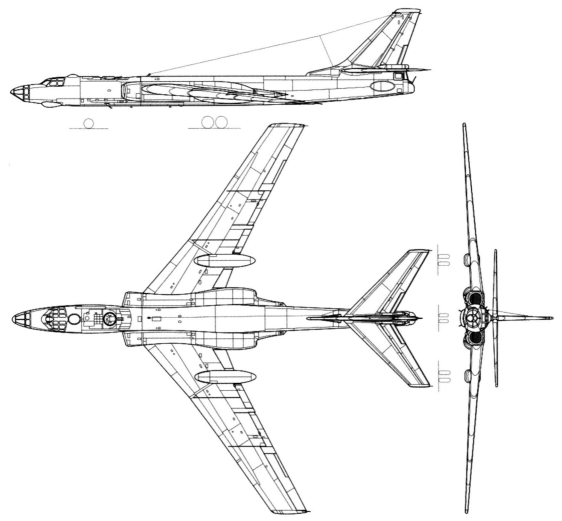

A three-view drawing of the Tu-16 with its sleek profile, pronounced 'area-rule' and teardrop main gear housings on the inboard wing sections. (Kaboldy)

With the NATO code name Badger, the Tu-16 was developed into many variants, including this reconnaissance model (Tu-16R) showing tail armament. (Author's collection)

A navalised Tu-16K10 adapted to carry cruise missiles. (DOD)

to the Kremlin. It must be remembered that even at this date, because of their unique specialities some engineers were still being released from gulags to work on defence projects.

In a directive of 10 July 1952 Tupolev was instructed to make preparations for serial production of Aircraft 88 and that it would be designated Tu-16, that it would receive the codename Topaz and that deliveries should commence in July 1953. It came as no surprise that the air ministry was impressed with the aircraft's rated performance, given that it had a range of 4,390km (2,728 miles) carrying a 9000kg (19,845lb) bombload – the weight of a Soviet A-bomb. Used as a nuclear bomber, it would have to survive a nuclear flash and air blast and the exterior surface of the Tu-16 was therefore finished with that in mind.

Despite its overweight condition, the first prototype Tu-16 was submitted for acceptance trials which began on 13 November 1952. A serious weight-reduction programme then began for the second prototype. Work focused on lightening non-stressed structural assemblies, redesigning joints and fasteners in the stressed components and changing materials. Moreover, a limitation on speed up to an altitude of 6,250m (20,500ft) reduced the maximum aerodynamic pressure and stress on the structure. Some delay ensued in getting blueprints for the lightened version ready and, risking his reputation, Tupolev ordered that version into production rather than the heavyweight design. All the necessary drawings were available by the end of 1952 but with a consequent delay in production until October 1953. Fast-tracking the process without going through the formal procedures came at a cost to Dmitriy Markov, the engineer responsible for lightening the aircraft, however. He was subjected to a formal public dressing down and had a notice of disapproval placed in his employment record. But his work provided an impressive aircraft and cut time in the certification cycle.

The lightweight Tu-16 second prototype, the 88/2, flew for the first time on 6 April 1953 and Tupolev completed its tests on 12 September. After a series of trials to determine the parameters for the pilot's notes, the 88/2 was cleared as the production model. Much more development lay ahead and over time more than a dozen variants of the Tu-16 would emerge. The initial production Tu-16 made its first public appearance at the 1954 May Day parade and again at the 1955 Tushino air display. None of these were yet able to actually carry nuclear weapons but that capability came with the Tu-16A, of which 453 would be built.

The Strategic Jet Bomber

The incentive for Russia to have a long-range, jet-powered strategic bomber in sufficient numbers to threaten the West originated with Stalin's perception that his country was under threat from attack. Fuel for that came from three separate directions.

The first was the consistent assertion from high-ranking German officers captured at the end of the war that they expected the British and the Americans to join with their depleted forces to press forward to expel Russian troops from Eastern Europe and to invade the USSR. However naive and incredulous that sounds today, to the ears of a paranoid autocrat it was noteworthy. Second, Stalin was aware that in April 1945 the then British Prime Minister Winston Churchill had asked the War Department to raise plans for a combined ground and air offensive against the USSR, should some form of military action be required by political events in Eastern Europe. Known as Operation Unthinkable, it was stimulated by Churchill's fear that the Russians would occupy Greece and unseat what he considered to be the foundation of Western democracy, however subjective an interpretation of history that was.

The final conclusion of the report handed to Churchill on 8 June 1945 was that such an operation would rapidly escalate into World War 3, although the successful detonation of the first atomic bomb five weeks later added plausibility to his belief that this would give the West incredible leverage over the numerical superiority of the Red Army. Stalin became

Egypt received 30 Tu-16 variants mostly for cruise missile or anti-radar use with weapons also provided by Russia. Two are seen here during the 1980 exercise Operation Bright Star. (DOD)

An F-16A of the Royal Norwegian Air Force 'escorts' a Tu-16 away from national airspace. (Author's collection)

aware of this report through informants working for the British government and it alone did nothing to dilute concerns when it specifically called for the use of German army and SS troops to bolster allied forces in any campaign against Russia.

Third, soon after the defeat of Japan the United States recognised the need for demobilisation and rapid conversion of a wartime economy into a domestic consumer marketplace. At the end of the conflict America had 12.1 million men and women in uniform, yet by June 1946 only 2.5 million remained in service. With not a little pressure from the British, who absolved the Americans of any moral reluctance to rely on nuclear weapons rather than massed armed forces, a rapid evolution toward the concept of massive atomic retaliation began to unfold.

Accepting this, in 1946 a secret US policy document began circulating under the code name Pincher as a strategy for engaging any Soviet incursion beyond the borders in Europe defined at the Yalta conference of February 1945. This was a defensive planning solution, as was a further study, Broiler, in 1947 which estimated the Russians could mobilise 245 divisions and achieve technological parity with the West including the use of nuclear weapons by 1952 – a prescient forecast, two years before Russia detonated its first A-bomb.

Mobilisation for war under Broiler stated the need for a major strategic offensive, with 34 A-bombs dropped on 24 Russian cities including seven on Moscow. In reality there were far fewer than 25 of the assumed total of 100 such bombs available, most of which existed only as components requiring assembly over several days. In the first few years after the end of the Second World War US atomic weapons programmes were anything but robust. The operational deployment of A-bombs came slowly, frequently with great confusion and uncertainty among service personnel and technicians not adequately prepared for their use. Nevertheless, the plans kept on coming.

Broiler was followed in 1948 by Halfmoon, renamed Fleetwood, which became the first war-

fighting policy document to fully integrate the use of atomic weapons in any future conflict. At the turn of the year it morphed into Trojan, in which it was estimated that 133 atomic bombs would be dropped on Russian cities. This in turn evolved into Offtackle, originating through a document from General Dwight D. Eisenhower, then chairman of the Joint Chiefs of Staff, calling for 292 A-bombs to completely destroy 85% of Russian industry. The belief that the threat of all-out atomic retribution would supplant the need for conventional armed forces would dominate the Eisenhower presidential years between 1953 and 1961.

Offtackle quickly led to Operation Dropshot, a 1949 plan for all-out war with the Soviet Union, triggering an escalation of intent from the US Strategic Air Command (SAC), custodian of the nation's nuclear attack instrument under the US Air Force. The opportunities afforded by these highly detailed plans were engaged by SAC commander General Curtis LeMay who consistently throughout his service career verbally endorsed the notion of a pre-emptive strike on the USSR. In 1954 he would tell a pilot who was shot at during an overflight of Russian airspace: "…if we do this overflight right, (maybe) we can get World War III started". Two years later LeMay began a round-the-clock full alert for SAC units.

If not in detail, all these developments were known to the Russians and unsurprisingly fuelled Stalin's concern over threats to the USSR, encouraging haste in the development of reciprocal atomic forces and urgency in developing ways to strike the United States and its Western allies. When the war in Korea began on 25 June 1950, it convinced the communist regimes in Russia and China that they were being challenged by the expanding capabilities of Western countries. It threatened China's hegemonic and long-term strategies for expansion and for a brief period united the Chinese political struggle with that of the Soviet Union.

Therefore, as early as 1947-49 the Soviet leadership was pushing for a strategic bomber capable of threatening airspace which for that period was largely dominated by American air power. In order to take any future conflict deep into the continental United States, the Russians needed a long-range jet bomber capable of carrying nuclear weapons. The only credible means of achieving that was the aging Tu-4.

The days of the piston-engine bomber had gone and the demise of that powerplant was rapid in the United States, with the B-29/B-50 generation and the post-war B-36 now on the way out. Even the B-35 flying wing could not survive and its jet-powered successor, the flying-wing YB-49 was similarly redundant. From the Soviet perspective, as noted previously, the early stages of the Korean War had vindicated the need for a fast, long-range bomber.

The Tu-16 was impressive but still lacked the range for strategic bombing missions against the United States. While it was being worked on, another Soviet designer was working in parallel on a much more ambitious project.

Back in Favour

Throughout his time at the Ministry Aviation Institute, Vladimir Myasishchev had worked with

TsAGI to study the challenges inherent in designing a high-speed intercontinental bomber and, with the help of his colleague Nazarov, drew up a concept with high aspect ratio, sweptback wings and jet engines. TsAGI was interested and this triggered a feasibility study for a strategichesky dahl'ny bombardirovschchik (strategic long-range bomber), or SDB. Although still employed at the MAI, Myasishchev could never be accused of thinking small – his preferred layout involved a high mounted, swept-wing configuration with four AMRD-03 turbojets, a take-off weight of 110,000kg (242,504lb) and a maximum bomb load of 20,000kg (44,092lb). With a 5,000kg (11,023lb) bomb load, range was calculated to be 12,000km (7,458 miles).

Support for his SDB put Myasishchev back in favour and, based on his earlier reputation, re-established him within the pantheon of Soviet airframe design teams, approval being given to proceed with his SDB concept under a directive of 24 March 1951. This alone attracted a wide range of new graduates to OKB-23 and support for the project came from

The Myasishchev M-4 was an advanced strategic bomber employing a range of materials and manufacturing processes new to the Russian aircraft industry. (Yefim Gordon via Tony Buttler)

The prototype M-4 made its first flight in January 1953. (Yefim Gordon via Tony Buttler)

the highest levels, for the real and imagined reasons discussed previously. When OKB-23 reopened it was located at Fili, then a suburb of Moscow but now totally embraced within the environs of the capital.

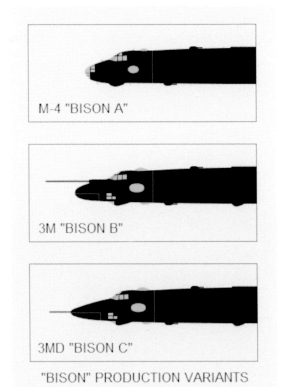

M-4 "BISON A"

3M "BISON B"

3MD "BISON C"

"BISON" PRODUCTION VARIANTS

Bearing the NATO code name Bison, the M-4 had several nose changes as shown here. (Greg Goebel)

Myasishchev called the project the VM-25 but it would eventually be redesignated M-4.

Project design was under the control of Leonid Selyakov and four months were allowed for the first draft. Several iterations of the original design were proposed, first with straight wings before reverting to the swept configuration, finally with engines placed in underwing pods, two per side in a common nacelle. After review a further configuration had eight TV-2F turboprop engines, each driving eight-blade, contra-rotating propellers. Mounted in tandem, the forward engines powered tractor propellers while the aft engines powered pusher propellers behind the wing trailing edge.In yet further revision, a swept-wing design featured six Lyulka turbojets, four buried in the wing roots and two on outboard underwing nacelles but this significantly increased the weight, which had a negative impact on predicted performance. The next iteration, the seventh by now, took the same design and mounted four AMRD-03 turbojet engines in the wing roots, marginally shaving off weight which had by now grown considerably beyond original expectations. The next design option was prepared with slightly shorter wings and a maximum take-off weight of 186,000kg (410,053lb) but engine choices narrowed to AL-5s or AMRD-03s.

The largest bomber yet to grace Soviet drawing boards, the M-4 brought unique challenges with materials and manufacturing techniques. Several specialist engineering bureaus were put to work developing new light alloys and heat-treatment furnaces were developed to fabricate large components. To reduce weight, large duralumin panels replaced conventional alloys sheets of small area so as to reduce the number of fastenings and connectors needed. The definitive prototype drawings were ready by 1 April 1952.

Great secrecy surrounded all this activity and the West had no indication from any of its intelligence services that a jet bomber of this size and capability was under development. For their part, the Russians had full knowledge of the Boeing B-52, which would

An M-4 at Ukrainka air base displays the acute nose-high pitch angle at rest on its tandem landing gear. (Boris Vasiljev)

Development work on the Myasishchev M-4 spawned the M-28/2M, with its engines in underwing nacelles, rather than built into the wings. The full-scale mock-up seen here. (Yefim Gordon via Tony Buttler)

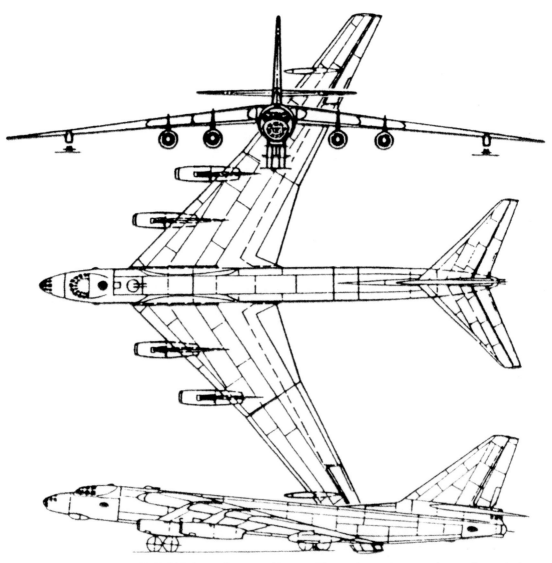

A three-view drawing of the M-28/2M shows the general layout with very large wing area, four pod mounted turbojet engines and a tandem landing gear with outrigger stabilisers. (Yefim Gordon via Tony Buttler)

make its first flight two weeks later. Contemporary documents and memoirs written long after these events speak of fears that NATO and the Western alliance would soon pose a major threat to Russia and the security of the Soviet state. The very existence of the B-47 and the B-52 brought accelerated plans for getting the M-4 into production.

Preparations for flight tests moved quickly, with the roll-out of the first prototype in December 1952,

after which it was dismantled and taken downriver to Zhukovsky. The first flight took place on 20 January 1953 but a range of modifications and changes were required, the schedule impacted to some degree by production of the Il-28. Acceptance trials did not begin until 4 May 1954, with an appearance at the May Day parade taking the visiting dignitaries and military attaches completely by surprise. Passing over the heads of the watching crowds, the

U-2 reconnaissance overflights of Soviet territory during the late 1950s marked a concerted effort to define the shape and size of Russia's nuclear weapons development programme amid US suspicion of a missile gap. (USAF)

prototype was escorted by four MiG-17 fighters. NATO code named the new bomber Bison. After displaying the M-4 in public and to the world, state trials were completed on 5 August 1954 but some shortcomings were apparent and the Air Force began to question the aircraft's suitability. With a full bomb load, maximum range was 6,500km (4,040 miles) or 9,800km (6,090 miles) with a 5,000kg (11,020lb) load. This was not quite the intercontinental bomber envisaged and a range of technical issues were revealed in the state examination of flight test results and engineering analysis.

However, on 3 July 1955 a further display of air power at Tushino worried the Americans a great deal

as they saw what they believed to be 28 M-4 bombers fly over. Former Secretary of the Air Force and a Missouri Democrat, Stuart Symington raised deep concerns that Russia had in production a long-range jet bomber capable of dropping nuclear weapons (he believed) on the United States. This triggered a major expansion of B-52 production, increasing output by 35%. Thus began the 'bomber-gap' myth.

What the Americans had actually seen was the first 10 aircraft fly around in a loop and pass over Moscow a second time, followed by eight different aircraft. Intelligence estimates, based on one U-2 spy flight over an airfield near Leningrad housing the entire complement of 30 M-4s, forecast a total fleet of

A line-up of Russian Tu-16s. More than 1,500 examples were built and the Chinese bought more than 230, badged as the H-6 of which about 176 remain in service today as China's only strategic bomber. (Author's collection)

600 such bombers within a decade. The production estimate was based on multiplication of that total over every Soviet airfield capable of operating an M-4 type aircraft.

Such was the intensity of the race for supremacy that 1954 and 1955 were pivotal years in which each side sought ways to outclass the other in nuclear strike potential. In the United States the decision had been made to develop an Intercontinental Ballistic Missile (ICBM) which would emerge as Atlas, deployed from 1959. An alternative design, Titan, wasn't far behind. In Russia, Sergey Korolev had been designing an ICBM since 1953 but progress was slow and few believed that it would be an effective system until flight tests began in 1957.

The Soviet air force was convinced that the only effective way to take the fight to the United States would be through a force of crewed bombers. It was a viewpoint mirrored by sentiment in the USA, where the Air Force diehards refused to accept that push-button warfare could ever supplant piloted aircraft. In the United States, the Air Force would take control of long-range rockets, including ICBMs, and they would be assigned to SAC from the outset, the Navy taking control of the Submarine Launched Ballistic Missile (SLBM) programme with Polaris.

But this would all come later. In the mid-1950s, as both superpowers sought to out-gun each other, America was shocked by the apparent surge in the deployment of Soviet jet bombers capable of striking the US and landing at a friendly base before returning home. The reality was that the Russians had no such capability and they knew it. The recognition by the Soviet leadership that they were still behind the technological and numerical superiority of intercontinental bombers operated by the US Air Force put urgency into preparations for a new generation of aircraft, realistically capable of surviving in a major conflict.

CHAPTER 4

IN SEARCH OF THE SUPERSONIC BOMBER

Myasishchev's M-4 was not the delivery platform it was designed to be and it would end up serving largely as a maritime reconnaissance aircraft, while the Air Force still sought a truly intercontinental bomber.

By now it appeared that there were two possible routes to the development of such an aircraft: using turboprop engines for a fuel-efficient, long-range subsonic bomber or using turbojets for a transonic/supersonic aircraft. The prospect of a supersonic bomber was particularly daunting, with technological leaps required for both materials and engines, it seemed essential to press for exactly that. Indeed, it quickly became apparent to the Soviets that the United States had already making substantial progress in this area. American trade journal *Aviation Week*, in its 8 December 1952 issue, published details of the Convair B-58 Hustler designed for Mach 2. It would be flying within five years and the speed of that development served to underline the differences between commercial companies in the West and the top-down system of control in the Soviet Union.

As related earlier, in Russia the development of jet and turbojet engines had a sluggish start, an initial use of Nene and Derwent engines going some way to plugging the gap. In many ways the MiG-15's performance during the Korean War of 1950-1953 had given a false impression of Soviet progress and it would be some time before this was realised by the West. Meanwhile, additional resources were ploughed into research, development and testing of more powerful, indigenously developed, engines.

Ilyushin, Myasishchev and Tupolev, the three design bureaus with experience in building large aircraft, came up with a range of proposals to provide a truly transonic/supersonic capability. Each would seek to provide a suitable bomber based on the more powerful engines that were gradually emerging from

Convair's B-58 Hustler was known to the Soviets as early as 1952 – long before it entered service – thanks to the laissez-faire attitude of American aviation trade journals to secrecy. (USAF)

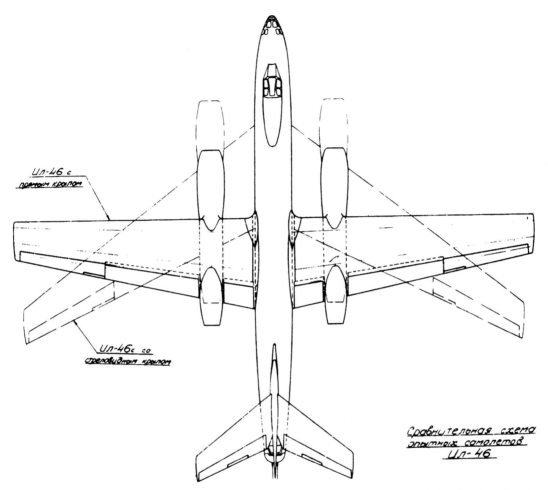

Ил-46 с
прямым крылом

Ил-46с со
стреловидным крылом

Сравнительная схема
опытных самолетов
Ил-46

In pursuit of a high-altitude, medium-range bomber the Ilyushin Il-46 began life as a straight-wing aircraft and was developed into the Il-46S with swept wings. It never flew. (Yefim Gordon via Tony Buttler

tests. The Council of Ministers had this requirement as a priority and all three design bureaus were encouraged to come up with concepts. That informed a directive issued on 29 December 1952 calling for Ilyushin to develop the Il-54.

The Il-54 was required to provide a dash speed of Mach 1.15 at 4,750m (15,584ft), demonstrate a range of 2,200-2,500km (1,367-1,554 miles) and to have prototypes ready for state acceptance trials in mid-1954. As had been so common with earlier concept proposals, a wide range of different configurations were examined. When Sergey Ilyushin gave the recommended concept his approval on 23 March

1953, it had a slender fuselage supporting swept wings at the mid-fuselage position, a swept T-shape tail and a three-man crew. Defensive armament followed the same general layout as that for the Il-28 with a tricycle landing gear, the main legs rotating forward and turning through 90 degrees into wing-root wells.

Ilyushin chose two TRD-1 (AL-7), axial-flow turbojets not by choice but availability, each placed on the fuselage above the wing root trailing edge. Satisfying the requirement, the design team estimated the Il-54 to have a top speed of 1,200km/h (746mph), or 1,255km/h (780mph) with an unspecified boost

Ilyushin further developed the transonic bomber concept from the Il-46S to the Il-54 which made its first flight in April 1955 but it never entered production. (Yefim Gordon via Tony Buttler)

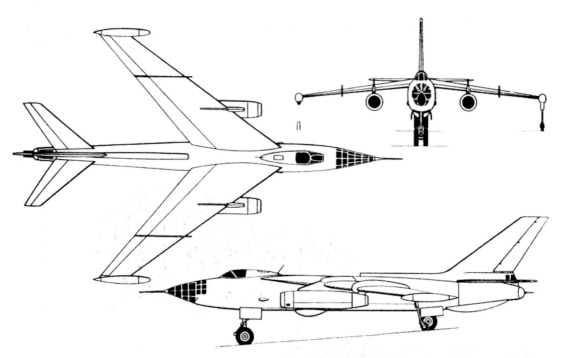

A three-view arrangement drawing of the Il-54, ultimate evolved configuration of the original Il-28. (Author's collection)

to the engines. With drop tanks it would have, said Ilyushin, a range of 2,750km (1,709 miles). The bureau gambled on the Lyulka engine being available; it was after all a contemporary of the Il-54 and without a proven record.

Frequently in the inspection of new aircraft concepts, minor changes cascade throughout the entire design to doom it to obscurity and that occurred when the Air Force objected to the landing gear as being inappropriate for use on dirt tracks. Larger wheels were needed and they could not be contained within the depth of the wings. Ilyushin therefore presented a revised design on 16 November. Now the wings were high-set and swept to 55 degrees at the leading edge with two wing fences; there was a low horizontal tailplane and the engines had been relocated to underwing pylon mounts for reduced drag. A bicycle landing gear was now fitted, with a small outrigger wheel at each wingtip.

This design moved rapidly into prototyping and the first flight of the Il-54 took place on 3 April 1955 followed by a second aircraft which joined the flight test programme in early 1956. But there were a few minor technical issues including the precise design and configuration of the landing gear which on one occasion caused the pilot to lose control on touchdown, damaging the airframe. The second aircraft introduced the AL-7F engines with an afterburner thrust of 98,000N (22,046lb) but the design and the concept would soon fall by the wayside.

The Il-54 was scheduled to appear at the 1956 Tushino air show but that was cancelled on 30 June. It was, however, displayed to a visiting delegation from the United States at the Kubinka air base just west of Moscow. Delegates saw that it was a tactical bomber and it was later given the name Blowlamp in the NATO lexicon of Soviet military types. Ilyushin had plans for a fully supersonic bomber project too and submitted them to the government. The ministry issued a directive on 28 March 1956 for its development as the Il-56, specifying a maximum speed of up to Mach 1.9 and a bomb load of 2,000kg (4,410lb) and with a maximum loaded weight no greater than 23,000kg

(52,920lb). Engine options included a single AL-7F or two of the new Mikulin AM-011s with afterburner and the latter won out. The AM-011 was the first twin-spool turbojet produced in Russia. With a thrust of 60,600N (13,635lb), it powered the Yakovlev Yak-25RV high-altitude reconnaissance aircraft.

The Il-56 was a high-wing monoplane, with a leading edge sweep of 45 degrees or 55 degrees

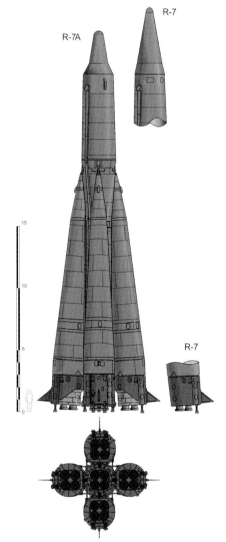

Russia's efforts to design and build a penetrating long-range bomber suffered when funds were diverted to Sergei Korolev's 8K71 (R7 Semyorka) ICBM. (Heriberto Arribas Abato)

depending on the preferred version, a high-set tailplane and a bicycle landing gear. The engines were located side-by-side with serpentine ducts, the intakes being located on the top of the fuselage and at the mid-wing position. It went no further than the drawing board though, and

by mid-1956 both the Il-54 and the Il-56 had been cancelled. Ilyushin was informed that he would no longer be developing manned aircraft but switching to cruise missiles.

This was when the Soviet rocket programmes were beginning to show real promise and Korolev was only a few months away from test launches with his R-7 Semyorka ICBM. Stalin had been dead for three years and paranoia had given way to pragmatism, a reality concerning the challenges faced as well as emerging opportunities. Few had been convinced by Korolev's claims concerning his rocket design but that was now put aside as the first test flights neared. The bomber programme would have to pass rigorous new standards with requirements shaped by the new mix of manned aircraft and a range of tactical and strategic rockets. Confidence in the rocket had been bolstered by the successful development of the R-11 Zemlya ballistic missile which first flew on 18 April 1953, entering production that December 1953. It would achieve notoriety under the NATO name Scud.

Seeking Speed

While working on the M-4 in 1952, Myasishchev started developing a series of proposals in parallel to those from Ilyushin for a transonic/supersonic bomber. Resources were stretched because the workforce was still engaged in preparing variants of the M-4. TsAGI was involved from the outset and worked up a range of concepts with Myasishchev under the designation M-30, balancing the weight introduced by a thin wing for high performance with the deficit in range that this incurred.

Based on wind tunnel results, a wing with a sweep of 55 degrees was selected and the first major design concept, the M-31, had a thickness ratio of 6% which required comparatively thick skins. Because of this,

Preoccupation with rockets produced a highly exportable battlefield/theatre missile, the Scud series attracting Kremlin support for comparatively low cost but taking further funds from manned aircraft. (David Holt)

two Dobrynin VD-5 engines would be mounted under the wings on pylons with two in the wing roots. The VD-5 had a thrust of 128,000N (28,660lb).

The M-31 was then superseded by the M-32, which adopted a delta wing with a 60-degree leading edge sweep and a highly sweptback T-tail. Various arrangements were considered for the four turbojets but when submitted to the ministry in March 1953 it was determined to be incapable of the strategic bombing role. Myasishchev had been working on delta configurations since 1951 and the M-33 concept was designed for specific research into the properties and handling of such a configuration but it was never built.

The ministry and the Air Force wanted a strategic bomber with a range of 13,000km (8,080 miles) and supersonic capability but the aerodynamic designs of

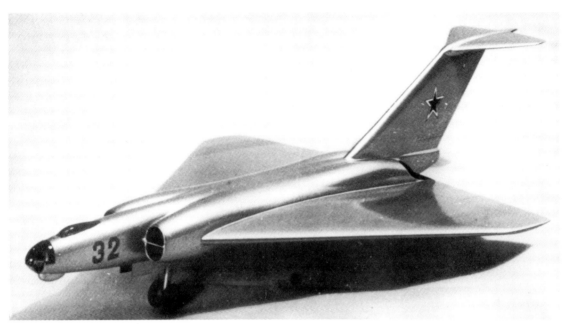

In parallel studies of the M-4, during 1952 Myasishichev proposed the delta-wing M-32 concept with a 60-degree leading edge sweep for improved supersonic performance. (John Hall via Tony Buttler)

the day and the available engines made this an almost impossible objective. Desperately searching for a solution, Myasishchev proposed a large aircraft with few crewmembers, minimum defensive armament, improved fuel consumption and the use of a purpose-built take-off trolley. Thus emerged as the M-34, with a single AM-13 or VD-7 engine hung on a pylon beneath each wing. It would have a maximum take-off weight of 80,000kg (176,367lb) which would have twice the range of the Tu-16 and 20% more speed.

Myasishchev solved the speed/range problem by shaping an operational flight profile to a cruise speed of 1,050km/h (656mph) and a dash over the target at 1,250km/h (777mph). This would conserve fuel and provide the mission requirement sought by the Air Force. There was capacity for a single 7,000kg (15,432lb) Kh-20 cruise missile carried in a recessed under-fuselage void with conventional bombs in the bomb bay and provision for two 23mm tail cannon.

The M-34 was soon cancelled however, leaving only Tupolev in the running for the first supersonic Russian bomber.

Tasked with this demanding requirement, Tupolev looked to an evolutionary development of Aircraft 88 (Tu-16), re-badged at the design bureau as Aircraft 98. Work officially began during January 1953 within the technical projects branch under S. M. Yeger, chief designer Markov and management of prototype construction under A. I. Zalesski. After discussion with Tupolev, the Council of Ministers issued a directive on 12 April 1954 defining requirements for a bomber capable of 1,300-1,400km/h (808-870mph) powered by two AL-7F turbojet engines, with a view to eventually swapping these for two AM-15s with a thrust of 111,700N (25,130lb), each AM-15 being essentially two paired AM-11s, or two VK-9s with a thrust of 117,600N (26,450lb). Initial development work was completed in July 1955, incorporating the new AM-23 cannon which could be operated using the PRS-1 Argon radar.

The first Aircraft 98 prototype took to the air on 7 September 1956 and flight trials progressed through the following year. The aircraft demonstrated a top speed of 1,238km/h (769mph) but never began state

Tupolev began an evolution toward the Tu-22 Blinder in 1953 with Aircraft 98 which made its first flight three years later. (Yefim Gordon via Tony Buttler)

trials due to reportedly numerous technological and manufacturing difficulties which could not easily be resolved. In particular, the Tupolev team were unable to raise the aerodynamic data they needed to refine its design. That had to come from the Central

Aerodynamic Institute with assistance from TsAGI. However, after Khrushchev summarily cancelled the project in 1958, Tupolev continued to progress the Aircraft 98 concept. It was adapted into the Tu-128 interceptor which was developed to serve in an

From Aircraft 98 came the Tu-128 interceptor, the largest aircraft in its class ever produced for operational use, the prototype being shown here. (Yefim Gordon via Tony Buttler)

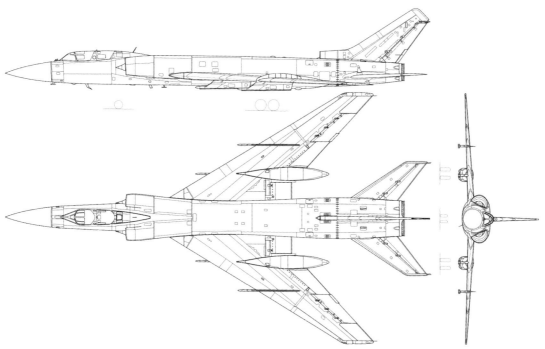

A three-view of the Tu-128 with its distinct area-rule design and aspects clearly evolved from Aircraft 98. (Kaboldy)

An ageing survivor, this Tu-128 carries the Bisnovat R-4 air-to-air missile of either radar-guided or infra-red homing capability. (Author's collection)

Never coming close to being a dogfighter, the Tu-128 was a difficult aircraft to fly, pilots receiving familiarisation training on the Tu-128UT. (Yefim Gordon via Tony Buttler)

air defence role on Russia's long frontier. With an area-ruled fuselage, it was the largest interceptor ever brought to operational status.

The Tu-128 had a length of 20.06m (98.6ft), a wingspan of 17.53m (57.5ft) and a maximum take-off weight of up to 43,700kg (96,342lb). It had a maximum speed of 1,929km/h (1,199mph) thanks to two AL-7F-2 afterburning turbojet engines. It also had a large internal fuel capacity offering a range of 1,560km (970 miles) and a service ceiling of 15,600m (51,200ft). This type was well suited to its purpose. And by the 1950s the Russian air defence forces

Equipped with four R-4 missiles, the Tu-128 was deployed to defend against the B-52 and other manned penetrating bombers. (Yefim Gordon via Tony Buttler)

This Tu-128UT is preserved at Monino outside Moscow. (Alexey Vlasov)

were capable of threatening intruders to a height of 15,240m (50,000ft) with 100mm anti-aircraft artillery (AAA), compared with 10,668m (35,000ft) using 85mm AAA during the previous decade.

Concern over the survivability of manned penetrating bombers contributed to a spate of proposals from Soviet design bureaus, some of which bordered on the bizarre. One of the more notable was the Tu-100 supersonic nuclear delivery concept, development of which began in 1953, not long after work began on Aircraft 98. The objective was to provide a very long range strike capability within the limitations of high fuel consumption with the turbojet engine.

Tupolev proposed a parasitic combination whereby a manned supersonic nuclear delivery system would be carried in a recessed position in the underbelly of a Tu-95, Tu-96 or Tu-108. The turboprop-powered carrier-plane would convey the vehicle to a range

of 6,500km (4,040 miles) before releasing it for independent flight. The vehicle would then fly a further distance of up to 1,000km (621 miles) before releasing its nuclear payload over the target and flying a further 500km (310 miles) at 1,500km/h (932mph). It would then cruise to a friendly base at 1,000km/h (621mph) and land.

This was a technologically advanced concept and would be a complex system to operate. Studies focused on the use of two afterburning Mikulin AM-11F turbojet engines for the Tu-100, a crew of two in a pressurised cabin and a bombload capacity of up to 1,500kg (3,307lb). A wide range of different configurations were proposed with the definitive configuration featuring air intakes beneath the cockpit and long ducts extending to the rear where the engines were located. Soloviev D-20 engines replaced the AIM-11Fs in 1955, providing a thrust of 58,847N (13,230lb) and giving the Tu-100 a top

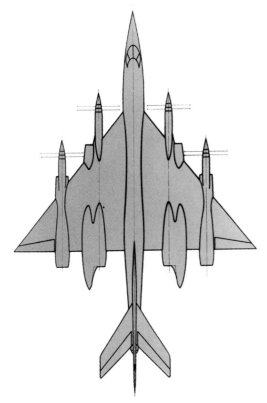

Tupolev responded to the requirement for a long-range strategic bomber with the series-100 design evolutions, the Tu-108 here proposed with P-8 turboprop engines. (Yefim Gordon via Tony Buttler)

A model of the Tu-96, an early attempt to perfect a high-altitude variant of the Tu-95 capable of reaching 17,000m (56,000ft) powered by augmented TV-16 engines and supporting a greater wing area.

speed of 1,800km/h (1,118mph). The project was shut down in 1958.

The search for a supersonic bomber, meanwhile, was simultaneously progressing along more conventional lines and Aircraft 98 also served as the starting point for a Tupolev design to replace the Tu-16, flying the same mission but at supersonic speed and with a shorter range.

Enter the Tu-22

Overlapping the chronological sequence of the Tu-100 concept's evolution, and powered by four VD-5 or VD-7 engines, Tupolev Aircraft 105 was the third contender, along with Ilyushin and Myasishchev, aiming to produce a viable supersonic bomber. It would have a streamlined fuselage and 45-degree

wing sweepback, this evolving into a 55-degree sweep and with engines outside the fuselage alongside the vertical tail. With help and support from TsAGI, Tupolev received a prototype contract for the design in December 1955. The now modified wing had a root thickness ratio of 9% tapering to 7% at the tip with a dihedral of -2.5 degrees. The wing sweep of the prototype design was 70 degrees at the forward leading edge changing to a 54 degrees at the tip.

Tupolev designed Aircraft 105's wing with integrally stiffened skins in rectangular strips with integral fuel tanks contained by spars at the 10% and 60% chord positions. Three additional spars were connected to a structural joint inserted at semi-span, bolted double ribs being set perpendicular to the rear spar. Two intermediate spars were positioned, the forward one blending in to the front spar at half span. There were no high lift devices at the fixed leading edge but the chord was increased at the trailing edge to accommodate the main landing gear.

Slotted flaps were attached to the trailing edge with ball-screw jacks extendible to 50 degrees for approach and landing. An outboard flap on each wing could be lowered to 30 degrees with a fully powered outboard aileron and a tab on an inner section. Anti-flutter probes extended the outer tips forward together with pitot heads.

A further derivative of the Aircraft 98 concept, Aircraft 105 had its two VD-7M turbojet engines placed on top of the tail either side of the vertical stabiliser. (Yefim Gordon via Tony Buttler)

Tupolev created a beautifully streamlined and remarkably low-drag fuselage profile with pronounced area-rule cross-section fabricated in six structural elements: the forward, conical nose section; the pressurised crew compartment for pilot and navigator/bomb-aimer; the centre fuselage section containing the forward landing gear, and two fuel tanks; the forward aft section housing fuel and the wing carry-through box structure; the rear aft section containing more fuel and the bomb bay below; and the tail section with more fuel and trimming tank, braking parachute, tailplane assembly and tail gun with ammunition magazines.

For longitudinal trim and pitch control, mounted low on the fuselage the horizontal tailplanes could act together or separately and had a leading edge sweep of 59 degrees. The vertical tail had an 80-degree sweep at the fuselage juncture, reduced to 60 degrees and supporting a single-piece rudder and tab. The tail surface area was large to compensate for the highly swept wing and to achieve optimum control over pitch and roll as well as general manoeuvrability and the overall impression was one of symmetrical design balancing performance with low drag characteristics.

Power came from the VD-7M turbojet, which had a dry thrust of 125,522N (28,220lb) and an afterburner thrust of 156,894N (35,273lb). Two were paired close together on top of the aft fuselage and with the exhaust nozzles either side of the vertical tailplane. This was optimal for maintaining control after losing one engine but it made life very difficult for maintenance crews who could only access the engines by using specially-designed trolleys and ladders.

The two Dobrynin VD-7M engines attached either side of a Tu-22PD Blinder's tail, with tail turret and radar clearly visible. This was a mid-air refuelling version of the Tu-22P electronic warfare variant. (Alex Beltyukov)

The Tu-22's remotely operated tail turret houses a 23mm R-23 cannon, here given scale by an engineer. (Igor Bubin)

The main landing gear had a wide track for stable landing characteristics, retracting inwards. The nose gear was taken straight from the Aircraft 98 design but strengthened and a steel-shod skid at the tail prevented damage on rotation. The capacious bomb bay was designed for a maximum load of 9,000kg (19,840lb) and could accommodate conventional, atomic or thermonuclear weapons but the aircraft was not designed for any external loads or stores. The only defensive armament was a tail turret equipped with two 23mm guns, each with 600 rounds.

The single prototype made its first flight on 21 June 1958 and a static test airframe was built, both of which were instrumental in a design revision known as Aircraft 105A. Additional refinements were made, the landing gear now retracting backwards into teardrop-shaped housings extending rearwards from the wing trailing edge. This allowed a further increase in the track width and that allowed designers to reduce the thickness of the wing root, reduce slightly the span and increase the area of the tail surfaces.

Reducing the wing thickness was key to achieving the required performance and the 105A was a considerable improvement on its predecessor with a much more pronounced area-rule applied to the wing/fuselage design. It first flew on

With wing fences added during development, the Tu-22 displays sleek lines indicative of its greatly improved aerodynamic efficiency over the Tu-16. (Bernhard Grohl)

The Tu-22U trainer version of the Blinder strategic bomber. (Pavel Adzhigildaev)

7 September 1959 at the hands of Yuri T. Alasheyev, the pilot who had also first flown the Tu-16.

This aircraft immediately began flight trials but crashed on 21 December during its seventh flight killing Alasheyev and the navigator I. Gavrilenko.

Only the radio operator K. Shcherbakov managed to eject safely. Caused by flutter, the crash showed handling problems and resulted in the design and installation of an all-flying horizontal tail powered by irreversible electro-hydraulic actuators serving both as

With full flaps, a Tu-22 comes in for a landing. (DOD)

trim and for longitudinal control. A pivot was placed at the 58% chord of the tailplane so that it could move up or down around the aft tailplane spar.

All of this resulted in the Tu-22B – the first serial production example of the type and the Soviet Union's first supersonic bomber.

The Tu-22B was a big aircraft, with a length of 41.6m (136.5ft) and a wingspan of 23.6m (77.5ft). It had a maximum loaded weight of 85,000kg (187,390lb) and a landing weight of 60,000kg (132,275lb). Maximum speed was 890km/h (550mph) at sea level and 1,510km/h (938mph), or Mach 1.45, at 12,000m (39,370ft) against a service ceiling of 11,700m (38,390ft). With a minimal bomb load of 3,000kg (6,615lb), the Tu-22B had a range of 5,850km (3,635 miles) which demonstrated the progress made over the previous five years in performance and operating capabilities.

Production got underway in mid-1960 when the first three were put through a gruelling sequence of test flights at Zhukovsky. The plan was to create five variants for specific applications. The Tu-22B made its first appearance to Western eyes during the 1961 Aviation Day parade where it was incorrectly assessed as a Myasishchev design. After some inappropriate and frivolous names – Bullshot, being deemed too rude and Beauty too complimentary – it was finally given the NATO code Blinder. Russian pilots liked the aircraft's handling qualities but had few words of praise for the cockpit, particularly the view through the heavy, angled windows. Pilot workload was high and it was consequently tiring to fly.

Despite its limited success as Russia's first operational supersonic bomber with provision for conventional or nuclear bombload, only 15 Tu-22Bs (known to NATO as Blinder-A) were built, formal acceptance into service following in September 1962. Nine aircraft had been on parade at the 1961 display but most Western observers, and those from pro-communist countries to which the Blinder would be sold, believed it to represent only some of the aircraft in service – adding further fuel to the bomber-gap myth perpetuated in America but infectiously reported elsewhere around the world. Along with satellites, big rockets and cosmonauts in orbit, the Blinder certainly played its part in persuading more than a few countries that Russia was the superpower of the future.

Authorised largely as a further development of the Tu-22's evolution towards a faster aircraft, Aircraft 106 filled the gap between the Tu-22 and its successor, the Tu-22M. Tupolev believed he could take the basic concept of the 105 and develop it into a Mach 2 bomber. Powered by two AM-17 or Dobrynin VD-9 engines with a thrust rating of 166,733N (37,485lb), it was projected to have a maximum speed of up to 1,800km/h (1,118mph), a range of 5,800km (3,604 miles) carrying a 3,000kg (6,615lb) bombload at an altitude of 16,000m (52,500ft) over the target. This was the requirement set by a directive from the Soviet Council of Ministers on 20 July 1954.

The project team were required to produce a definitive specification by February 1955, enabling

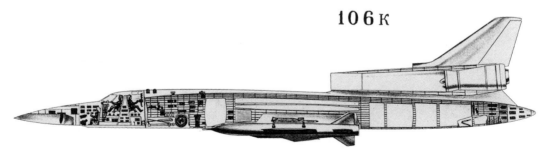

The Tu-106 profile view shows the recessed under-fuselage space for the Kh-22 missile which was designed for this aircraft but adapted for other bombers later. (Yefim Gordon via Tony Buttler)

a decision on further development the following month. If the project was approved, flight tests were to start in 1958. Where the 105 had morphed into the 105A, which had VD-7M engines, the 106 was similarly improved with NK-6 engines, producing a take-off thrust of 210,868N (47,407lb). In this period Russia was keen to develop an operational air-to-surface missile (ASM) capability. The subsonic Raduga KS-1 – more commonly known in the West as the AS-1 Kennel – became operational in 1953 and the Mikoyan K-10S, AS-2 Kipper appeared in 1961 with a range of up to 185km (115 miles), carried by Tu-16s in an under-fuselage position.

The directive of 17 April 1958 which authorised work on what would become the 105A (Tu-22) also formalised the 106 with the NK-6 engines. Those were further uprated to 215,772N (48,510lb) and raised the predicted maximum speed to 2,000km/h (1,243mph). Range dipped to 3,000km (1,864 miles) carrying a 3,000kg (6,615lb) bombload at maximum speed, or 6,000km (3,728 miles) at a subsonic 1,000km/h (620mph). Service ceiling was now 17,000m (55,777ft) over the target. Flight tests were to commence in 1960 and Tupolev believed that uprated NK-6 engines would eventually give the 106 a top speed of 2,500km/h (1,553mph) and a ceiling of 20,000m (65,620ft).

Delays to the Kh-22 nuclear ASM it was being designed to carry (see below) and further work priorities on the 105A/Tu-22 delayed progress but in 1960 Yeger's team got back to technical development of the concept. They looked at two development paths: the 106R for pure reconnaissance work and the 106K carrying the ASM. The ASM variant was further split into a proposed 106B, which had a refined fuselage, and the 106A with the engines moved to underwing locations. A succession of design options were examined, alternatives including three or four VD-19s or Tumansky R15B-300 turbojets, different wing shapes and even the incorporation of lift-engines located in the landing gear wells for reducing take-off runs. After five years of intensive work, a definitive 106 concept emerged sporting very thin wings with a

60-degree swept leading edge plus NK-6 engines – a configuration to be verified through flight tests using a Tu-95LL test aircraft. The 106 at this point had a calculated top speed of 2,200km/h (1,367mph), a subsonic range of 6,750km (4,194 miles), reducing to 4,000km (2,485 miles) when flown at a supersonic speed, and a ceiling of 30,000m (65,620ft). There would be three crew and no defensive armament – only electronic countermeasures.

Doubts about the viability of the 106 and the NK-6 engine began to grow and in 1964 Tupolev decided to quickly build a prototype. This was have been essentially a Tu-22 with NK-6 engines. However, Tupolev ran into strong opposition and Kuznetsov was struggling to get the NK-6 into a sufficiently viable stage of development for testing. In 1965 the bureau was told to stop work on the 106 and anything further involving the Tu-22. Some of the rationale for its demise was Tupolev's own fault, existing work which had emerged as the Aircraft 145 showing greater promise for what would become the Tu-22M.

Change of Use

Early in the Tu-22's development the Air Force planned for both reconnaissance and range-extension capabilities through in-flight refuelling and other techniques. As such, the type was cleared for development as the Tu-22R reconnaissance variant and changes were made to the interior of the bomb bay so it could carry electronic and optical equipment. Several cameras could be contained on a single pallet which would be installed in the forward section of the bay, photo-flash magazines being contained aft of the pallet. Following tests between 1960 and mid-1963, around 60 such aircraft were so configured, NATO code name Blinder-C.

The Tu-22RD was the designation applied to reconnaissance aircraft from 1962, the 'D' indicating Dalniya, or long range, capability with a refuelling probe. These aircraft also had the more powerful RD-7M-2 engine with a thrust of 161,800N (36,376lb). Further enhancements were

Equipped with a Kh-22 missile and refuelling probe, this Tu-22KD is seen at the Poltava Museum in Ukraine. (Author's collection)

grouped into the Tu-22RDM which appeared in 1975 and incorporated better cameras, infrared line-scan equipment and wider options for sensors and optical equipment. The Tu-22RDK derivative added a side-looking airborne radar (SLAR).

The most prolific variant was the Tu-22K standard production aircraft, aka Blinder-B. Around half of the more than 300 Blinders built were of this type, with deliveries from early 1965. This variant was more operationally flexible in that it could be rapidly switched between roles, the semi-recessed Kh-22 cruise missile being removed and a standard bomb bay installed. It was theoretically capable of also carrying a single Kh-22 under each wing but the weapon was too heavy for that to be practical.

The Kh-22 which was married to the Tu-22K had been under development since 1958 as an anti-ship missile. Known as Burya (Storm) to the Russians it

was designated AS-4 Kitchen by NATO and, along with the Blinder, at the time it was considered a long-range system. Built by A. Berezhnyak's Raduga group, which had shifted away from the Mikoyan OKB and become an independent group in 1957, the Kh-22 had an active radar guidance system and a selectable range of 80-330km (50-205 miles). A range of variants evolved over time with inertial guidance or active-radar homing capability for the terminal stage. By the late 1960s the Kh-22P anti-radiation missile would have homing capability for use against enemy radar. Paradoxically, the missile far outlived the Tu-22, eventually being configured for use against a wide range of land targets as well as aircraft carriers and battle groups with a nuclear or conventional warhead.

Recognisable by its larger radome bulge on the underside of the nose, to accommodate the Rubin-PN radar and its larger antenna, Blinder-B had a protracted introduction to service. It would not be fully operational until 1967 due to the complexity of work required to fully test the advanced electronics equipment it boasted.

Perhaps the most unusual variant was the Tu-22U (Blinder-D) trainer – which had a second, raised, cockpit behind the original one for an instructor but lacked defensive armament and was not combat capable. The final member of the original Tu-22 family was the Tu-22P (Blinder-E). Configured for electronic warfare in support of Tu-22K missile carriers and carrying a range of jammers and other countermeasures, this entered service in 1968.

Going Nuclear

Russia, like the United States, considered the possibility of fitting a bomber with its own, small, nuclear reactor. This would supply sufficient power to give the aircraft unprecedented range and endurance but would, as might be expected, cause a host of problems.

It was initially believed, during the 1950s, that such an aircraft could be operational by the second half of the 1970s. The principle was deceptively simple: the reactor would produce heat which would then, via a heat exchanger, power two jet engines – taking the place of their usual chemical fuel. This nuclear-powered bomber would conduct the same mission as that envisaged for the Tu-22 but it would be necessary to adopt a layout which shielded the crew from radiation. The proposed solution was to put the reactor in the rear fuselage and the crew in a heavily insulated forward fuselage section. Wingspan was to be 24.4m (80ft), fuselage length was 30.7m (100ft) and wing area was 170m² (1,829ft²).

The strategic bomber thus described was given the designation Tu-120 and the project was extended to encompass a possible low-level, tactical bomber designated Tu-132 and a large strategic bomber for which there is no known designation. This latter proposal had a wingspan of 30.6m (100ft), a fuselage length of 40.5m (132.8ft), a wing area of 320m² (3,444ft²) and a maximum take-off weight of 153,000kg (337,365lb). It would have been

powered by six Kuznetsov engines of which two were to be powered by the nuclear reactor. Research and development costs would have been astronomical and there were more practical means to achieve the same objective.

The surge in funding for ICBMs and SLBMs during the second half of the 1950s, and the burgeoning development of theatre and battlefield ballistic missiles, meant there was no money for such seemingly outlandish ideas. The concept of nuclear propulsion evaporated but the desire for a powerful, long-range supersonic bomber never went away.

After the distraction of bizarre and unworkable concepts such as the nuclear-powered bomber, Tupolev proposed a concept which it unofficially designated Tu-125. This was envisaged as a replacement for the Tu-22 and got the attention of Yeger's design team during 1958. The calculations involved were based on known aerodynamic principles and the required amount of power came from turbojet engines. Yeger defined the required minimum lift/drag ratio as 6:1 for supersonic flight and as much as 12:1 for subsonic flight. It would have a take-off weight of 124,000kg (273,240lb) and a total thrust output of 392,314N (88,200lb). Moreover, fuel efficiency would have to greatly exceed that of the Tu-22.

Yeger understood that operational requirements would push the Tu-125 to high cruising speeds at moderately low altitude and that brought concerns about temperature and stress on materials. Aluminium alloys were no longer plausible and blends of traditional materials with titanium alloys were considered. This generated a lot of discussion between Tupolev, TsAGI and various specialist metallurgical research institutes. Prolonged supersonic flight would necessitate the optimum aerodynamic properties and the kind of wing suitable for high speed flight was not conducive to operations into or out of most Soviet air bases.

Development started with the former 105A and 106 projects and

Yeger selected a canard configuration as optimum for high-speed flight, just as the Tupolev bureau

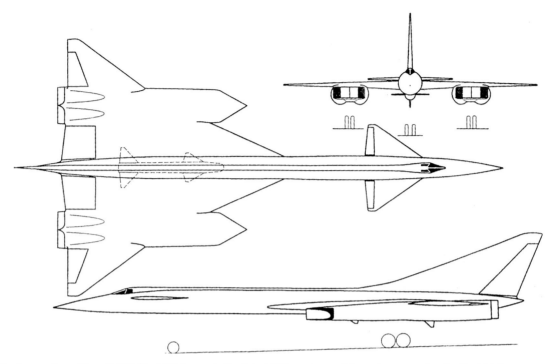

Design work on Aircraft 125 (Tu-125) began in the late 1950s as a possible replacement for the Tu-22 Blinder, this version powered by four engines in two nacelles with a single cruise missile in the under-fuselage bay. (Yefim Gordon via Tony Buttler)

would for the Tu-144 supersonic airliner. A large range of alternative configurations were examined and these merged with another design flow, the 135 strategic strike concept. But Yeger kept the Tu-125 requirement focused specifically on long-range penetration at high altitude and at supersonic speed against land or sea-based targets; the Russians were very aware of the large US carrier battle groups which became a cornerstone of power projection.

Had it been built, the Tu-125 would have been powered by two NK-6 or NK-10 turbojet engines which were at various times placed in the rear fuselage with intakes beneath the forward wing sections or in underwing nacelles. The delta-wing was to have extended forward root sections and there would be a prominent, large-area canard between the wing root and the nose. The design made liberal use of duralumin and titanium and was believed capable of 2,700km/h (1,678mph), a range of 6,000km (3,728

miles) and a ceiling of 25,000m (82,000ft). Subsonic range was calculated to extend to 9,000km (5,592 miles).

The Tu-22M and Tu-160 would emerge from these studies much later but the prevailing view now shifted from the manned penetrator to the concept of a platform for launching supersonic cruise weapons while remaining distant from the target. This was of interest to the Soviet government for two reasons.

First, the Kremlin saw that the United States was investing heavily in bases across Western Europe and the UK, either as staging posts or as deployment centres with tankers extending the range of bombers and strike aircraft. This actually made it easier to strike at US forces – formerly withdrawn to the continental United States – without having to cross the North Polar regions and down into North America. Not until the 1960s would the expanding Soviet ICBM and SLBM forces make it possible to threaten the continental US with an unstoppable deterrent. Second, the ability to threaten all of Western Europe became increasingly important in the Soviet view as a means of maintaining parity and reducing the risk of the pre-emptive war they feared. With the realisation that they would be facing advanced US air and land-based weapons by the end of the 1950s, the importance of tactical and theatre weapons to the Kremlin increased. This led directly to the burgeoning proposals for supersonic strike systems where survivability, not necessarily range, moved up the agenda.

The Tu-125 was quietly overtaken by other priority projects at the Tupolev factory, including the Tu-127 supersonic strike aircraft which had been under development as an idea since the beginning of 1958. Yeger's team drafted an outline concept for a two-seat, single-engine ASM carrier with a 55-degree swept wing, pronounced area-rule powered by a VD-7M turbojet fed by an air inlet on top of the fuselage. The requirement stipulated a maximum speed of 1,880km/h (1,168mph) at 11,000m (36,090ft), a 2,000kg 4,410lb) bombload and a supersonic range of up to 1,100km (683 miles) or 2,400km (1,490 miles) subsonic.

The Tu-127 was designed to be compatible with the P15 ASM, later designated SS-N-2 Styx by NATO. Designed from a requirement issued in 1958, the Raduga P-15 first appeared in 1960, primarily intended for shipboard deployment but with an air-to-surface role too. It was powered by a liquid propellant rocket motor boosted by a solid propellant rocket which gave it a maximum speed of Mach 0.95 and a range of 40km (25 miles). The P-15 was fast-tracked into production on the basis of lost cost and ease of assembly, upgraded variants remaining in widespread use today, but its selection for the proposed Tu-127 ensured it a broader, airborne application. The chunky missile was to have been carried within the weapons bay beneath the wing centre-section.

The Tu-127 led to a development identified as the Tu-129 but that was abandoned at a very early stage in favour of the Tu-135, which was brought about by a change in the structure of the manufacturing industry.

On 3 October 1960, the Council of Ministers informed Tupolev that Myasishchev's OKB-23 was to be merged with Vladimir Nikolayevich Chelomei's OKB-52 and that work on the M-56 missile-carrier was to be terminated. Tupolev was to proceed with its own proposal for that requirement and to consider a production schedule. Thus began another flurry of different design concepts and both Myasishchev and TsAGI were involved in the wide range of ideas examined over the next five years.

Composite Bombers

Myasishchev had already assembled a backlog of unsuccessful supersonic bomber designs including the M-50, which got as far as becoming a flying prototype and which many have hailed as the most outstanding aircraft of its time. Triggered by concerns over the emerging Convair B-58A Hustler in the United States, a Council of Ministers directive of 30 July 1954 for a composite-bomber of the same general layout as that of the US design set Myasishchev on the road to building the M-50. It evolved through a range of almost 40 different concepts before the bureau settled on an ambitious configuration which stretched the capabilities of the Soviet aircraft industry and challenged engineers to their limits.

The M-50 had a thin delta-wing layout with a highly swept tail, two engines being carried on underwing pylons and two more at the wingtips. The design was so complex and demanding that it took nearly five years to complete. New types of steel alloy were researched and developed, completely new manufacturing techniques being required for the panels and large stringers. Difficulties were encountered with finding ways to accommodate the large amount of fuel required and a fuel-displacement management system was essential for maintaining the centre of gravity as the weight shifted. By keeping the crew down to just two, automatic control systems were made essential and Myasishchev developed unique electronic systems to that end.

With design work completed in 1955, a mock-up was prepared. A formal inspection the following July

The Myasishchev M-50 was a desperate attempt to produce a supersonic bomber but only one was built and the project failed, despite the rash interpretation of the US technical press that it was a nuclear-powered bomber! (Yefim Gordon via Tony Buttler)

This impressive view of the M-50 shows the nose-high static attitude on its tandem landing gear with four turbojet engines. (Alex Beltyukov/RuSpotters Team)

An early design concept for the M-50 with engines mounted on pillars attached to the aft fuselage. (via Tony Buttler)

found, to the manufacturer's surprise, that it failed on predicted range and on the long take-off run which was said to require RATOG to get it into the air. Moreover, the commissioning inspectorate said it had an unacceptable vulnerability to enemy defences in a subsonic, low-altitude profile. Nevertheless, despite it requiring two mid-air refuelling passes to reach its target, the OKB was given authority to build two prototypes to a slightly amended design. With two non-afterburning VD-7A engines on the wingtips and two on short pylons under the wings, each delivering a thrust of 107,800N (24,250lb), the first prototype M-50A took to the sky on 27 October 1959.

It had been hoped to replace the two inner engines with the afterburning VD-7MA engines delivering a thrust of 156,800N (36,273lb) but these were only ever used for take-off. The added thrust was intended to give the M-50A a top speed of Mach 1.7 but reheat was only used for take-off. Far too complex for even the test crew to handle effectively and certainly unsuitable for any operational role, both this and the successor evolution, the M-52, were cancelled in 1960. The M-50A was, however, displayed at the 1961 Tushino air display shortly after the Myasishchev OKB had been shut down.

The story does not end there. Two more highly ambitious projects were developed before OKB-23 was shut down – the M-54 and the M-56. If any

concept from Soviet design bureau came closest in performance to the B-58A Hustler it was the M-54, which would have been powered by four RD-16-17 turbojet engines, delivering a thrust of 181,300N (40,785lb), on pylons beneath a large delta wing but no tail to save weight. In appearance it would have been dominated by the Kh-22 cruise missile carried as its single offensive load. Initially, the total weight of the Kh-22 was 5,700kg (12,568lb) for a conventional or 330KT nuclear warhead. The M-54 only got as far as wind tunnel tests before it was superseded by the M-56, which had its origin back in 1957 as a spur off the M-52. The conceptual requirement looked to a speed of 3,200km/h (1,988mph), a ceiling of 20,000m (65,617ft) and a range of up to 16,000km (9,944 miles). It was conceived for two roles: the M-56K cruise missile launcher and the M-56R for dedicated reconnaissance duties.

With an expectation of service entry in the late 1960s, the M-56 dispensed with a tail for its all-delta configuration, which reduced the shift in the centre of lift from 28% to 15%, and adopted a canard for trim and longitudinal control. The canard would be moveable at subsonic speeds but fixed for supersonic flight, which moved the centre of lift forward, the elevons ensuring longitudinal control. Power was to be provided by four Kuznetsov NK-10B engines but the performance projected at the final stage of preliminary design fell a little short of expectations.

Approval for the M-56K was granted by the Council of Ministers on 31 May 1958 and an order was issued for four prototypes which would be powered by the RD-17-117F. Further studies led to two 1/25th scale models used for evaluating aerodynamic performance characteristics, where the engine arrangement was verified. There is disagreement as to whether a mock-up was actually built, aiming toward a first flight during the summer of 1963. However, other considerations fed in to the fate of this programme.

On 4 July 1960 the Scientific and Technical Committee (NTS) and the State Committee for Aircraft Development (GKAT) met in a wide ranging debate regarding the state of Soviet military preparedness for war. Under discussion was nothing short of the total balance between all existing and candidate strategic systems including ICBMs, SLBMs, manned penetrating bombers and cruise missile carriers. There was strong support for missiles but many attendees warned about the unreliability of ICBMs, so evident in the numerous test failures during this period.

By the date of the NTS/GKAT meeting, the M-56 had been revised yet again, now powered by six Klimov VK-15 engines with a thrust of 98,000N (22,050lb), a change brought about by the imminent cancellation of the NK-10B. The six engines were grouped in two banks of three integral to each outer wing section with delta-shaped tips outboard of those housings. The highly swept delta wing had the advantage of a modest compression lift akin to the XB-70A Valkyrie, with elevons on the trailing edge and a single vertical stabiliser added.

This was a very large aircraft, with a length of 44.25m (145.2ft), a wingspan of 27.16m (89.1ft), a top speed of 3,500km/h (2,175mph), a maximum range of 11,000km (6,837 miles) and a calculated ceiling of 25,000m (82,020ft). The cruise missile would itself add 2,000km (1,243 miles) to the range of the entire system. In the final proposed version, six afterburning RD17-117F engines each producing a thrust of 171,500N (38,580lb) would power the M-56K. It was an impractical behemoth in every sense, with a maximum loaded weight of 210,000kg (462,963lb), some 30,000kg (66,150lb) in excess of the maximum that the built Soviet runways of the day could physically support.

The Council of Ministers cancelled work on the M-56 in a directive dated 3 October 1960 but some additional work was conducted, using the study as the basis for research studies. Specifically, the Tumansky VK-15 version of the M-56 formed the basis for a derivative alternative configuration which was conducted alongside the mainstream M-56 and before its cancellation. The M-57 was an ambitious derivative expected to carry two Kh-22 SAMs.

A wind tunnel model of the twin-fin Tu-135 configuration with canards. (Yefim Gordon via Tony Buttler)

Cancellation of the advanced Myasishchev projects opened the path for Tupolev to begin work on the Tu-135 as a development of the Tu-127 and Tu-129, work on which had been underway since 1958. Much of this was in parallel with the M-56 requirement and is best considered in that regard. For two years activity proceeded at a languid pace until the M-56/M-57 designs were abandoned and Tupolev was given three months to absorb the Myasishchev work and come up with a long-range, supersonic project capable of conducting deep-strike work and reconnaissance.

Design work was led by S. M. Egera but in 1962 the Myasishchev design leader L. L. Selvakovka was transferred to Tupolev, bringing knowledge and experience from the M-50 to the M-57 projects. A wide range of engines were selected as optional for the Tu-135 and even a nuclear plant was considered, albeit only briefly. In general, driven by the thrust of each type, four to six engines were planned in a wide-range of configurations. A variety of wing arrangements were examined before a double-delta wing with variable sweep on the leading edge was chosen. There would be a single tail fin and twin engine nacelles on underwing pods. There was provision for a wide range of cruise and gravity bombs, both conventional and nuclear.

Duralumin was to be widely used in the airframe with thermal protection an essential prerequisite for

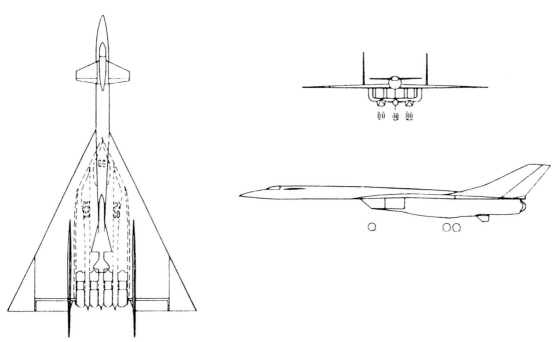

With a configuration similar to that of the XB-70 Valkyrie, this version of the Tu-135 would have had a constant delta wing, two fins and four engines grouped together in an underbody. (Yefim Gordon via Tony Buttler)

the skin; heat-resistant alloys and special materials being evaluated. The definitive design utilised NC-6 turbofan engines, with which the Tu-135 was calculated to achieve 3,000km/h (1,864mph). Some 10-20% of the flight distance could be conducted at Mach 2.82, a speed determined by the temperature

The Tu-135 went through a series of design iterations, this configuration displaying a cranked-arrow wing leading edge. (Yefim Gordon via Tony Buttler)

limits on usable materials. Its mission was to destroy aircraft carriers and large surface battle fleets as well as attacking harbours and logistical supply ports with cruise missiles, some of which would have a range of 500km (311 miles). For that it needed a range of 5,000km (3,108 miles).

The Tu-135 was also required to loiter on patrol for up to eight hours, 2,000km (1,243 miles) from base. On top of which it was required to operate from unpaved strips and low-grade runways. But the Tu-135 was also to carry air-to-air missiles for attacking enemy air transport and resupply aircraft, to harass logistical routes and to attack small, heavily defended strategic targets with cruise-type weapons or air-launch ballistic rockets. The Tu-135P reconnaissance version was expected to swap offensive equipment for optical and sensor packages, making it capable of electronic intelligence gathering and mapping.

Always with one eye on progress with the XB-70A Valkyrie, tweaks and changes to the design were a constant strain on finding a truly definitive configuration, dozens of different shapes and sizes being proposed. But eventually work on the project was suspended in favour of a Sukhoi development – the T-4.

Enter the Push-Button Era

Work on Sukhoi Project 100 (denoting the desired gross weight in tonnes), more commonly known as the T-4, began in September 1961 with the bureau's Oleg Samoilovich very much in charge of design.

The formal requirement for it had originated in the spring of 1962 as Tupolev was being given the task of developing the Tu-135 and Yakovlev the Yak-33. The real contest began when the Yak-33 was dismissed as being too small and incapable of meeting minimum requirements.

The T-4 was to have a range of up to 6,000km (3,726 miles) and a maximum speed of up to 3,200km/h (1,988mph), pushing the technological boundaries of the early 1960s. Weight and range were driven by the need for rough field operation and for deep strike, respectively; the maximum speed was constrained by the thermal properties of materials, as it had been for other supersonic bomber projects from Myasishchev and Tupolev.

A commission created by the Russian Air Force was assigned to conduct a detailed analysis of the Sukhoi

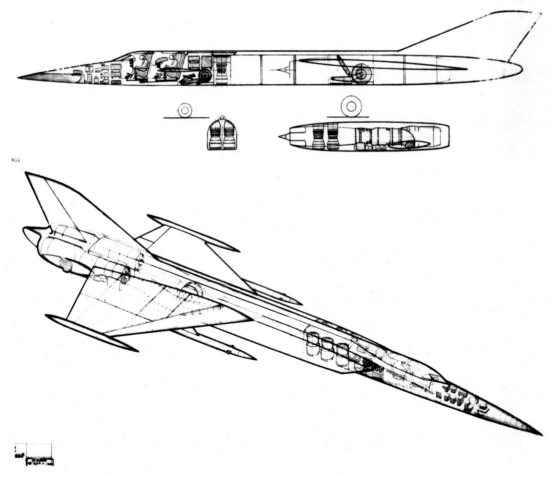

The supersonic VTOL Yak-33 never progressed beyond the design stage. Note the separate lift engines. (Yefim Gordon via Tony Buttler)

The Sukhoi 100/T-4 on view at Monino, a failed attempt to produce a Mach 3 strategic bomber fabricated in titanium and stainless steel. (Alan Wilson)

Powered by four Kolesev RD-36-41 afterburning turbojet engines, the T-4 never exceeded Mach 1.3 and exhausted considerable resources prior to cancellation. (Sergey Dukachev)

study from 23 May to 3 June 1963, following which conditional approval was given to proceed to final detailed design and the construction of a prototype. The T-4's projected performance was considered to be within expectations, powered by two Tumansky R-15BF-300 or two Zubets RD-17-15 turbojets, either of which would be suitable. The Council of Ministers had given their agreement to the project by the end of 1963 and it was expected that flight testing would begin within five years.

During the period following initial approval, Sukhoi had considered around 130 different configurations, throwing the net wide across all forms of propulsion and conceptual layouts, including nuclear propulsion, but it did not stop at the required

role. Pavel Sukhoi saw his star in the ascendant and had plans drawn up for a T-4 with variations on the basic design being suitable for long-range interception of incoming threats or even for application as a supersonic airliner. This latter consideration mirrored contemporary Anglo-French efforts which would eventually produce Concorde.

In further analysis of the Project 100 design, another inspection was made by the commission between February and May 1964 with GKAT examining the concept in June that year, receiving approval four months later. Further design changes were introduced, significantly the adoption of four Kolosev RD-36-41 turbojet engines, developed by OKB-36 and manufactured at the Rybinsk Motor

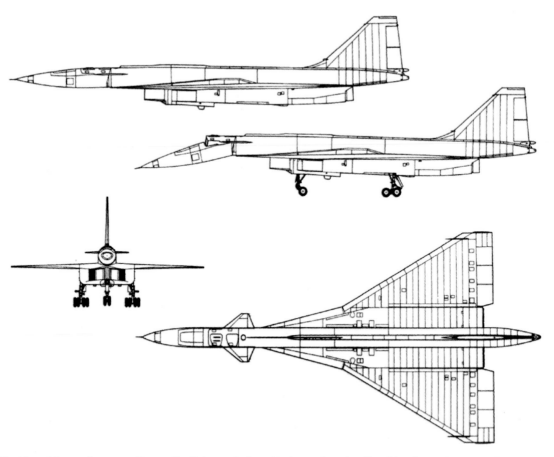

The hinged forward nose section on the T-4 was designed to lower for takeoff and landing to improve pilot visibility. (Author's collection)

Sukhoi T-4 seen here with its droop-nose in the cruise configuration. In this mode the pilots would be flying exclusively on instruments. (Yefim Godon via Tony Buttler)

Impressively futuristic in profile, only 10 flights were made with the T-4. (Yefim Gordon via Tony Buttler)

The T-4 comes in for a landing after one of its flights conducted from 27 August 1972 prior to cancellation two years later. (Yefim Gordon via Tony Buttler)

Building Plant, instead of the previous options. In January 1965 the T-4's engines were relocated to the back of the delta wing in much the same arrangement as that on the XB-70A, each producing a thrust of 156,800N (35,275lb). With these, the aircraft was believed to have a maximum speed of 3,200km/h (1,989mph) at 20,000m (60,617ft) and a top sea-level speed of 1,100km/h (684mph).

But there were still several changes to come for the overall design and layout, some innovative concepts being examined based on reports about the Lockheed SR-71, which had taken the Russians by surprise. Throughout, studies concerning the T-4's aerodynamics had occupied much wind tunnel time and TsAGI focused a lot of resources on the project. Reviews of the mock-up took place in December 1966 and between 17 January and 2 February 1967; final design details were evaluated through the mock-up commission.

At this stage, approval had been granted for a static test article and a single prototype (101) before the second prototype (102), with a reconfigured structural arrangement and with composites replacing alloys, was used for testing the navigation/attack system. Two further prototypes (103 and 104) would conduct

weapons tests and range evaluation and avionics would be tested on a fifth prototype (105) before a pre-production demonstrator (106) was built for full evaluation of the entire aircraft and its systems.

The mock-up had a cranked-delta wing area of 291m² (3,132ft²) and a leading edge sweep of 70 degrees on the inner section with 60 degrees on the outer panels. Wingspan was 22m (72ft) and fuselage length was 43.7m (143.3ft). The wing had a thickness ratio of 2.7% but the maximum take-off weight had grown to 146 tonnes (230,600lb), belying the 'Project 100' designation. Nevertheless, it promised a maximum speed of 3,000km/h (1,864mph) and a range of 6,200km (3,853 miles). The T-4 by now enjoyed widespread support, despite Pavel Sukhoi's tetchy relationship with the Tushino fabrication facility where the giant bomber was to be built.

During preparations for the initial hardware fabrication stage, Project 100 expanded to embrace a wide range of aircraft adapted for specific test roles, including a Su-9 converted to evaluate handling characteristics with the type of wing the T-4 would have. Over time, other wing planforms were tested on this aircraft to determine their suitability or otherwise. Additional aircraft contributed by the Air Force were used to test and evaluate some control system concepts such as fly-by-wire (FBW), electronic navigation sets and autopilots. Despite never having previously designed a missile, Sukhoi developed the Kh-45 anti-ship missile specifically for the T-4. It weighed 4,500kg (9,922lb), had a range of up to 600km (373 miles), a speed of 7,000km/h (4,350mph) and carried a nuclear warhead. It was eventually cancelled but not before being considered for the Tu-160 Blackjack.

Fabrication of the T-4 began in 1969, with the centre and forward fuselage sections transferred to the Sukhoi assembly shop for installation of equipment and aircraft systems. The first aircraft was moved across to the Sukhoi test facilities in December 1971 while the structural test article (100S) was fabricated at the Tushino factory and taken from there to TsAGI. Of some concern was the drooping nose section which was given special thermal testing to ensure its viability. Prototype 101 arrived at the Zhukovsky flight test facility on 30 December 1971 and was accepted for trials on 20 April 1972.

An extraordinary amount of pre-flight testing and 12 taxi runs prevented the first prototype flight from taking place until 22 August 1972, when it was piloted by Vladimir Ilyushin accompanied by navigator Nikolai Alferov. The initial phase of testing comprised 10 flights. The second prototype was finished in 1973 and expected to fly by the end of the year with the third prototype in 1974 and successive aircraft up through 106 thereafter. The Air Force had great plans for the T-4 and requested resources for 250, which was unexpected. In its brief period of flight testing the T-4 showed promise, demonstrating a speed of Mach 1.28, and its advanced autopilot and FBW proved successful.

However, the size of the aircraft, the resources required to manufacture it and the infrastructure needed to operate it brought strong criticism. For these and other issues concerning cost and its impact of the overall inventory, support for the Sukhoi T-4 began to slip away and acceptance for a limited production run never came. There were other contenders, less sophisticated, closer to existing production line

Marshall Andrei Grechko prioritised fighters over bombers due to concerns about the perceived threat from the US Air Force Strategic Air Command. (Author's collection)

designs and cheaper. Moreover, Defence Minister Marshal Andrei Grechko wanted money for a new generation of MiG fighters and fighter-bombers and the Sukhoi T-4 threatened to drain the coffers.

As mentioned previously, the only other contender in this period was the Yakovlev Yak-33 which was designed to a revised view of how to deliver conventional and nuclear bombs. Yakovlev chose to concentrate on a Mach 2 bomber capable of low-level intrusion. The bureau received approval for a range of studies grouped under the Yak-33 designation, the most prominent among which involved exhaust efflux deflection plus six lift-engines augmenting the main turbojets. This, thought Yakovlev, would allow a wing of short span for operation out of dispersed airfields or short runways. However, proving unsatisfactory, none of these proposals were accepted.

CHAPTER 5

THE UBIQUITOUS BEAR

None of the aircraft described previously are now in front-line service and very few were developed as realistic possibilities for operational deployment. But three bombers today form the mainstay of the strategic, long-range, naval and reconnaissance aviation units of the Russian Air Force which are each capable of confronting, and seriously challenging NATO and Western nations. Foremost of these is the generation of turboprop bombers of the Tupolev Tu-95 series and their numerous successor variants and versions.

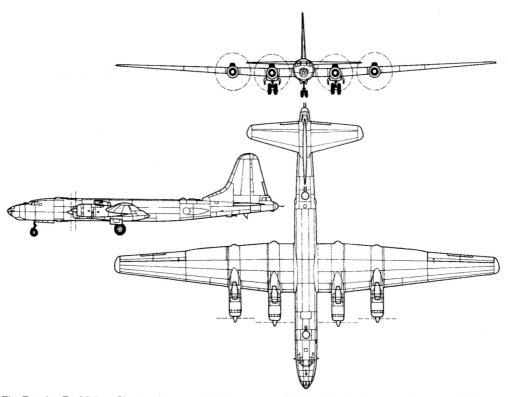

The Tupolev Tu-85 (see Chapter 1) was a failed development of the Tu-4 but an important step in the evolution to the Tu-95. (Author's collection)

A contemporary of the turbojet-powered Boeing B-52, and as long in its service, the Russian aircraft that NATO codenamed Bear is as frequent an intruder along the borders of Western airspace as it ever was. Having survived several changes in strategy and function, the Tu-95 and its derivatives have evolved along with the shift in how power projection is played out and how the manned penetrating bomber has adapted to new threats and found new applications to keep it current.

The requirement for an aircraft of this type originated during the Korean War when, in 1951, the Kremlin judged it had three years before a nuclear war with the United States would commence. It already had the atomic bomb and had made great progress with developing a system for dropping that by air – though this still fell short of actual operational capability. At the time, Russia's only long range bombing capability rested on the Tupolev Tu-4, with very little real chance of threatening targets in the United States. Aware of the development of the B-47 and the B-52, jet bombers significantly outclassing anything the Russians had as a viable equivalent, the requirement for a fast, long-range bomber was taken up by Myasishchev and Tupolev.

As noted earlier, the turbojet-powered contender emerged in production as the Myasishchev M-4, which served a political purpose but little else. Tuopolev made an early judgement to the contrary, that long-range would depend upon fuel economy and that this could best be achieved by the turboprop engine, albeit at the cost of a lower speed. Work on what would become the Tu-95 really began in early 1950 when the concept was first developed by B. M. Kondorski's team.

Taking the Tu-85 as the starting point, a very wide range of possibilities were examined for an aircraft which had to be capable of carrying a 5,000kg

Nikolai Kuznetsov and German engineer Ferdinand Brandner designed the TV-12 (NK-12) engine, then the most powerful turboprop in the world. (Peterbutt)

The twin exhaust outlets for the NK-12 engine on a Tu-95. (Vasily Zimin)

(11,025lb) bomb load, possessing a top speed of at least 900km/h (559mph) and a range of 13,000km (8,078 miles). When balancing speed against range and carrying capacity, it was clear that only a marginal reduction in speed using turboprop engines over turbojets would provide the required range. Following final deliberations, a simple but relevant design was chosen embracing swept wings and tail, four turboprop engines each delivering at least 8,948kw (12,000hp), a specific fuel consumption of 0.25kg/hp (0.55lb/0.7457hp) and a gross weight of 200,000kg (441,000lb). It would have a maximum range of 14,000km (8,700 miles).

Turboprops would afford the Tu-95 a range some 55% greater than that claimed for the M-4 – but at the time, the early 1950s, no turboprop existed with a greater power output than the TV-2F, which had a take-off rating of 4,660kw (6,250hp). The solution was to fit early aircraft with a pair of TV-2F engines mounted in tandem, located on the swept wings and

driving contra-rotating tractor propellers. In fact, the decision to use the turboprop engines had determined the wing configuration together with its leading edge sweep of 35 degrees.

The TV-2F was an ingenuous design whereby the integrated engine consisted of two power sources, the left-hand one driving the front set of four-bladed propellers by a shaft which passed through the drive from the right-hand power source connected to the rear set of propellers. In the definitive layout, the opposing outer engines had a displacement of 24.4m (80ft) in their thrust lines. This was a sophisticated and complex arrangement and many aero-engineers predicted trouble. Tupolev also planned to use the TV-2F for initial test flights and then switch to the TV-12 engine for production aircraft.

Then in advanced development at Kuznetsov, the TV-12 promised a shaft power of 9,312kw (12,500hp) from a 14-stage compressor with pressure ratios varying between 9:1 and 13:1 depending on the altitude and the position of variable inlet vanes and blow-off valves. Cannular combustion chambers were fitted with centrally mounted flame tubes to an annular aft section. A five-stage axial turbine drove the contra-rotating propellers and the engine displayed a mass flow of 65kg/sec (143lb/sec). The propellers ran at 750rpm and the characteristic sound was produced by the supersonic tips. The engine began full tests in October 1952 and remained the most powerful turboprop engine built until the appearance of the Europrop TP-400 engine in 2005.

The basic wing profile came straight from the Aircraft 88 design, with a thickness chord of 12.5% at the root and 10% at the tip and the reduction at the outer panels allowed leading edge sweep to be reduced to 33.5 degrees at that location. The high aspect ratio of 8.39 for the swept wing brought its own structural challenges, three very strong bridge spars being placed across the fuselage with three main spars attached to the root ribs and extending out to the tip. A fourth spar was placed at the structural interface with the rear spar outboard of the outer engines and a further spar was positioned between the outer flap and the aileron. No moveable lift surfaces were placed at the

Even as development of the Tu-95M with its NK-12M engines, of which only 12 were built, was under way, Tupolev was developing the Tu-142 for maritime operations. (US DOD)

leading edge and while the trailing edge had a straight and uniform sweep from root to tip, the wings had an anhedral of one degree.

The trailing edge supported large, slotted flaps which were located inboard and outboard of the landing gear fairings and these were supplemented to advantage by the slipstream from the propellers. The four flaps were driven by ball-screw jacks to a maximum droop angle of 35 degrees. To accommodate the expected degree of flexing, which was considerable with the high aspect-ratio wing, the ailerons were in three sections with a trim tab on the inner set. A single, power-driven spoiler was situated ahead of each inboard aileron and these doubled as an air brake and roll modulator. Flight tests revealed the need for three fences on the upper surface of the wings, aft of the leading edge to the trailing edge, between the draught propeller wakes and at the gap between the centre and outer ailerons.

Vibrations from the engines and the contra-rotating propellers were a problem in that the Russians, uniquely among worldwide aircraft design engineers of the time, were particularly concerned with fatigue life and also with the comfort of the crew on what would be very long flight times. Considerable pains were taken, particularly by TsAGI, over these issues and several departments were set up by whom future studies related to these issues could be undertaken,

Defined by its high aspect, high-set wing, the Tupolev Tu-95 would become the most enduring aircraft produced for front-line service with Russian air forces. (Author's collection)

A Tu-95M displays the rear fuselage and tail turret arrangement highly reminiscent of a 1950s design. (Author's collection)

Engels air base is the cultural home of the operational deployment of the Tu-95 and is the primary operating location from which tests and trials take place. (Marina Lestiva)

A Tu-95RT adapted from an early production aircraft into a reconnaissance and naval intelligence gathering variant. (DoD)

requirements drawn up and information disseminated to design bureaus as appropriate. The cockpit of the Tu-95 was quite small and there was little room for moving around from assigned seat locations.

Much about the Tu-85 was retained in the design of the fuselage for the Tu-95. It had a 2.9m (9.5ft) circular diameter but with a much greater length,

The Tu-95 demonstrated long-range capabilities from the outset and its deployments were closely monitored by NATO. (Author's collection)

construction requiring consideration of the larger bending moment. Expansion rivets were provided for accommodating flexure during flight and thick layers of thermal insulation were provided. The interior layout was dictated by requirements for a six-man crew including two pilots, navigator/radar-operator, a second navigator, flight engineer and radio operator/gunner in a single pressurised compartment in the fuselage nose. Two gunners were carried in unpressurised rear compartments, one to operate blister defensive positions either side of the fuselage and an aft gunner operating the tail barbette.

A benefit of the swept wing was the forward positioning of the transverse fuselage bridging spars ahead of the centre of gravity which allowed a large bomb bay to be incorporated in the centre fuselage unimpeded by carry-through structures. The bay had to carry conventional and nuclear weapons, the largest being the 9,000kg (19,840lb) nuclear bomb. Maximum bomb load was 12,000kg (26,455lb). Aft of the bay were ejector tubes for pyrotechnic target indicators and the centre-section of the fuselage also housed fuel cells and dinghies. The forward pressurised crew compartment afforded escape from

A revealing view of the main and nose leg landing gear with the tail bumper to protect the underside of the aft fuselage in the event of a nose-high pitch on takeoff or landing. (DoD)

a doomed aircraft down through a hatch in the floor operated by hydraulic rams. The tail gunners had manually operated floor hatches.

Tupolev leaned on the Aircraft 88 project for the Tu-95 tail assembly, with the horizontal stabilisers spanning 14.78m (48.5ft) with rods and bell cranks controlling movements and hydraulically boosted elevators with trim tabs. The vertical fin had a leading edge sweep of 40 degrees and a boosted rudder with tab. The tricycle landing gear took its design from Aircraft 88 but with stronger and improved leg design, each main bogie carrying four wheels with

hydraulically-powered expanding brakes. An electric screw jack controlled the rearward retraction of the main legs and the steerable nose leg carried two wheels. A tail skid was provided for protecting the underside of the rear fuselage and two parachutes were provided for braking after rollout on landing.

The design and the rationale for its deployment allowed full integration with Soviet warfighting plans using atomic and later thermonuclear weapons. On 11 July 1951 the Council of Ministers issued a directive for detailed design and fabrication of two prototypes of the Tu-95. Tupolev had personally

Side-view of the Tupolev Tu-95MS Bear-H. (Flanker)

The sole surviving example of the Tu-95LAL used for special propulsion experiments and now on display at the Monino museum. (Aeroprints)

convinced Stalin that the urgency of the requirement justified a major effort. Initially, as recommended by Tupolev personally, the first prototype would have coupled TV-2F engines and the second would be fitted with the TV-12. With an ever-watchful eye on the requirement to have it operational by 1954, flight tests were expected to begin in September 1952 followed by trials with the more powerful prototype exactly a year later.

Four days after granting approval, the Council of Ministers sanctioned production which was expected to commence at Factory No. 18 in early 1953. Also on 11 July 1951, S. M. Yeger put his technical projects team to work on the detailed blueprints. Shortly thereafter, and somewhat after the fact, based on how it wanted to integrate the aircraft into its operational plans, the Air Force issued its own sheet of expectations for the Tu-95. It was to have a service range of 15,000km (9,320 miles), an extended range of up to 18,000km (11,185 miles), a maximum speed

of up to 950km/h (590mph), a service ceiling of up to 14,000m (45,934ft) and a take-off run no greater than 1,800m (5,905ft).

Turboprop propulsion brought its own, unique challenges. The decision to adopt contra-rotating propellers was forced upon the design team by the requirement for a propeller with a diameter of 7m (23ft). Ground clearance would require an unacceptably tall landing gear and the only workable solution was to reduce the length, and double the number, of blades on the single shaft. This contra-rotating transmission system was new in Russian aero-engine design and the performance expected from the aircraft called for efficiency levels of 0.78-0.82 but that had never been achieved before. Crafting the new technology was K. I. Zhdanov at OKB-120 and he was able to provide that shaft output.

When the preliminary design was examined in the autumn of 1951 it fell close in performance to that specified and a full-scale mock-up was prepared prior to assembly of the first prototype starting that October. Much work had been accomplished through TsAGI and the Air Force expressed interest in the design of the flexible wing which, due to its high aspect ratio, had received special attention from A. M. Cheryomukhin. With a necessity for lightness of structure, a series of static load tests were carried out to ensure safety margins – contributed by Myasishchev from that bureau's similar work on the M-4. Despite the shared information required by TsAGI there was a distinct air of competition, each design bureau knowing that priority would go to one at the expense of the other.

Despite the pressure of time and the urgency placed upon the programme by the Air Force, this was no simplified layout. The Tu-95 would carry sophisticated flight test and navigation equipment and new technology incorporating aluminium wiring to connect electrical systems. This became a standard on all Russian aircraft. Efforts were made to introduce an automatic engine control system to relieve the crew of excessive workload but in saving weight ejection seats were not fitted. Irreversible hydraulic actuators were not installed either and this also raised questions but Tupolev stuck with that decision and it proved to be correct.

From the outset it was clear that a massive challenge existed to integrate and control all the many departments, organisations and supply companies and N. I. Bazenkov took charge of that in addition to his primary role of chief designer – for the initial Tu-95 and subsequent variants. His successors over the years were N. V. Kirsenov from the 1970s and D. A. Antonov a decade later, work on the derivatives and especially the Tu-95-derived Tu-142 maritime reconnaissance and anti-submarine warfare aircraft (NATO code name Bear-F) continuing apace.

Flight Tests

By the autumn of 1952 assembly of the first prototype had been completed and it was cleared for flights tests on 20 September. So concerned were the authorities over the possible leak of the aircraft's existence that

the state security police, the MGB (forerunner of the KGB) restricted access along the Moskva River to prevent farmers and agricultural workers from getting a glimpse of taxi trials. Movements with the aircraft were also timed to avoid traffic along the Kazanskaya rail network and the use of freight wagons was limited.

Piloted by A. D. Perelyot, with M. R. Marunov as co-pilot and a crew comprising flight engineer A. F. Chernov, navigator S. S. Kirichenko and chief engineer N. V. Lashkevich, the first flight of the Tu-95 prototype occurred on 12 November 1952. Airborne for around 50 minutes, the large and powerful aircraft appeared to handle well and reached a height of 1,160m (3,700ft) on what was a conservative test of its flying characteristics and handling qualities. It flew on two more occasions before the end of the year and was followed by a fourth flight on 13 January 1953. Tests went well until 17 April when a gearbox failure on one of the TV-12F engines caused a loss of pitch control and almost brought disaster, avoided only by the skill of the pilot, Perelyot.

Less than a month later, on 11 May the seventeenth flight of the first prototype began as usual, on this occasion Tupolev himself being in the control centre at the Zhukovsky airfield talking with the crew. Reporting back that he was at the Noginsky district and at an altitude of 7,300m (23,944ft), suddenly Perelyot announced that the No. 3 engine was on fire. One of the two power sources had failed and was burning fiercely. Perelyot's first instinct was to request clearance for an immediate landing which was granted but not before that engine had burned itself off the wing, falling in flames to the ground near the town. As the wing itself continued to burn, Perelyot levelled off at 5,000m (16,400ft) and ordered the crew to escape but the aircraft plunged to the ground where it exploded.

Perelyot and three engineers were killed but other crewmembers managed to escape, jumping from 5,000m (16,400ft). The pilot was later awarded the title Hero of the Soviet Union for remaining at the controls to turn the burning aircraft away from a residential area. Tragically, A. M. Bolshakov, a technician from the Institute of Aircraft Equipment, jumped out but had not been briefed on the specific type of parachute carried and he fell to his death. First on the scene was Tupolev himself who rode across the marshes on a horse while the others made their way across the boggy ground on foot. The crash shocked Air Force and industry officials as well as security services keen to discover the reason and apportion retribution as appropriate.

Initial reports appeared to place the blame on poor management, sloppy quality control and even a flawed design, which led to calls for certain individuals to be removed from office and punished – a not uncommon response in Russia – and some criminal charges were brought. Those initial reactions were tempered sometime later by the official report issued to relevant parties on 15 October 1953 in which it was determined that the intermediate reduction gear had failed due to the material having insufficient strength and the overall design having low fatigue tolerance. The fire, it concluded, had been allowed to propagate due to an inefficient extinguishing system.

Both the jet-powered Myasishchev M-4 and the turboprop-powered Tu-95 were vital programmes for the Soviet Air Force and both were affected by the crash. Each company was required to meet higher inspection and quality control standards and major decisions were made regarding the Tu-95. Added to existing concerns about the concept of the eight contra-rotating propellers, the incident brought added efforts to fully evaluate the operating principle and thorough testing which added changes to the design of the gearbox. Those were displaced by a decision to move directly to the TV-12 engine for the second prototype and to delay further flight trials until that could be made ready for evaluation.

Much hung in the balance regarding this aircraft, its clearly demonstrated potential contrasted by the worsening geopolitical situation, to which had been added the death of Stalin on 5 March, two months before the crash. Extraordinary attention was paid to the detail of the incident, the design of the transmission and the overall inspection of

quality control during the manufacturing phase. The identification of the responsible company, which had provided inferior materials, got the solid attention of the security police. Tupolev had great influence in the Kremlin, but that failed to prevent his own bureau from being on the receiving end of a deep scrutiny. What emerged, however, was a clear determination from the Air Force to get the Tu-95 into its inventory.

Work on the second prototype had been underway since February 1952, intensive effort having been exerted to significantly reduce its weight. The first prototype had been 15% overweight, the second reducing that to just 3%. Moreover, the modified engine nacelles for the much more powerful TV-12 engines were a great improvement, with an annular intake around the propeller boss for the contra-rotating propellers. Significant changes too were made to preparations for flight with this aircraft. Kuznetsov was required to test the engine in the air on a converted Tu-4 with extensive and long-duration ground runs on a test rig. New requirements were raised regarding integrated fire extinguishers and Kuznetsov designed an almost fail-safe system which established new ground rules for this and for aircraft from other manufacturers.

The second airframe was completed in November 1952 but delays in the development of the TV-12 engine kept it grounded beyond the period of the crash and its investigation. A succession of changes and modifications were made as a result of this and the time available while waiting for the new engines helped transform the second prototype into a much more reliable aircraft. By November 1953, reports from initial flight trials with the engine indicated that the power output of the TV-12 was 2-3% up on expectations and better by the same value on specific fuel consumption.

The extensive schedule of static runs and flight testing raised confidence and the decision to enter full-scale production pre-dated the first flight of the second prototype. By August 1955 two engineless production model Tu-95s had been built, awaiting completion of flight trials with the TV-12. Around this date the engine received its new designation of NK-12, which it retains today. There was a further effort to develop a new engine for the Tu-95, the D-19 which promised 11,190kw (15,000hp) shaft power for take-off and 9,175kw (12,300hp) on cruise power, but it was never fitted and the NK-12 remained the most powerful turboprop engine ever built for a production-line aircraft.

The first NK-12 engines were installed on the second prototype in December 1954. The following month the aircraft was moved to the Zhukovsky airfield and on 21 January it was cleared for flight operations. Piloted by M. A. Nyukhtikov and co-piloted by I. M. Sukhomlin, the first flight with this aircraft took place on 16 February 1955. Successfully completed, it opened the way for a total of 68 test flights in 168 flying hours with the last manufacturer's flight on 8 January 1956. Only one came close to disaster when the landing gear failed to deploy. It would be virtually impossible to belly-flop the Tu-95 and Tupolev himself organised a rapid failure analysis with a small team of specialists. Suspecting a stuck relay, they ordered the electrical system to be recycled, whereupon the gear extended and the aircraft landed without trouble.

The second prototype was used to 'fly the flag', beginning with General Secretary Nikita Khrushchev getting a special introduction to the aircraft while seated in the cockpit along with defence minister Zhukov, salient aspects of its design and controls being personally pointed out by Andrey Tupolev. Already a favoured plane-maker, Tupolev capitalised on his popularity at the Kremlin and used the Tu-95 to extend his influence, which would see the turboprop eclipse the jet-powered M-4, which was only 70km/h (43mph) faster and had less than half its range. In July 1955 the Tu-95 made its first public appearance at that year's Tushino air display and shocked the foreign dignitaries in attendance, presenting a formidable threat.

During one flight of the evaluation phase, the prototype achieved a distance of 13,000km (8,078 miles) and dropped its 5,000kg (11,025lb) bomb load

The NK-12MV engine eventually made its way into the Tu-95, delivering 11,033kW (14,795hp), also employed on the Tu-126 and Tu-142. (Vadim Kondratiev)

at a designated range. For this particular test the Tu-95 had a take-off weight of 167,200kg (368,676lb), a cruising speed of 750km/h (466mph), a maximum speed of 880km/h (547mph) and a ceiling of 12,150m (39,864ft). Refinements to the NK-12 engine were made. Confidence was boosted by one flight involving the new NK-12M engine in the state trials series which demonstrated a range of 15,040km (9,346 miles). This had a take-off weight of 182,000kg (401,310lb) with fuel load increased from 80,000kg (176,400lb) to 90,000kg (198,450lb). Designated Tu-95M, this became the template standard for the later, evolved production machines.

Manufacturing was centred at Factory No. 18 with the production Tu-95 having NK-12 engines but with its fuselage extended by 2m (6.5ft) and a 5% increase in empty weight to incorporate a full suite of instrumentation and electronics. The first two off this block were deemed ready for flight tests on 21 August 1955 with a manufacturer's flight test schedule from 1 October 1955 to 28 May 1956. The state trials started in May 1956 involving the second prototype and the two production aircraft, during one of which a Tu-95 completed a flight of 15,040km (9,345 miles). But this was less than had been required in the Council of Ministers directive of 1951.

To address the range deficit, Tupolev used the second production aircraft and ran it through a modification programme from 20 August 1956 to 21 February 1957. This involved integration of the new NK-12M engine and evaluation with modifications to the airframe and the flight control surfaces as well. With a shaft output of 11,185kw (15,000hp), the Tu-95M had a maximum take-off weight of 165,154kg (364,000lb) and fuel capacity increased from 73,258kg (161,400lb) to 81,243kg (179,060lb). Factory testing on this type was completed in September and October 1957 during which it demonstrated a speed of 905km/h (562mph) and a service ceiling of 12,150m (39,852ft). With the improved NK-12M, the Tu-95M had a maximum range of 16,750km (10,042 miles) and an operational range of 13,000km (8,073 miles).

Tupolev received acceptance for the Tu-95 on 26 September 1957, the operational range cited in those documents being 13,200km (8,202 miles). With verification and full production clearance, the aircraft, which would receive the NATO code name Bear, became the first genuinely intercontinental strategic bomber fielded by the Soviet Air Force. Capable of carrying conventional or nuclear war loads, it would eventually be on strength supporting long-range probing flights far beyond Russia's borders, and still does to this day as a highly credible bomber, reconnaissance aircraft and cruise missile carrier, also supporting anti-submarine and maritime warfare roles.

When it was first eyed by foreign visitors invited to the 1955 Tushino air display, interpretations were varied. The trade press were undecided about its true worth, seeing in it a propeller-driven bomber more reminiscent of the immediate post-war Tu-4 era than a serious long-range threat. Initially, experts believed it to be an Ilyushin product and only a few were seriously concerned regarding its capabilities, which were assessed based on Western capabilities of the day. British aero-engine specialists were consulted by the Americans, since it was they who had led the way with turboprop engines, and when it was realised that this was the type of propulsion carried by the Tu-95, their views were crucial to an interpretation as to its capabilities.

There were familiar British turboprop engines in service with production aircraft. With a shaft output of 1,484kw (1,889hp), the Rolls-Royce Dart powered the Vickers Viscount and the 3,320kw (4,450hp) Bristol Proteus was installed in the Bristol Britannia. Incredulous British experts explained that the power output required to give the Tu-95 the performance it was reported to have was both unlikely and experimental at best. Initially, it was by these standards that information on the Tu-95 was assessed. Quite quickly, however, the magnitude of the challenge posed by the Tu-95 began to influence defence strategy across all NATO countries, particularly North America, now threatened by the real possibility of a trans-polar attack. It is the influence of the Tu-95 that is so infrequently mentioned in studies about the early years of Soviet long-range aviation. The transformation was seminal.

The Dew-Line

During the Cold War, NATO believed that any land attack on its member countries would, logically, come

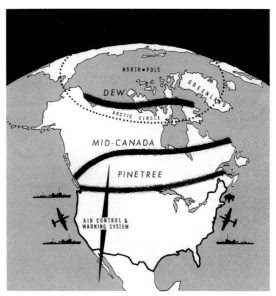

The Defense Early Warning (DEW) line stretched across the North American continent by the early 1960s – for acquisition and tracking of incoming hostiles, primarily airborne attack forces from Soviet Russia. (DoD)

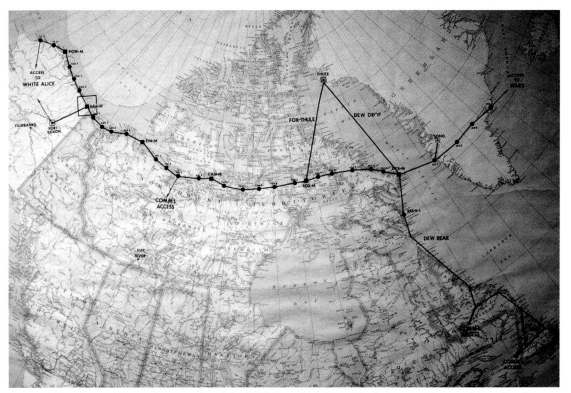

Thirty-eight radar tracking stations populated the DEW line which increasingly integrated ground-based early warning with aircraft and missile systems to knock down approaching enemy bombers and long-range strike aircraft. (DoD)

across the division between East and West Europe as defined by the Soviet occupation of countries liberated from the Nazis and probably across the north German plains. An attack by air on the contiguous United States would follow the shortest route – over the North Pole from Soviet bases across Russia and the northern regions of Siberia. The distance between Moscow and Washington DC is 7,800km (4,846 miles) and from Moscow to Los Angeles it is 9,770km (6,070 miles). All these air routes provide entry points to North America across Iceland and northern Greenland, respectively.

Not long after the Second World War it was concern over the future potential for Soviet Air Force long-range bombing raids that triggered the establishment of a series of defensive radar stations across North America which would, over time,

become the Distant Early Warning (DEW) line, eventually stretching 5,800km (3,600 miles) from Alaska, across North America to Greenland. There did not exist at the time a plausible threat from Soviet bombers but the immediate appearance of the Tu-4 signalled intent that the Russian Air Force might soon acquire the means to attack the continental United States.

Formed in 1946, US Air Defense Command had responsibility for protecting the air space of the United States, and through an agreement in 1951, the establishment of the Pinetree Line, a series of radar stations across southern Canada, followed in 1954 by agreement to build two lines of radars across Canada. One, called the Mid-Canada Line was built by the Canadian government across the 55th parallel, a second establishing the DEW line was built by the

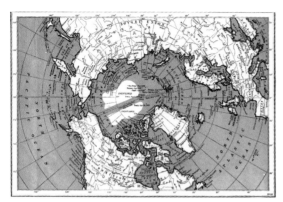

This 1947 polar projection map shows the shortest flight routes from Soviet airfields to targets in the United States and was used to familiarise SAC recruits on strategic tutorials. (Author's collection)

United States to cover the northern regions roughly contiguous to the 69th parallel. On 1 September 1954, the US Continental Air Defense Command (CONAD) was formed to coordinate anti-aircraft artillery, anti-aircraft missiles (mostly Nike rockets), fighter stations, radar sites and command posts.

The operational introduction of the Tu-95 Bear urged upon the NATO alliance the expansion of this defensive network of radar stations and associated units of Continental Air Defense Command. The

In its most pre-satellite developed form, the air defence of North America was the culmination of agreements between the USA and Canada on radar acquisition strings. (DoD)

impact that this aircraft had upon the deployment of defensive measures began in 1957 and would build over the years to also include the Ballistic Missile Early Warning System (BMEWS) for providing alerts to attack from ballistic missiles. The threat from ICBMs overshadowed the immediately preceding concerns regarding the threat from the Tu-95.

Combined with concerns about the Tu-16, Tu-22 and the M-4, the response to the Bear had a major impact on the defensive policy of the US Air Force. The Americans had not expected this aircraft and analysis of its likely performance prompted changes to the USAF's fighter fleet inventory and structure. That inventory increased from around 3,600 in 1950 to more than 9,300 in 1956, partly in response to the need for a robust air defence policy, those numbers falling to 4,500 in 1962, by which date a greater reliance on rockets and missiles took over, remaining at that level for the rest of the decade.

This period also signalled a major shift in funding for the Air Force, increasing from 12% of defence spending in 1949 to almost 49% in 1957, the balance going to the Army, the Navy and the Marine Corps.

Commensurate with that was a major shift toward stockpiling of nuclear weapons, the US increasing its arsenal from 250 in 1949 to 5,400 in 1957, an increase several orders of magnitude above that known to have been in the Soviet inventory. Even in the mid-1950s it was believed that US bases and weapons stores were vulnerable to Russian attacks by air, the obvious 'overkill', recognised only in closed circles at the time, being a prerequisite for ensuring sufficient would be available to inflict unacceptable losses on the USSR.

To ensure that, the active bases available for Strategic Air Command increased from 17 in CONUS in 1949 to 38 in CONUS and 30 overseas by 1957. Over the same period the strategic bomber force of the USAF increased from 525 to 1,655, moving from an all piston-engine force to an all-jet force, bar the last B-36s being retired within a year. Moreover, the organisational command of SAC ensured an increasingly higher state of alert with various improvements to readiness. By the end of 1957, SAC had 11% of its force including tankers and bombers armed with nuclear weapons ready to get airborne within 15 minutes of a scramble. By 1960 that increased to 33%. By the following year B-52s were performing airborne alert training.

The impact of Soviet strategic threats on US Air Force plans and policies since the Second World War passed in three phases: the first Russian atomic bomb in 1949; the Tu-95 in 1955; and the first ICBM in 1957, exemplified by the first tranche of Sputnik satellites. The Bear contributed to the bomber-gap myth, which could not be effectively lanced publicly due to the highly classified clandestine intelligence net cast out by President Eisenhower. Nevertheless, it was soon supplanted by the missile-gap myth, both of which accelerated a major expansion of US capabilities in aircraft and ballistic missiles at the expense of conventional forces.

With the pending availability of an ICBM and the production and service introduction of the Tu-95, late 1957 proved a turning point for Russia in beginning the shift toward equivalence. It would be a long and expensive transition from isolation to the potential for direct engagement with strikes against the North American continent, expansion which would not be completed for 20 years. That starting point was marked late in 1957 with the first aircraft from Factory No. 18, the first 19 production Tu-95s signalling a major increase in capability for the Russian Air Force following an intensive series of tests and evaluation flights.

The initial Tu-95 and Tu-95M production run saw four aircraft completed in 1955, 23 in 1956, eight in 1957 and 14 in 1958. Eight Tu-95Ms were apportioned flight test trials and in a definitive report in late 1958 the Air Force rated the aircraft with a take-off weight of 165,154kg (364,000lb) carrying a bomb load of 5,956kg (13,125lb), which was the mass of a production 1MT thermonuclear warhead. The Air Force required mission range to leave at least 4% of fuel in the tanks for contingencies and with that it noted an operational range of 13,200km (8,202 miles), which was the same as that recorded

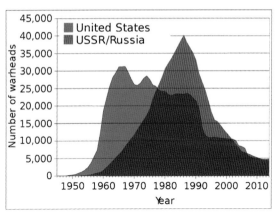

Russia would not exceed the numerical superiority of the US nuclear weapons arsenal until the late 1970s, totals here including land, sea and air delivery systems. (Author's collection)

at acceptance in 1957. The maximum speed was 902km/h (560mph) and a cruising speed of at least 720km/h (447mph) was available. These were the metrics used as a baseline against which all future Tu-95M aircraft would be measured.

In operation, there was very little difference between the Tu-95 and the Tu-95M, notable only for the additional air intakes on top of the engine nacelles which contained additional electrical cooling equipment. The initial tranche of aircraft, all of the Tu-95 and Tu-95M configuration, were subject to a wide range of minor modifications and improvements, many to the interior of the forward pressurised cockpit area and to the console displays. By the late 1970s these aircraft were reaching the end of their fatigue lives and many were switched to training and familiarisation roles, all of them serving in that capacity by the late 1980s. Only 31 of the Tu-95 type were built, the last in 1957, with 19 Tu-95Ms by 1958. The Tu-95 entered service with the 106th Heavy Bomber Aviation Division at Uzin in late 1955, replacing the Tu-4, with the vital responsibility for carrying the nuclear deterrent until the advent of reliable ballistic missiles in large numbers.

To the surprise of many who planned an all-jet bomber force, the Myasishchev M-4 was a great disappointment, only 31 being completed at the Fili plant between January 1955 and June 1956. Each had been handmade and brought troubles with them to the operational units to which they were delivered. Nine major accidents were logged between 1955 and 1958 causing the Air Force to withdraw them from service for a while. When they returned in the early 1960s, the 25 surviving examples were converted into tankers.

Reluctant to discard a bomber which had absorbed so many resources and cost so much money, a major redesign of the M-4 was conducted during 1956 with the introduction of the 3M and the M-6. Dubbed Bison-B by NATO, the 3M was the first variant equipped for aerial refuelling, extending its range to 15,000km (9,321 miles) for the first time. But it had poor reliability and troublesome engines, rarely achieving 100 flying hours between major overhauls. It was, however, the first Soviet bomber to carry electronic jammers for countering the DEW-line defences and it also became the first aircraft to carry 'stealth' radar-absorbent paint which had been developed from German wartime research and technology used for coating wing leading edges and other surfaces.

By 1960, 116 Myasishchev bombers had been built although never more than 60 were ever operational at the same time. At peak strength in 1962 there were 57 of the 3M variant and 24 M-4 tankers. But its use was highly limited due to poor reliability and persistent engine problems. All the Myasishchev bombers were located at Engels with the 22nd Heavy-Bomber Aviation Division. The Tu-95M was with the 79th Heavy Bomber Aviation Division at Semipalatinsk and the 106th Heavy-Bomber Aviation Division at Uzin in the Ukraine, one regiment of that division being located at Mozdoc. But the crews had mixed views about the Bear.

The cockpit was dark in its overall black paint, frequently dank and odorous with no toilet or galley and virtually no room to move around. Recorded as the noisiest propeller-driven aircraft ever built, it had frequent problems, especially with the propellers, and a lack of experience in operating aircraft in the Arctic

regions took its toll on crew and ground personnel alike. This too had its effect on aircraft equipment, oil frequently freezing up which called for special heaters to prepare it for flight. So dire were the facilities at many of these bases that crews had to start the engines every few hours to prevent the entire aircraft freezing over. This forced changes to the chemistry of the oil delivered, to the benefit of other units operating different aircraft at such locations.

Perhaps surprisingly, morale was high due to the exalted regard for the long-range bomber units and their personnel operating the country's strategic deterrent. Many crewmembers were experienced and appreciated the modest benefits that came with their assignment. The Russian Air Force always prided itself on acknowledging the arduous conditions their personnel frequently endured and allowed them special privileges. Training and familiarisation became a hallmark of these units, much like their counterparts in SAC. Tu-95 crews routinely flew two 10-hour night operations a week, logging 1,200 flying hours annually.

The Nuclear Card

Soviet bomber units never flew armed nuclear weapons on training flights, unlike the Americans, but they undertook long flights over the Arctic wastes practising to cross the Pole and attack the United States. Neither did the Soviet Air Force ever operate to the advanced level of readiness employed by the US Air Force.

Nuclear weapons were routinely kept in specially protected bunkers and were initially under the control of the KGB, formed in 1954 out of the old MVD. That changed in 1959 when the army took over control and handling. This was part of the reorganisation of strategic forces presaged by Khrushchev's firm conclusion that bombers could not survive in any future conflict with the West and that they could never justify their expense and the resources they required. Moreover, the slow emergence of a nuclear weapons production industry was shaped much more toward the requirements of ballistic missiles and the bombers had little integration with weapons or support infrastructure.

The first Soviet atom bombs were developed for deployment with the Tu-4. The initial bomb was the RDS-4 Tatyana with a yield of 40KT, roughly twice that of the Hiroshima bomb. It was to have been replaced with the RDS-6S, a thermonuclear device which never worked to expectations and was cancelled. The RDS-37 was a thermonuclear bomb with a yield of 2.9MT and this was produced widely throughout the late 1950s and the 1960s. That yield was oversized for dealing with the operational targets many would have been assigned to, so work began on smaller devices, the RP-30 and the RP-32 with a 200KT yield, much more useful in that the electromagnetic impulse (EMP) was less likely to affect Soviet forces in theatre or on the battlefield.

Armed with these bombs, Tu-95s were deployed to a wide range of locations in the Arctic region including Anadyr on the Chukotsky Peninsula. None of these aircraft were ever on airborne alert and the separation of bombs and aircraft, and the complex procedures for enabling and arming them, made it impossible to bomb-up the Tu-95 or the M-4 in less than several hours. Operating these aircraft in such remote and inhospitable locations was, as related earlier, wearing on crews and aircraft alike. Probably worse still, for any integrated force equivalent to Strategic Air Command, the few bombers in the inventory prevented implementation of a consolidated integration and combined operational training programme.

Aircraft went out on patrols, came back and the crews recycled to another sequence of training flights but while morale remained high at unit level, very few knew the integrated plan by which they would be required to fly – probably with a high risk of never coming back. For example, flight crews were not told that the thermonuclear RDS-37 could never be dropped by a Tu-4 with any possibility that the flight crew would survive the blast and the shock waves. A weapon with an explosive yield 242 times that of the bomb dropped on Hiroshima would overwhelm any departing bomb flying at less than Mach 1.5.

US spy flights using the Lockheed U-2 took place over the USSR starting in the late 1950s, with a select few pilots flying missions for the CIA and the Air Force. Among them was Francis Gary Powers. (DoD)

The introduction of the second-generation bomber force to Soviet long-range aviation in the second half of the 1950s offered little improvement in the way the force structure was organised. Big changes were in the offing which threatened the very survival of the manned strategic bomber. In the United States, given the brouhaha surrounding fears of Soviet domination and the suspected bomber gap during the Eisenhower years, there was universal fear among the general public.

During the president's time in office (1953-1961) the Russian Air Force never had more than 151 strategic bombers while SAC had built an all-jet strategic force approaching 1,500 aircraft comprising B-47s, B-52s and B-58s. Information which raised suspicions concerning the true level of Soviet capabilities was top secret and never subjected to public scrutiny.

They were, however, only suspicions. There was no way of accurately assessing the true extent of Soviet aircraft production and operational deployment. The closely kept secrets of production and force readiness levels prevented the collection of meaningful intelligence information, which is why right at the end of the 1950s, Lockheed U-2 spy-plane overflights were made in a bid to obtain reliable data. But that was sporadic and ended after the shooting down of Francis Gary Powers in 1960.

A new branch of the Soviet armed forces, the Strategic Rocket Forces, was created in December 1959 and the following year a complete reorganisation of long-range aviation began by dismantling the air armies which previously had been under the jurisdiction of the Supreme High Command. From 1960, strategic bombers were assigned to aviation corps subordinated to the Air Forces Command structure. Priorities at the design bureaus hitherto focused on aircraft shifted to rockets and missiles in

Operation Grand Slam had Powers fly a U-2 from Peshawar, Pakistan, to Bodo, Norway on this route to gather missile intelligence during which he was shot down on 1 May 1960. (Author's collection)

the belief, from the Kremlin down, that aircraft would be subordinate to these systems. The shift in emphasis resulted in a lean period for manned bombers and disinterest in speculative designs overwhelmed previously judged opportunities for new types.

As noted earlier, the Russian Air Force had never invested in strategic bombers and long-range aviation was an adjunct to rather than a component of military aviation in the Soviet Union. Two areas of development kept the bomber force alive and operationally relevant: aerial refuelling operations for extending the range of existing aircraft and the use of these bombers as cruise-missile launch platforms. Objections to manned aircraft based on their perceived vulnerability to air and ground defences were mitigated to some degree by their use for carrying large, or multiple loads of smaller, stand-off weapons. The development of these two technologies kept the Soviet bomber forces in being during the fallow period until their reconstitution began to appear in the 1970s.

Development of the probe-and-drogue system had been a major programme, urged on as a means of keeping the manned penetrator relevant. Recognising that the range limitation of the early Tu-4 meant it was only suitable for the European theatre of war, V. S. Bakhmistrov began work in 1948 to develop a system to considerably extend the range of the manned bomber force. He used the Tu-4 to explore possibilities in techniques based on the American probe and drogue concept, tests beginning on 16 June 1949. By 1952 some Tu-4s were being adapted as aerial tankers but only on a limited scale.

With the operational debut of the Tu-95 and the Tu-95M, Tupolev proposed a longer-range version of the Bear incorporating additional fuel tanks. The added weight would require a take-off power of up to 14,920kw (20,000hp) and some work was conducted to achieve that, in the belief that the aircraft could achieve a range of up to 20,000km (12,420 miles) without refuelling. To help get to that, three additional tanks were placed above the wing centre-section, theoretically making possible nonstop flights of up to 24 hours. It nearly worked; in 1958 the modified aircraft with advanced NK-12M engines remaining aloft for 23 hours 40 minutes. The compromise in additional engine power and reduced bomb load due to the extra fuel swung the decision to achieve extended range through air-to-air refuelling.

The Tu-95KD was a variant configured to carry the Kh-20 cruise missile, initially proposed for the Myasishchev M-34, and also the first equipped with a refuelling probe. A mid-air refuelling capability compensated for a range reduction of 4,200km (2,608 miles) due to the weight of the missile. Designed by Mikhail Gurevich, lacking a place on the defunct M-34, the Kh-20 was specifically developed for the Tu-95KD in a programme funded from 1954. The configuration was based on the MiG-17 and MiG-19 fighters with power from a single Lyulka AL-7FK turbojet producing a thrust of 67,100N (15,100lb) and a speed of Mach 2, rendering it unassailable by manned aircraft while in flight.

Tests conducted between 15 October 1958 and 1 November 1959 proved less than successful, range and speed being lower than anticipated, seven of eleven fired failing to achieve their goals. As deployed, the Kh-20 had a range of 380-600km (240-370 miles) depending on the warhead, which was selectable between 0.3MT and 3MT. When known in the West it received the NATO name AS-3 Kangaroo, entering service in 1960 when plans anticipated two missiles for each Tu-95M or Tu-95K. This was eventually reduced to one missile per aircraft, due to the effect on the Bear's range and speed. Accuracy of the missile was poor, manual guidance achieving better results than the inertial system, and the initial decision to use this against targets in the United States quickly proved untenable.

As with all Soviet atomic and thermonuclear devices, the laborious preparation time hindered the missile's use as a first-strike weapon and, as related earlier, it was never effective in that role. ICBMs and

The front end of a Kh-20/AS-3 cruise missile. (Pavel Adzhigildaev)

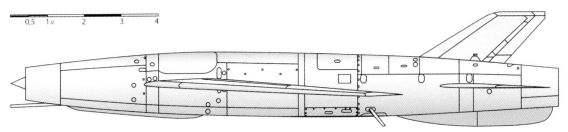

The Kh-20 (AS-3) cruise missile was developed for the Tu-95 and carried a thermonuclear warhead with selectable yield of 0.3-3.0MT. (Allocer)

SLBMs were considered to be the first-response or first-strike weapons. With integral warheads installed, only the preparation and firing time of the missile determined how quickly they could be fired. The R-7 ICBM had been under test since the first was fired successfully from Baikonur on 21 August 1957. But it was incapable of rapid launch due to its liquid oxygen oxidiser for combustion with T-1 fuel, a form of kerosene. LOX must be kept at -182.8C (-297F) and is continuously boiling off as the temperature rises. The consequences had a significant effect on the strategy of Russia's airborne nuclear deterrent.

The R-7 was declared operational on 9 February 1959, a realistically insignificant date due to the slow installation of launch sites, initially at Plesetsk in north-western Russia. It required a 22-hour launch preparation time with the LOX tank only maintaining a readiness level for 24 hours before essential draining and reloading. Not until 1962 were all R-7s operational, with no more than eight at Plesetsk and a single launch pad at Baikonur in Kazakhstan. The ICBMs which put such fear into US citizens when publicly displayed for the Sputnik flights from October 1957 were at best only second strike weapons which would, due to their exposure and vulnerability, be unlikely to survive the first hours of a major war with NATO or the United States. Not until the development of storable propellants could the ICBM force begin to complement, and then supplant, the manned bomber for direct attack.

The first of those was the R-16 which made its first flight on 2 February 1961 with initial deployment before the end of that year. With two rocket stages

R-16U

Developed during the late 1950s, the first truly effective Soviet ICBM, the 8K64 (R-16) was declared operational from the end of 1961 but at the time of the October 1962 Cuba Missile Crisis fewer than 30 were ready. (Heriberto Arribas Abato)

A briefing chart for President Kennedy shows evidence of Soviet missile deployments in Cuba, October 1962. (DoD)

Presiding over the land and air nuclear deterrent, headquarters of Strategic Air Command, Offutt AFB, as it appeared during the Cuba Missile Crisis. (USAF)

and hypergolic propellants which ignite on contact, the propellants were stored in the rocket at room temperature but only up to three days, before they had to be de-tanked due to the corrosive properties of the nitric acid oxidiser. Like the R-7, a laborious procedure was required to make them ready for launch, a process lasting up to three hours to remove them from protective hangars and erect on the adjacent pad. Even at the time of the Cuban Missile Crisis in October 1962, the Russians had fewer than 30 R-7 and R-16 ICBMs available for use.

Development of warheads for the missiles and bombs for the Tu-95 and M-4 accelerated during the second half of the 1950s, driven largely by the commitment to deploy large numbers of ballistic missiles. The bombs available for the long-range aviation units were variants of designs primarily configured for the rockets but the initial testing zone at Semipalatinsk raised concerns regarding the radioactive fallout on adjacent cities and rural communities. On 31 July 1954 a decree shifted the test site to Novaya Zemlya in the Barents Sea, the first detonation occurring there on 21 September 1955.

High-yield tests began in 1957, driven by the inaccuracy of the R-7 which had a circular probability of 10km (six miles), defined as a radius within which 50% of rounds fired are likely to fall. High yield was to compensate for low accuracy, devices used initially for deployment on the bombers. Khrushchev's obsession

with ICBMs and SLBMs dominated nuclear weapons production while reducing priority for the manned bomber and, to a very great extent, starving it of the limited funds available. By the end of the decade more than 10,000 scientists were employed in the nuclear industry at ten closed-off cities, many of which were not shown on official maps. Such was the expenditure on this work, under the rule of Council Minister E. P. Slavsky, that its budget was exceeded only by the state budgets of Russia and the Ukraine.

As quickly as relations with the United States thawed at the end of the decade, they were to chill again after the Powers incident in May 1960. A unilateral moratorium on nuclear testing between 1958 and 1961 was revoked and a crash programme of super-bomb development began. Designed by a team of nuclear physicists including Andrei Sakharov, the AN602, sometimes referred to as the RDS-220, was developed with a de-rated explosive yield of 50MT, some 3,125 times that of the Hiroshima bomb. A specially prepared Tu-95N was adapted to drop this device both as a test and a demonstration to the West of Russia's scientific and military prowess.

The need to patrol the Arctic coastline of northern Russia and Siberia to prevent incursions by NATO aircraft brought a requirement to track and jam electronic eavesdroppers. Plans to convert the Tu-

Andrei Sakharov played a major role in the development of the Soviet atom bomb, working closely with Igor Kurchatov who was the principle scientist in planning and organising the programme. (Author's collection)

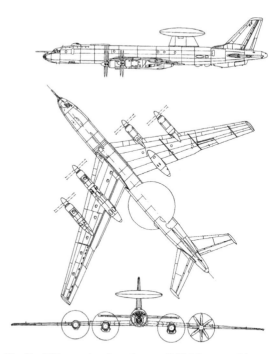

The Tu-126 was developed as an AWACS to provide advance warning of a US air attack over the North Pole but only 12 were built. (Martin Zielinski)

95 into this role were thwarted by its slim fuselage, a development of the Tu-114 airliner being adopted and designated Tu-126. With a wider fuselage, itself a derivative of the Tu-95, the Tu-114 was large enough to carry extensive and bulky electronic jamming equipment. The powerful Liana radar in an 11m (36ft) diameter radome mounted above the fuselage was capable of detecting aircraft at up to 350km (217 miles) or large warships at a distance of 400km (248 miles).

Development of the Tu-126 to serve as a general AWACS aircraft was ordered by the Council of Ministers on 4 July 1958 and the prototype made its first flight on 23 January 1962. Only eight production aircraft were built, the first becoming operational with an AEW unit based at Zokniai in Lithuania in 1966. Five flight crew and eight radar and systems operators were carried in the defenceless

aircraft which had a range of 7,000km (4,350 miles) or considerable longer with in-flight refuelling. It was replaced by the Beriev A-50 which first flew in 1978 and entered service in 1985.

When the Tu-126 retired its work was transferred to the Beriev A-50 Mainstay introduced in 1985. (Author's collection)

CHAPTER 6

RUSSIA'S BIG STICK

The Tu-95N programme began in 1955 as plans to create a carrier-plane for a supersonic strike system developed by design engineer Pavel Tsybin at OKB-256. The system would have a Tu-95 carry in its bomb bay an RS supersonic reconnaissance system which, when released, would be capable of 3,000km/h (1,864mph). Powered by two ramjet engines it would have had a range of up to 13,000km (8,384 miles) and following presentations the Council of Ministers approved the project on 30 July 1955. The RS was married to the Tu-95 because that was the only aircraft capable of carrying it.

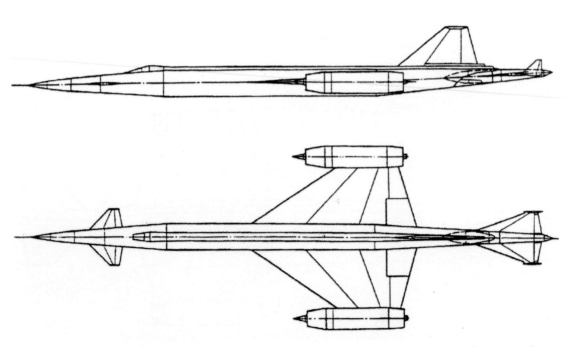

Inspired by the Convair B-58 Hustler, on 4 March 1954 Pavel Tsybin proposed a similar composite supersonic bomber in the RS (Reaktivnyl Samolyot), Reaction Aircraft, concept. (Yefim Gordon via Tony Buttler)

In the 1950s Russia began development of high-yield thermonuclear devices capable of being air-dropped on urban centres and military facilities, culminating in 'Tsar Bomba'. (Author's collection)

With a weight including all the support equipment predicted to be up to 36,298kg (80,000lb), the RS required considerable modification to the bomb bay. During 1956, the internal layout of the centre-fuselage section of the Tu-95 and most of the design required was shared between OKB-256 and Tupolev, the assigned aircraft then receiving the Tu-95N designation. Tupolev's chief designer Nezval was in charge of aircraft modifications and manufacturing changes were conducted at Zhukovsky. By early 1957 it was decided to modify several aircraft to the Tu-95N configuration but later that year, largely due to over-zealous optimism for ICBMs, the entire programme was dropped. The sole Tu-95N completed was the aircraft selected for dropping the colossal RDS-220, rebadged as Tu-95V.

Bearing the code name Vanya, the AN602 (RDS-220) has also been known as the Tsar Bomba. The CIA tagged it as Joe 111. Development began in

1956 and resulted in the RDS-37, first tested on 22 November 1955 when its nominal 3MT yield was descaled to 1.6MT for that initial event. At this date

The Tsybin RS concept incorporated a delta-wing 244Kt thermonuclear weapon in the aft fuselage, both carried aloft by a Tu-95N. (George Cox via Tony Buttler)

A practice case for the Tsar Bomba, the largest thermonuclear device ever detonated. (Author's collection)

the USSR had no delivery system in place to pose a serious threat to the United States but the Kremlin believed that they needed a propaganda weapon to counter the burgeoning US long-range SAC bomber force.

Another development, Project 202, led to a bomb design with a yield of 150MT. It was postulated that it would, in theory, be possible to design a bomb with a yield of 1,000MT, a device more than 60,000 times the yield of the Hiroshima bomb. This could have no useful military function other than as a propaganda vengeance weapon and that was the reason for developing a de-scaled version with a predicted yield of 50-58MT for that purpose. On 10 July 1961 it was agreed that a demonstration test should take place

involving a weapon which was experimental in that it utilised several untried and innovative techniques.

For carrying a bomb weighing approximately 27,000kg (59,535lb) with a length of 8m (26ft) and a diameter of 2.1m (6.9ft), the Tu-95V was extensively modified, its bomb bay being removed along with fuel tanks from the fuselage. The bomb carried an 800kg (1,800lb) parachute to retard the fall of the device. This was to allow the bomber and an accompanying Tu-16 instrumented for observations and measurements to get to a predicted distance of 45km (28 miles) which would provide a chance of survival. With a crew of nine, the aircraft flew with the bomb from Olenya to test site No. 6 on Novaya Zemlya.

The Tu-95V was considerably modified to accommodate the 27 tonne (12,250lb) bomb, 8m (26ft) in length with a diameter of 2.1m (6.9ft) attached to a 1,600m² (17,000ft²) retardation parachute. (Author's collection)

A Tu-95V dropped the Tsar Bomba thermonuclear device with an explosive yield in excess of 50MT, achieved on 30 October 1961. (Author's collection)

Russian pride in its technological achievements today includes a schools education programme highlighting military successes with a large range of exhibits related to its nuclear weapons industry. (Author's collection)

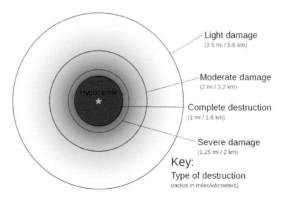

Key:
Type of destruction
(radius in miles/kilometers)

Light damage
(3.5 mi / 5.6 km)

Moderate damage
(2 mi / 3.2 km)

Complete destruction
(1 mi / 1.6 km)

Severe damage
(1.25 mi / 2 km)

Hypocenter

Detailed analysis of the damaged caused by the Hiroshima and Nagasaka A-bomb attacks allowed Russian strategists to evaluate the size of bomb yield required for air-drop weapons to achieve defined military objectives. (Author's collection)

The bomb was dropped on 30 October 1961 from a height of 10,500m (34,449ft) about two hours after take-off and detonated 4,000m (12,123ft) above the Mityushikha Bay range at 11:32am Moscow Time. At the time of detonation the Tu-95V had escaped to a distance of 39km (24 miles) and the Tu-16 was 53.5 (33.2 miles) away. The crew of both aircraft wore light-filter eye shades and the exterior surfaces of the aircraft were coated in thermally reflective paint. The shock wave from the bomb prevented the fireball from reaching the ground but it caught up with the Tu-95V at a distance of 115km (71 miles) from the point of detonation, reaching the Tu-16 at 205km (127 miles). Both aircraft survived despite the Tu-95V dropping 1,000m (621ft) when the shock wave hit.

The fireball alone had a diameter of 8,000m (26,248ft) across and, because it was detonated above the surface, reached an altitude of 10,500m (34,450ft), the height of the two aircraft. The mushroom had a stem about 40km (25 miles) wide and a cloud around 95km (59 miles) across, rising to a height of 67km (42 miles) above the ground. The fireball was seen 1,000km (620 miles) away and created a series of earthquakes recorded around the globe, the shock wave travelling three times around the world. The pressure wave shattered windows at a distance of 780km (480 miles) and the EMP cut off all contact with the two aircraft for some time, causing widespread concern for the crew from those monitoring the test.

Scientists used the opportunity to calibrate a scale of effects on animals and flora produced by various nuclear weapons tests. The Russians had already carried out more than 100 nuclear tests and this provided a unique opportunity to gauge effects of a very large yield. All wood and brick buildings in the village of Severny at a distance of 55km (34 miles) were totally destroyed as were all the wooden houses several hundreds of kilometres away. The heat of the fireball could have caused third-degree burns at 100km (62 miles) and witnesses felt the heat at 270km (170 miles). Some windows were broken at a range of 900km (560 miles) while reflected blast waves smashed windows in Norway and Finland. The seismic shock was equivalent to a magnitude 5.25 earthquake.

It is perhaps sobering to conclude that the reason why the 100MT device enthusiastically sought by scientists after this test was cancelled lay in the effects analysis which showed that no aircraft releasing it could escape its own destruction and that the fallout would render the test site unusable for decades.

In-flight refuelling and tanker operations greatly extend the Tu-95's range, allowing it to fulfil the nuclear role for which it was designed. (Author's collection)

A simulated tanker operation as a Tu-95MS flies in formation with an Il-78 during the 2009 Moscow Victory Parade. (Sergey Ashmarin)

Because of that the Proton, an ICBM being designed to carry such a device, was considered the only practical delivery system apart from the N-1, which could also have carried a 100-150MT warhead. But the propaganda effect had worked and in any event by this time the Cuban Missile Crisis of October 1962 had reset the balance between the manned bomber and unmanned rockets. The Proton rocket was used as a satellite launcher and the N-1 was used in a flawed bid to put cosmonauts on the Moon. The Tu-95V was pivotal to crucial, if not key, decisions during this period of the Cold War and the tests which it supported were many and long. Novaya Zemlya is now uninhabitable in large areas because of these tests but the extended and concentrated data-gathering at a single site did itself demonstrate the infallibility of the use of manned bombers for gravity-drops of

such high-yield devices. The ability to flexibly assign stores and munitions proportionate to the mission at hand opened a new way of thinking among Soviet Air Force planners and this infrequently discussed and largely underrated part of the Russian bomber story is equal in importance to that of the aircraft themselves.

Many and Varied

As the first Bear to carry a mid-air refuelling system, the Tu-95KD (NATO designation Bear-B) became the standard by which this and all future bomber requirements would evolve. In designing the type, Tupolev had been aware of the potential for range-extension through mid-air refuelling but that had never been built in to the Tu-95 or the M variant. On 2 July 1958 the Council of Ministers stipulated aerial refuelling as an essential feature of future aircraft. But

A fine shot of the air refuelling probe on this Tu-95MS at Engels-2 air base. (Author's collection)

Details of the mid-air refuelling probe and nose area are clearly visible in this shot of a Tu-95K22. (Pavel Adzhigildaev)

there was considerable debate about the most effective method.

A few months previously, on 28 April the Military Manufacturing Commission had proposed a wingtip to wingtip concept much as that employed by the Tu-16. This appeared to be the preferable way to proceed and engineering analysis began but the probe and drogue systems was already being tested on the M-4/3M and that was selected when the wingtip concept proved unsuitable for very large aircraft. The Council of Ministers approved that choice in a directive dated 20 May 1960 and the Konus system was to be installed, the first being on a converted Tu-95M in May 1961 at the Tupolev factory.

The Konus system was capable of transferring 4,537kg (10,000lb) of fuel per minute and required a permanent refuelling boom installed in the upper nose of the fuselage, with a fuel line running down the outside to a mid-fuselage tank. Compressed air would be used to operate the mechanical components of the probe and a scavenging system was provided. Communication between the Tu-95KD and the tanker aircraft went through the Pritok equipment installed for that specific purpose.

Long duration flight tests ran from 5 July to 8 September 1961 with 18 flights each averaging 38 hours. In a second sequence from 17 October 1961 to 30 January 1962, 16 flights averaged 43 hours each. For all 34 test operations, a Myasishchev M-4/2 served

as the tanker. They were a complete success and the equipment served as a template for all future bombers but mid-air refuelling would itself be a stumbling block in future arms control talks when applied to the swing-wing Tu-22M Backfire, as explained in the next chapter.

Thanks to aerial refuelling, the Tu-95 could be flown with maximum bomb load over great distances using M-4s converted to a tanker role. Line production began in 1962 and 23 aircraft were completed in this configuration by 1965, added to which were 28 Tu-95Ks retrofitted with a probe. In addition, a refuelling capability was added to the Tu-22 with converted Tu-16Z aircraft employed as tankers for them. But they never had the range to be classified as long-range strategic bombers and were only useful in a theatre context.

The operational deployment of the aerial refuelling concept married to the cruise missile gave the Bear a completely new role. Development ran in parallel with the deployment of Hound Dog with SAC in the United States, where a stand-off capability was being forced by Soviet SAMs, and in the UK where from 1963 Blue Steel was extending the flexibility of the RAF V-bombers. But development of a stand-off capability had, as mentioned, began in the USSR a decade earlier, when the vulnerability of the manned bomber was seen as inevitable.

Production of the Kh-20 cruise missile followed an improvement in its performance and a resolution from the Council of Ministers on 9 September 1960 sanctioning integration of this weapon with the Tu-95K. The system had been extensively tested in the Barents Sea in an operationally simulated environment against electronically masked targets and moving vessels. In all, 47 production Tu-95Ks were built of which 28 were modified to the Tu-95KD configuration for aerial refuelling. The operational aircraft continued to serve until the 1980s.

Cruise missiles were not new to the Tu-95 and a proposal emerged in 1958 that this aircraft could carry four Kh-10 under its wings while also retaining a capability for carrying nuclear weapons in its bomb

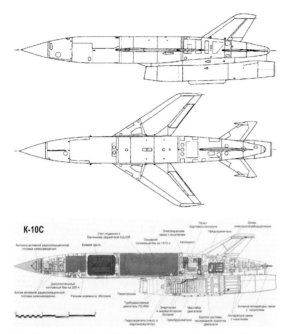

K-10C

The Raduga Kh-10 (AS-2 Kipper) as developed for the Tu-16 but proposed for the Tu-95. (Author's collection)

bay. The Kh-10 (AS-2 Kipper) had been designed specifically for the Tu-16K-10 and entered service in 1961 following a six-year development period. Like most early Soviet cruise missiles it adopted the shape of a small jet fighter and had a total weight of 4,553kg (10,039lb) with a conventional or 350KT nuclear warhead, possessing a cruise speed of Mach 1.7 and a range of up to 325km (202 miles).

Its application to what would have been designated the Tu-95K-10 failed when studies showed the aircraft would suffer an unacceptable drop in performance. Moreover, by the end of the 1960s the K-10 was judged unsuitable for high-value targets and it was dropped in favour of the much more advanced and survivable Kh-22. In several respects, the Kh-22 had been the first fully effective cruise missile application and had kept prospects for the Tu-22 alive during the second half of the 1950s when Khrushchev became obsessed with rockets. But that aircraft was unable to provide it with its full potential.

Described in detail earlier in this chapter, the Kh-20 pressed the need for aerial refuelling to compensate

for a reduction in range caused by the weight of the missile and the drag induced by its external carriage suspended beneath the bomb bay. By the end of the 1960s the Tu-95KD was put through an upgrade programme identified by redesignation of type to the Tu-95KM variant. Modifications included a new radar gunsight, the option for an improved passive reconnaissance system, the new SPO-2 radar warning system, new navigation equipment, an updated radar altimeter, an automatic compass and greatly improved radio equipment.

When partnered with these upgrades, the modified Kh-20, identified as the Kh-20M, rendered a further Bear redesignation as the Tu-95K-20, the maximum radius of action increasing to 8,250km (5,123 miles) as the theoretical launch point, the missile adding a further 600km (373 miles) to the target. But in reality, the aircraft had to get to within at least 380km (236 miles) of the impact point to ensure acceptable accuracy. The need for guidance added to the system's vulnerability and the constant threat of electronic countermeasures (ECM) gave concern to Russian Air Force planners. It was not an ideal match.

By the early 1970s, significant progress with ECM added to these worries and even as early as 1963 Tupolev had been studying the possibility of adding to the stand-off range and protecting the system from electronic threats. Not for another 10 years was the decision made to integrate the Kh-22 with the Bear and that came at the beginning of 1973 when the Council of Ministers approved it and the first production Tu-95KM arrived at the Kuibyshev factory for modifications. A further 17 months lapsed before the necessary drawing and technical information on the missile arrived at the works in May 1974.

Changes to the airframe were extensive, the tail gun was removed and in its place an ECM package was installed, a new Yard radar unit was fitted, control equipment for the preparation and release of the Kh-22 was installed and a special carriage unit for the missile was built in to the bomb bay. For external placement of two additional missiles, two underwing pylon mounts were installed. The work to ready the

The KSR-5 seen here under the port wing of a Tu-16KSR Badger G was found to be a misguided fit for the Tu-95. (DoD)

first aircraft took another 17 months before it was completed on 30 October 1975. Initial flight trials followed by extensive testing ensued and it was not before 1981 that the first launch of a Kh-22 from a Tu-95KM took place. The system was formally integrated into the front-line operational inventory in 1987.

Other missiles were considered as well, not all successful in marriage with the Bear. Decidedly in the latter category, the KSR-5 emerged as a scaled-down version of the Kh-22, smaller and weighing around 4,000kg (8,800lb) with a top speed of Mach 3.5 and a range of up to 700km (435 miles). It could carry conventional or nuclear warheads and was specifically

designed for the Tu-16, series production beginning in 1969, in service with the Badger the following year and the Backfire from 1974. The target is identified by the radar on the launch aircraft and the accuracy has a circular probability error of 46m (150ft).

A decision was made in February 1973 to fit out 33 Tu-95 and Tu-95M aircraft with this missile together with its dedicated launch system for a single missile under each wing, lifted almost directly from the installation on the Tu-16s. Modifications very similar to those carried out for the Tu-95KM were completed at the Kuibyshev factory in October 1976, the Tu-95 re-identified as a Tu-95M-5. The first flight occurred shortly thereafter but tests were halted in May 1977 when they showed it had little or no advantage over other aircraft equipped to carry the missile.

A further, as yet then unfulfilled, requirement for a long-range reconnaissance aircraft was sought to extend the capabilities of optical and sensory data acquisition carried out by the Tu-22RD. On 20 May 1960, the Council of Ministers authorised modifications be made to the Tu-95 to fulfil that function. Designated Tu-95MR-2, it was hurriedly prepared and made available for flight testing by the end of the following year. Modified at Factory No. 18 using Tu-95M No. 410, it incorporated a special station for operating the reconnaissance equipment with a dielectric fairing installed in the aft fuselage just ahead of the horizontal tail. The bomb bay incorporated a range of optional photographic equipment. The flight test programme began on 12 November 1964 and went extremely well, including trials with a flight refuelling system using a Myasishchev M-4-2 tanker. Day as well as night trials took place; on one nocturnal top-up the MR-2 receiving 45,372kg (100,000lb) of fuel. The tests were completed on 19 December and it was accepted by the Air Force, three more following of which one had no mid-air refuelling capability. The Air Force used these four aircraft extensively on some very long flights, primarily hunting naval vessels and conducting their own clandestine activity close to the borders of NATO countries. The UK was not exempt from these visits and the popular press frequently misidentified the aircraft as bombers – to dramatic effect! They remained in service throughout the 1970s and 1980s and were then converted into Tu-95U trainers into the early 1990s.

Service Life

Operational use of Tu-95s had begun in April 1956 with the first division based at Uzin in the Ukraine and the second at Semipalatinsk. As their use expanded territorially, operations in the Middle East revealed advantages for their application in a tactical, rather than strategic, role. This led to changes from their initial role as nuclear bombers and modifications were made to the configuration of bomb-racks and

weapons carriers in the bomb bay. The most useful adaptation allowed the carriage of up to forty-five 250kg (551lb) bombs for use against enemy airfields, runways and marshalling yards.

The Cuban Missile Crisis of October 1962 did much to open new maritime support roles for the Tu-95, the Tu-95M and, later, the Tu-142. This work was pioneered using Tu-95 being flown in pairs, one pure reconnaissance, as they monitored and kept close eye on US movements. This tactic was used to shadow the British naval operations against the Argentine occupation of the Falklands Islands in 1982. By this date both Tu-95 and Tu-142 operations worked in concert with intelligence provided by Soviet reconnaissance satellites, which frequently provided an initial orientation as to areas of interest, especially during regional conflicts such as those in the Middle East.

Over time, the gradual shift toward priority for the Soviet strategic nuclear deterrent going to ICBM and SLBM forces relieved the Tu-95 from that function and allowed the Bear to operate in the anti-ship role, the big bombers going against the large US carrier battle groups operated around the world. These

A three-view drawing of the Tu-95MS, developed from the Tu-142 as the prime carrier for the Kh-55 cruise weapon. (Kaboldy)

With a turbofan engine, the Kh-55 (AS-15 Kent) missile was a significant improvement on the cruise weapons fielded heretofore and provided the Tu-95MS with a credible warload of six missiles. (George Chernilevsky)

became realistic targets for simulated attack, testing not only the performance of the bomber crews but also to precisely record how the US responded as they approached the edge of the air defence perimeter. These frequently led to close encounters of a particularly dangerous kind, a game also played by the Americans, who would paint the Russian bombers with their missile radars in a threatening game of 'chicken'.

As confidence grew in its capabilities, the aircraft was adapted to new roles, one of which included its use as a cruise missile carrier. Not for supersonic missiles but a new generation of subsonic weapons with extended range for greater stand-off capability at much less cost. Developed by MKB Raduga beginning in the early 1970s, the RKV-500A missile, also known as the Kh-55 and AS-15 Kent to NATO, was a significant step forward, providing the first in an evolving series of increasingly advanced weapons which continue in frontline use today. The shift

toward a greater number of smaller cruise weapons had a tactical advantage in that by being launched in large numbers they could saturate air defences, offer greater operational flexibility and, arguably the most important factor, possess outstanding range and greater accuracy compared to a supersonic weapon.

A R-95-300 turbofan engine placed the Kh-55 in the same operations category as the USAF's Air Launched Cruise Missile (ALCM). (Author's collection)

Detail on this Tu-95MS clearly shows the nose landing gear as a Bear is manoeuvred out of its maintenance hangar. (Russian MOD)

The Kh-55 was equipped with a turbofan engine providing a cruise speed of Mach 0.7 and a range of about 2,500km (1,553 miles). It could support a conventional or nuclear warhead and was most closely matched in the West by its contemporary, the Air-Launched Cruise Missile (ALCM). The US equivalent had evolved from SRAM/SCAD attack/decoy devices carried by the B-52 and the Russians sought the same functional purpose for their new missile. For carrying the new weapon, the long-range Tu-95 was an obvious choice. Having evolved through the supersonic Kh-20 and Kh-22 eras, in the late 1970s Tupolev began work on the Tu-95MS configured for the Kh-55. It was based on Tu-142 No. 42105, being the airframe used for initial conversion.

The aircraft was extensively modified with a new cockpit and forward fuselage, a remodelled nose area for the radar installation, shorter fuselage, additional carriage points and provision for rotary launchers

in the redesigned bomb bay. Additional ECM and radar instruments were installed in arguably the most thorough single upgrade to the type since its operational introduction. To improve performance, the more powerful NK-12MP engines replaced the earlier MV variant with more powerful generators

The Tu-95MS introduced the Leninetz Obzor, a nav/attack radar which is also claimed to have synthetic aperture capability. (Leninetz)

The Azovsky MAK-UT missile approach warning system is an addition to the Tu-95MS. (Miroslav Gyurosi)

A Tu-95MS poses for a public relations shot, simulating a mid-air refuelling operation which would never be conducted for real at such low altitude. (Author's collection)

producing dc power. Changes to the Tu-95MS would transform the operational capabilities of this aircraft and render it as the primary strategic airborne component of the Soviet and post-USSR Russian air forces.

Surprisingly fast, the first Tu-95MS was ready at Taganrog in little more than a year, the first flight occurring in September 1979 at the start of tests which would last until late 1981. Production that

The Tu-95K-22 was provided with two inboard BD-45K launchers for the Kh-22 in addition to the single BD-45F launcher on the fuselage centreline replacing the conformal station for the Kh-20 carried previously. (Author's collection)

had begun at Taganrog was supplemented through a second line at Kuibyshev from 1983, that facility taking over full production thereafter. With all development work supported through the flight tests, production at Taganrog followed two variants: the Tu-95MS-6 which could carry six Kh-55 missiles in the internal rotary launcher and the Tu-95MS-16 with an additional six missiles under each wing, three on each of two pylons in tandem and close to the fuselage.

The original tail armament was eventually replaced by a GSH-23 with four 23mm guns which was the same as that developed for the Tu-22M2 Backfire. Standard for all Tu-95MSs was a crew complement of

Development of the capable Tu-95MS, seen here, blurred the line between the Tu-95 and the Tu-142 for naval operations. (Tupolev)

Mid-air refuelling became a vital element in operational readiness for strikes against North America. Here, an Il-78 flies with a Tu-95. (Sergey Ashmarin)

seven including a commander, second pilot, first and second navigators, flight engineer, systems engineer and tail gunner. Over time, a considerable range of modifications and improvements were made to a variant which would rapidly become the enduring mainstay of Soviet strategic forces. Production included 32 of the MS-6 variant and 56 of the MS-16.

The first unit to operate the Tu-95MS was at Semipalatinsk in early 1983 and in 1985 a second unit at Uzina was formed and a third at Mozdok in 1987. Training exercises included a flight completely around the perimeter of the Soviet Union using tanker aircraft while another from Semipalatinsk crossed the North Pole and flew up to the Canadian border. But it was the Tu-95RT that became the most frequent visitor to North America, to the UK and to US bases in South East Asia. NATO intercepts frequently encountered familiar faces peering at them through the aft blisters, friendly and sometimes not so polite signs displayed against the windows. Dubbed the 'Eastern Express' it became a routine exercise in testing the tactics, response times, noting radar frequencies, etc.

Over time, the aircraft gained a good reputation for safety, capable of absorbing damage due to accidental collisions with refuelling tankers, such as the Il-78. Pilots found value in the turboprop engines, especially on landing where reverse-pitch brought the huge propellers into good use, shortening the roll-out distance considerably. Capable of absorbing lightning strikes and surviving a long flight home with large chunks of the tail missing, Russian pilots remained confident in their aged aircraft.

When the Soviet Union collapsed in 1991, the Soviet Air Force had about 84 Tu-95MS variants listed in the inventory. In addition there were 63 Tu-95Ks, all equipped to carry the Kh-20, plus 11 Tu-95U trainers. Of the 147 bomber variants, 23 were in Uzina, 22 in Mozdok, 40 in Semipalatinsk and 61 in Ukraine. There was also one at Kuibyshev. The Tu-95Us were at the training centre at Ryazan and some unidentified examples remained at the Zhukovsky airfield but these were not assigned to the operational inventory. Arms control agreements limiting the number of nuclear weapons carried by a single bomber would reduce the offensive load of the MS configuration, the external pylons of the MS-16 being eliminated. Hard points are retained for conventional loads, however. Transitioning to the use of the Tu-95 as the prime strategic conventional and nuclear arm of Russia's long-range strategic forces passed seamlessly across the transitional divide from the communist era to an ostensibly democratic federation of independent republics.

The size, range and operational capabilities of the Tu-95 provided opportunities for some non-military applications. Several older aircraft were modified for the search and rescue (S&R) role supporting Russia's Vostok manned spacecraft programme. Tests with unmanned capsules began on 15 May 1960 followed by a further six flights before the first manned Vostok on 12 April 1961 carrying Yuri Gagarin into orbit as the first human to enter space. Designed to recover on land, in cases of emergency the Vostok spacecraft could come down anywhere along its flight path and that included water. The order to develop the S&R capability was issued in September 1960 and the aircraft were ready with appropriate communications

through the Pritok transceiver. They would continue to serve the programme for many years.

Naval Bears

Shortly after the end of the Second World War, Russian development of jet and rocket propelled cruise missiles provided Soviet naval forces with a means of attacking enemy surface fleets far from home. Eventually, from the late 1950s, SLBM-equipped Project 629 (Golf-class) submarines would threaten the eastern seaboard of North America. Without a credible intercontinental bomber force until the arrival of the Tu-95 and its derivative variants, the ability to creep up on the US rested solely with the submarine force.

The Russians had a long history of submarine design dating back to the First World War but after 1945 great efforts were made to capitalise on German submarine technology, particularly the Type XXI which appeared right at the end of the war and was considered the outstanding design of its time. That evolution emerged through Russia's Project 611 (Zulu-class) submarine which leaned heavily on the

Integrated with the overall Soviet strategic plan, Juliett-class submarines would rely on Tu-95s to deliver targeting information. (Author's collection)

P-5 missile tubes on the Juliett class which would attack US targets from off the eastern seaboard. (Author's collection)

Type XXI in several key design aspects and entered service in 1952. Success with that led to a wide range of different submarine types and the development of cruise missiles which could be launched against surface targets.

Maritime patrol and surveillance of international shipping lanes was considered vital to Russia's national security, the ability to supply beleaguered countries with goods and equipment from far-off allies having been pivotal to Britain's success in both world wars. In time of conflict, the Russians were aware that blocking supply lines between North America and the European conflict could prove crucial to Soviet success on the battlefield. But it was with the Soviet attack submarine that the long-range Tu-95 was to play a highly significant role in reconnaissance and mid-course radar targeting for anti-ship missiles launched by submarines. The variant supporting

Whiskey-class submarines also carried the P-5 and would have integrated with other forces attacking the United States in the event of war. (Author's collection)

In service from the early 1960s, Echo II-class submarines carried eight P-6 missiles and similarly rely on navalised Tu-95s and the Tu-142. (Author's collection)

partnered anti-ship submarine operations was the Tu-95RC, an evolution to enhance operational capabilities supporting the diesel-electric Project 651 and the nuclear powered Project 675 submarines. It was essentially an adaptation of the Tu-95RT supporting maritime operations.

Project 651 (Juliett-class) boats were initially planned as a means of striking surface fleets or, just conceivably, directly at the continental United States from submarines off the eastern seaboard, using cruise missiles launched from surfaced boats. Each boat initially carried four P-5 turbojet-powered missiles

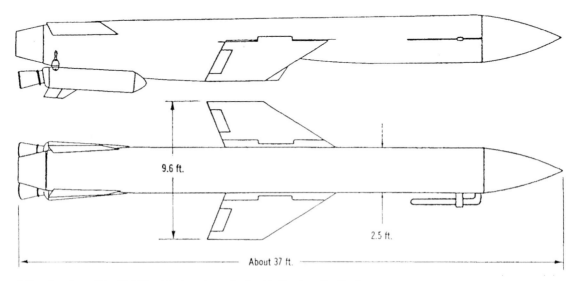

A line drawing of the P-6 Shaddock cruise missile. (Author's collection)

with a range of 500km (310 miles) capable of carrying conventional or 300KT warheads. Later, the two-stage, rocket-powered Chelomey P-6 was introduced as a more effective means of attacking targets inland. Project 675 (Echo II-class) boats carried eight P-6 missiles with a range of 300km (186 miles) and they appeared in service during the early 1960s.

A persistent problem with this generation of missiles lay in their targeting and guidance, which could not be achieved by the submarine itself. Moreover, the American aircraft carriers had an air defence perimeter of 150-200km (93-124 miles) which pushed development of the P-6 to prevent turbojet powered cruise weapons from being shot down. Project 675/P-6 originated on 17 July 1956 with the Council of Ministers as an anti-ship programme with adaptation to a later development of the P-6 for attacking coastal targets, around Europe or on the North American continent. A major drawback required the surfaced submarine to elevate each missile tube – four on each side of the Echo-II hull – through 14 degrees for launch. This operation required up to 30 minutes for preparation, tube elevation and launch.

The operational need for accurate targeting inspired development of the Success aero-intelligence system using suitably converted Tu-95RT and Tu-16RC relay aircraft. The Kyiv Research Institute of Radio Electronics was given the task of designing a system which would allow these aircraft to locate suitable targets and pass this information to submarines for specific target allocation. The submarine system Argument would control the launch of up to four missiles at a single salvo with a full complement of eight sent to saturate fleet air defence systems.

Using a trailing wire communications system the submarine would receive a direction to fire its missiles, rise to periscope depth and make contract with the relay aircraft which would send target data to the submarine. The operator's console would display this information and a specific set, or sets of targets would be selected and those would be entered into the missile firing computer for range and bearing.

The integrated concept of submarine, missile and relay aircraft was recognised as an enabling capability dependent on the effectiveness of the reconnaissance and target designation and relay aircraft. Work on the Tu-95RC began through a directive from the Council of Ministers on 21 July 1959 with Tupolev given two years to complete the work. In early March 1960, a further directive approved conversion of Tu-95M No. 510 by removing the bomb bay doors for installation of the Success equipment, a unique fairing being designed and added, the existing flare system replaced by a Square-2 antenna system and radio communication equipment installed for relaying data to the submarine.

Flight tests began on 21 September 1962 under the command of test pilot I. K. Vedernikov. Completed on 4 June 1963, the first series comprised 23 flights logging 107 hours 23 minutes out of Kuibyshev and Zhukovsky and also additional trials from Belay, Cerkov and Uzin. These revealed serious deficiencies in operating the Success system and with the radar as well as with the electrical distribution between new equipment added for the role. A second sequence of tests was completed by December 1964 which resolved many of the operational issues, increasing the reliability of the integrated variant and submarine. These tests also allowed full evaluation at maximum range.

The Soviet Navy considered the type to be in operational use during August 1964 and it would remain in use for 25 years. Production that began with two aircraft in 1963 continued until the last of 52 Tu-95RC aircraft, excluding the original modified Tu-95M, was handed over in 1969. The target designator aircraft were fitted with aerial refuelling probes and these were converted Tu-95MR types. Officially, the Council of Ministers declared the Tu-95RC to be at operational readiness on 30 May 1966, by which date a great number of flights had taken place, not all of which were successful.

Highly complex and with equipment which was still in the development stage, the Tu-95RC suffered more than its fair share of accidents. Opened in

August 1963, the naval base at Fedotovo near Kipelovo, about 40km (25 miles) north of Vologdva hosted many of these aircraft as crews were trained on the role and familiarised with the variant. From there they joined the 392nd ODRAP (long-range reconnaissance regiment) which was assigned support operations with the Navy's Northern Fleet. Their range of tasks extended from monitoring the activities of foreign navies in international waters around the Arctic Circle to providing civilian maritime operators with ice cover information. The majority of sorties supported pure reconnaissance and surveillance rather than the specific role of supporting cruise missile targeting.

From the 1970s, this regiment supported general maritime reconnaissance activity around Angola, Cuba and Guinea. Long duration flights over the West Atlantic and the South Atlantic were supported by Myasishchev M-4/3MS-2 tankers or through refuelling stops in friendly countries. During the second half of the 1970s, increased patrol requirements extended the frequency of sorties and that took its toll. In 1971 two aircraft were lost with all crewmembers, one crashing into the Barents Sea after a fire broke out in mid-air, and another crashed on landing at Kipelovo air base. In 1976 another Tu-95RC was lost after a long flight in the West Atlantic close to US shores and in 1984 another carrying a full fuel load crashed on the Kola Peninsula. The 392nd was finally disbanded in the early 1990s, after the loss of four aircraft and 61 crewmembers.

The application of Tu-95 derivatives to naval operations also extended beyond the reconnaissance and targeting role into a pure anti-submarine warfare (ASW) operation. In the early 1960s, Tupolev proposed a Tu-95 PLO variant which would carry a weapons load of 8,167kg (18,000lb) including bombs, mines and torpedoes in addition to omnidirectional sonobuoys. The sorties envisaged for this variant would involve on-station loiter times of 3.5-10.5 hours and provide a fully integrated network service involving Russian surface ships and submarines. In researching potential mission roles, equipment essential to the role was either deficient or missing from the inventory. Powerful surveillance radar, infrared search and track systems and the necessary magnetometer were just not available at this date and the proposal got nowhere. But the requirement never went away.

Tu-142 – Dedicated ASW Hunter

The October 1962 crisis over the deployment of Russian missiles on Cuba identified an urgent need for resilience in naval operations. In one exercise of brinkmanship, a Russian submarine came within seconds of firing a torpedo at a US naval vessel during the quarantine of the island. When a US destroyer dropped practice depth charges signalling the malfunctioning submarine to surface, its crew already suffering from the build-up of carbon dioxide, the political 'minder' on board ordered an officer to fire a nuclear-tipped torpedo at the ship. The officer refused but the criticality of the episode sank deep in to the Soviet consciousness; had that nuclear weapon been fired the outcome would have been very different.

Admiral Sergey Gorshkov made it a priority to expand the Russian naval forces at sea and to integrate that with support from long-range aviation. The Soviet Navy was traditionally divided into the Northern Fleet, the Black Sea Fleet, the Baltic Fleet and the Pacific Fleet, each with their own air regiments. It needed the extended support of long-range aircraft to

Tu-142s preparing for a winter training flight from Fedotovo air base. (Russia MoD)

Long-range aviation is the cornerstone of the Russian air force and naval operations, integrated with submarine patrols and networked target location. (Author's collection)

complement the expansion of Soviet naval forces. The options were few but the Tu-95 had the range and carrying capacity to provide that support.

Requirements that underpinned the development of the Tu-95RC were exceeded by an order from the Council of Ministers on 28 February 1963 for a long-range ASW aircraft which would be designated Tu-142. Based on the Tu-95RT, it was in effect an advanced variant of the Bear, adapted to carry an ASW weapons load and special search, track and destroy electronics. The capacity to carry out basic reconnaissance duties would be provided by Kvadrat-2 and Kub-3 electronic systems.

The expanded requirement got the attention of the Air Force, which decided to incorporate a secondary range of modifications, including a capacity for the aircraft to operate from rough fields and unprepared airfields. The landing gear for the Tu-142 would have a six-wheel bogie on each main leg which necessitated a larger retraction well. Changes would be made to the wing, the area being expanded to 289.9m² (3,120ft²), with double-section flaps and bellows wing tanks

replaced by steel tanks comprising part of the main torsion box. The elevator area was enlarged by 14% and irreversible hydraulic actuators installed.

At one point it was suggested that boundary layer control systems should be installed as a way of reducing take-off and landing speeds but the magnitude of the work involved and the cost was not approved. Nor was a proposed crew seat ejection system installed. Some changes were made to the defensive armament, an ECM package being installed alongside the tail armament. But the quantity of electronic equipment added to the cockpit area forced an elongation of the cabin by 1.7m (5.6ft), a modification applied to the second prototype.

Because the Tu-142 was essentially a variant of the Tu-95 it was misguidedly believed that the type could be ready by the end of 1964 when it would begin flight tests. The work was driven largely by the additional electronics and the operational requirement to configure the capabilities so that it could hunt for and track enemy submarines – techniques which were, and are today, highly classified and with mixed and uncertain results. By 1968 serious questions were raised in the Kremlin about delays and although fabrication of the prototypes was progressing, development and breadboard testing of the electronics and sensor suites was not.

Further investigation of progress was made in early 1969 and several changes were required in the cockpit and on the flight deck in particular. Engineers fitted a new forward glazed section to improve vision and changes to the seats were required for comfort and endurance on very long sorties. The cabin extension proved difficult and called for several items of equipment to be relocated. But some delays were down to misdirected requirements rendered unnecessary on further analysis.

Case in point was the stipulation for rough-field operation. The extensive changes to the inboard engine nacelles to accommodate the large bogies prompted Tupolev to complain to the Ministry of Defence that rough-field operation would never be appropriate for such a large aircraft. The Minister summarily agreed and on 6 October 1970 promptly rescinded that requirement; the Tu-142 got the original landing gear back but only after a lot of wasted time and money, the Minister never quite discovering who had made the stipulation initially.

The first prototype (No. 4200) had been completed by mid-1968, with many similarities to the Tu-95RC and the basic Tu-95RT having been the template for modifications and adaptations to the role, the Tu-142 carrying the same side-looking radar of the latter in the ventral, mid lower fuselage section. Both dorsal and ventral gun turrets were removed and the large dielectric radome was replaced with a smaller fairing which enclosed the infrared search system. Also, the Arfa system's antennas on the Tu-95RT were replaced with new antennas on the tip of each horizontal tail.

The first prototype made its initial flight on 18 July 1968 followed by the second prototype on 3 September with its extended cabin but without a full set of equipment. When the third prototype flew on 31 October it was fully equipped with all the systems required by the Navy and stipulated by the Air Force.

Flight testing proceeded without major incidents, the aircraft was essentially a modified variant of the Tu-95RC but with very different electronics and support equipment. It was the latter that occupied most of the flying hours involved and the first production aircraft were evaluated by the Navy's ASW units during May 1970.

In the interim, a considerable amount of work was required to make essential changes brought about by the role the aircraft would conduct. Tests with the ECM and SIGINT equipment were taken out for a series of basic tests which had weight reduced by 3,700kg (8,157lb) but the outcome was disappointing. The subtle changes to the wing, the tail section and the general control of the aircraft required longer take-off runs but the range was greater than expected. But installation of the equipment which would really transform the aircraft into the role for which it had been built was still some way off.

The perceived submarine threat worried Russia's war planners and sophisticated ways of evading detection posed serious problems for scientists seeking technical solutions. Submarines were getting quieter and the equipment previously used to find them was getting less effective. The United States placed similar priority on detecting Russian submarines. The deployment of the Greenland-Iceland-Faroes sonar detection line allowed NATO to keep an ear on Russian submarines transiting into and out of the Atlantic Ocean.

The Russians used sonobuoys with trigger devices operating in the 3-10Hz acoustic band but multi-blade submarine propellers could generate waves of up to 100Hz. Detecting submarines in deep water involved the use of an explosive sound source (ESS) which propagated waves reflected from the hull of submerged boats. By the mid-1960s, Soviet research scientists were integrating this with existing sonobuoys and developed the Berkut search radar with the Udar programmes. This resulted in the development of the Tu-142M, which became the primary platform for submarine detection when initial plans for using the Ilyushin Il-38 ran into problems due to its limited onboard computer equipment.

Berkut was soon exposed as technically flawed and operationally ineffective and the concept of ESS was dropped but the upgrades to the aircraft were valuable when a replacement was planned. Known as Korshun, the new target acquisition system was also hampered by technical bugs and delay piled on delay as the entire project fell far behind schedule. Authorised on 14 January 1969, the Tu-142M made its first flight with the Korshun system in place on 4 November 1975. Suffering from one of the most protracted and delayed projects in its history, the Ministry of Defence could only satisfy seven out of 31 requirements after extended periods of flight testing using the three prototypes at various locations.

By October 1978 when the last of three test periods involving 138 flights ended, further delays ensued, the Council of Ministers finally approving operational deployment in a decree on 19 November 1980. The search radar (STS) was persistently unreliable, only marginally effective and was only recognised as needing a significant upgrade programme in 1979. Moreover, on 6 December 1980 the Ministers approved awards to 2,000 specialist workers for their contribution to the aircraft and its STS search radar – clearly dysfunctional as understood by crews assigned to operate this equipment on the Tu-142M.

The aircraft itself was marginally improved over the basic Tu-95M, with an additional 3,000kg (6,613lb) fuel load which compensated for the increased take-off weight due to the additional electronic equipment plus bombs, torpedoes, sonobuoys and sea-mines. Range remained the same at 12,000km (7,457 miles) at a take-off weight of 185,000kg (407,925lb) while aerial refuelling extended that by 2,000km (1,243 miles). The new role increased the crew complement to eleven which included two sonar systems operators, a communications officer, chief flight engineer, tail side barbette gun operator and tail gunner in addition to the two pilots, two navigators and a combat navigator.

Integration of the information feeding the crew displays included data concerning friendly activity in the air differentiated from potential hostiles.

The Korshun-K system did provide the necessary discrimination and early evaluation returned more positive results. As designed, it allowed the crew to identify and destroy submarines at sea, to exchange tactical information with surface ships' command and control centres, to conduct tactical searches as requested and to conduct wide area surveillance for encroaching hostiles. The new equipment incorporated tactical information displays with a lot of control operations already stored in the computer memory, relieving the crew of many manual input tasks.

A great advantage was with the revised displays that allowed identification of the aircraft's position together with simultaneous indication of flight path heading, sonobuoy location, the position of identified submarines and additional parameters selected by the operator. It could also present all this detail while conducting attack operations by selecting appropriate weapons for the targets addressed and in that the system was ahead of some of its equivalent contemporaries in the West. The Korshun-K search radar could support four separate sonobuoy types, all of which would be used on any one flight, two (RGB-75 and RGB-15) identifying the existence of a submarine in the water and two (RGB-25 and RGB-55A) tracking it and plotting its movements.

The RGB-15 could operate with the ESS detonators and, with a range of 10-15km (6.2-9.3 miles), serve to identify and locate the position of submarines directly targeted by the Tu-142M. The ESS charges could be set to explosively detonate at various selectable depths between 25m (82ft) and 400m (1,312ft), the specific setting determined by the shape of the propagated wave and the desired reflected wave. This information would be passed to the patrolling aircraft. Each aircraft could carry a variety of different ESS charges, three types being available for a range of water depths and seabed conditions.

An advantage of the Korshun-K system was its integration with the Tu-142M's NPK-142-M avionics suite providing automatic or semi-automatic flight control modes, data taken from the search radar and the navigation system relieving the crew of workloads during levels of high activity. It also worked in concert with the defensive and offensive weapons systems, the trajectory control settings for the torpedoes and bombs and the settings for each item of munitions. The offensive weapons suite was operated by the tactical computer. During en route operations to the target area, command and control was effected by the navigation software, management switching to the search radar in the area itself.

The effectiveness of the sonobuoys and the ESS depended upon the speed of sound in the water, which is determined by temperature and current. To get this information, the Tu-142M carried two small buoys which when dropped in the water would provide this information at various depths. Offensive weapons on the aircraft normally included two 23mm cannon in the tail barbette, an optical sight and an aiming computer which could receive inputs from the Krypton gun-laying radar. The considerably improved communication system connected all crew members, maintained contact with command and control centres, with other aircraft and with surface ships, all of which was recorded on board.

During a typical operation, the Tu-142M would enter a designated search area, defined usually by reports of ship or boat movements indicating subsurface activity, dropping the selected sonobuoy and deploying additional buoys in a sinusoidal pattern for maximum effect. This process, however, could be detected by submarines in the area. Submarines could go 'quiet' for several hours without revealing their presence until the aircraft had withdrawn. The Soviet Navy never exercised an aerial refuelling operation within the search area and only conducted those operations far from the hunting zone. If detected, the air crew would be instructed as to conducting an attack or carrying out extended surveillance.

From the outset, operations were complicated by technical issues related to faulty sonobuoys, trouble with the avionics suite and difficulties in the way operational use of the equipment was poorly set out. The magnetic anomaly detector (MAD) was difficult

to operate and, due to its location in the airframe, several systems had to be switched off before it could be turned on. A dense thicket of classified information about the sonobuoys prevented crews being familiar with their operation. When they were finally declassified, disparities and anomalies with the data recorders prevented effective discrimination between real submarines and false signals. Neither was it possible to interpret the data to show when targets were using electronic or acoustic veiling techniques to evade detection.

From 1985 Tu-42M crews got improved magnetic data recorders with higher efficiency and effectiveness levels. Upgrades and improvements were not always a complete success, crews being trained often having more experience and a better working knowledge of the equipment than their tutors. Operational difficulties were more frequently caused by desk-bound planners setting down procedures without any real-world flying experience and the assignment of crew roles frequently conflicted with a more logical allocation of tasks. This had been a stalling problem since the start of production and typified the top-heavy bureaucracy of the communist regime.

In Service

Preparations for the operational debut of the Tu-142 began as early as 22 June 1969 when the Northern Fleet started filtering crews to man the aircraft. Training began at the Nikolayev facility in southern Ukraine supporting orientation activities in the Black Sea on 4 March the following year. Within three months the first crews were ready for operational trials. The second inductees did not begin their training before the end of 1971 but the operational deployment could not start until adequate production lots had been delivered and they were slower than scheduled. Only 12 of a promised 36 were delivered during 1972 and these were the early configuration with the 12-wheel main leg bogies.

The reason for these production delays lay with decisions made by the air ministry, included among which was one to shift assembly of the Tu-142 from

Kuibyshev to Taganrog. Located on an inlet to the Sea of Azov, Taganrog was already an established assembly facility but had little work when the decision was made. This was good on paper but bad on delivery because the place had little infrastructure for producing such a large aircraft which needed to incorporate specialised and relatively sophisticated equipment.

Taganrog had little going for it. It required the construction of a new airfield, erection of new assembly facilities, new machine tools and jigs, improved test equipment and completely retrained mechanics, engineers and managers. The delays in production and pre-flight testing had a major impact on the operational deployment of the type. As they built up the facility to the standards found at Kuibyshev, managers established a reputation for good work, minor improvements being made to the aircraft and subtle upgrades added without changing the standard training manuals, such as they were.

Production from Kuibyshev had been slack due to the shift to Taganrog, the old facility delivering two aircraft in 1968, five in 1969, 1970 and 1971 and their last one in 1972 for a total of 18 aircraft. But the aforementioned preparations for production delayed the first aircraft from Taganrog until 1975, the last one from Kuibyshev being the template for the first from the new assembly facility. It identified them merely as Tu-142M but that designation disappeared when they entered service, the Soviet Navy referring to them simply as the Tu-142. Production at Taganrog continued for two years.

The first operational unit with the Tu-142 was the 76th Independent Long Range ASW Air Regiment formed on 15 August 1969. Based at Kipelovo in the northern part of Russia, it was within close flying range of the eastern Baltic Sea. Training flights from there began in March 1970 and involved additional familiarisation at Nikolayev, on the Black Sea, before the first operational flight on 15 April, the early aircraft fitted with 12-wheel bogies. As the first two operational aircraft arrived, the first ASW flight took place on 7 July, in reality still a training exercise. The

unit was joined by additional crews that summer and night flights began before the end of 1970.

Although full operational capability was claimed during early 1971, the gradual induction of new crews brought increasing need for familiarisation sorties. One of those took place over the Sea of Norway on 27 July when two aircraft gave crewmembers their first taste for flights across international waters. It lasted 13 hours 50 minutes and provided some real-time rehearsal of the activities they might be called upon to perform against NATO ships and submarines. The second squadron of the 76th stood up in 1972 and both units participated in the Northern Fleet exercise that year beginning on 6 April. The surface fleets were integrated and quite quickly the Tu-142 began to impress with an ability to seek out unidentified 'targets' set out by the simulation supervisors.

The effectiveness of the unit and its aircraft was only reliably measured by the interaction it had with the surface and subsurface fleets and here there was increasing confidence in their value. During one operation in the Barents Sea during late August 1974, four Tu-142s on a semi-operational training exercise shadowed a NATO submarine in Soviet waters for two hours 55 minutes before it departed. This was the only method by which the boat was known and identified. Tracking it for that entire period demonstrated the value to more conventional naval operations and provided verification of the equipment's effectiveness, albeit after a protracted and much delayed development period.

Over the next several years, the Tu-142 participated in several naval exercises, some in international waters where non-Russian submarines were located, identified and tracked. Several very long duration flights took place and operational effectiveness gradually increased and expanded. Operational flights extended across many areas of the globe, submarines being tracked in the Philippine Sea, the Atlantic Ocean, the Baltic, the Barents Sea and the Norwegian Sea. On one sortie, 13 non-Russian submarines were located and tracked without previous knowledge of their presence.

Tu-142MK, a significantly improved and upgraded variant of which 43 were produced by Tagonragog. It is equipped with the Korshun radar, new avionics and ASW devices. (Russian MOD)

The Tu-142M was introduced in 1979, the first solo flight of this type occurring on 20 February, followed on 14 April by a test dropping the torpedo with the aid of the Korshun-C radar. Later that year, another NATO submarine was located and shadowed for more than an hour. The effectiveness of the system grew commensurate with practice and that year the Tu-142 operated 64 combat sorties, identifying 10 submarines and logging almost 3,000 flying hours. Confidence grew and in a cooperative venture with the 392nd Maritime Reconnaissance Squadron operating Tu-95RT aircraft and jointly based at Kipelovo, a probing operation was undertaken into the airspace of Iceland and the Faroe Islands. Much useful information was obtained about air defences, acquisition and target identification frequencies.

Following the Vietnam War, the late 1970s and the 1980s saw an escalation in the interaction between NATO and Russian aircraft. After several years of lacklustre military upgrades and replacement cycles for the US inventory, a new and increasingly proactive approach during the early years of the Reagan administration (1981-1989) put US forces into a more dynamic contact with their Russian counterparts. The margins between national and international airspace once again became blurred and indistinct. The Tu-142 was again at the forefront of that shift. Throughout this period the number of annual sorties ran at 70-90 for the Tu-142, on one occasion dropping sonobuoys and depth bombs to warn off NATO ships.

As friendly relations with Vietnam grew, a naval air detachment was set up in Da Nang with the older

Early Tu-142s from the Kuibyshev plant were fitted with 12-wheel landing gear bogies. This was found to be ineffective and was replaced with four-wheel units. (Igor Bubin)

From 1988 to 2017 the Indian Air Force operated eight Tu-142MK-E types, this one seen at Hansa, Goa, with an Il-38 May in the background. (Andrea)

Tu-142 aircraft going to the Pacific Fleet as the Tu-142M was introduced to the 76th ASW regiment. This presence in the region had been steadily growing since 1975 but in the aftermath of the war conditions were so poor that operational effectiveness was a fraction of what it was with the Northern Fleet. Where planners anticipated around 40 sorties a year to patrol the seas around the Philippines, barely 10 were possible, supplies being late and fewer than requested, naval surface liaison being negligible and morale poor. Nevertheless, Tu-142s at Da Nang flew patrols along Japan's east coastal regions conducting reconnaissance right up to the Aleutian Islands.

As with the Tu-95, upgrades were introduced for the Tu-142 and some equipment which qualified for new variants were introduced. Driven by a more focused development of specific operational roles, the Tu-142MK (Bear-F Mod 3) was configured as a dedicated ASW aircraft. Appearing during the early 1980s, it had an infrared, side-looking radar, towed magnetometer, an infrared seeker, and a greatly improved NPK-142M flight navigation system which operated closely with the flight control system to control the aircraft during active sub-attack operations. Initial pre-production aircraft entered service in November 1980, operations aided by a new magnetic anomaly detector.

One of India's Tu-142MK-Es from the Soviet inventory on patrol. (Author's collection)

An Indian Naval Air Arm Tu-142MK-E escorted by a Grumman F-14 Tomcat. (USN)

A Tu-142M with stretched fuselage, Big Bulge target-acquisition radar and relocated antenna with a fairing for electrical wiring connecting avionics packages running along the starboard forward fuselage. (Author's collection)

A further evolution introduced the Tu-142MZ, which NATO identified as Bear-F Mod 4, appearing in the late 1980s. With the more powerful NK-12MP replacing the original NK-12MV engines, it had more advanced ASW equipment including the latest Korshun-KN-N search radar and an improved solar navigation system. The overall improvement greatly enhanced performance during sub-hunting sorties and reduced the cost of the sonobuoys, submarines now being detected down to a depth of 800m (2,625ft) in seas up to Force-5.

Again, development was tediously slow and the collapse of the USSR came before it could be declared fully operational; not until 1993 did it support the Russian Navy. By this time a few additional upgrades had crept in which provided a better ECM suite and improved search radar elements. In the closing years of the Soviet regime, which came to an end in 1991, Tu-142 units were unable to conduct the same number of sorties, a lack of fuel restraining flying hours.

An intelligence-gathering Tu-142M escorted by a P-3 Orion of the US Navy. This particular Orion was transferred to the Republic of China in 2010. (US DOD)

A Tu-142 patrols high above the clouds. (DOD)

Improved Tu-142M produced at Kuibyshev. (US Navy)

Various one-off derivatives were proposed by the Taganrog facility including the Tu-142MZ-C cargo transport which offered a range capable of accessing all districts in the Soviet and post-USSR federation, and a Tu-142MP would have had advanced ASW equipment. To provide a dedicated communications relay between submarines, the Tu-142MR (Bear-J) was a variant of the MK and several of these were produced from Taganrog and used with the 76th Regiment operating from Kipelovo. They had some equipment stripped out and replaced the side-looking radar with a trailing wire antenna.

Other, less successful, derivatives included the use of the Tu-95 as a testbed for a new engine assigned

to the supersonic Tu-22. In July 1957 work began to adapt the second prototype Tu-95 for carrying the turbofan NK-6 equipped with afterburner promising a thrust of up to 37,300kW (50,000lb). Designated Tu-95LL, over time it would also be used for testing a range of other engines including the NK-144A for the Tu-144 supersonic transport, the NK-144-22 for the Tu-22M and the NK-22 for the Tu-22M1 and M2. For these activities, the subject engine was mounted to the underside of the fuselage with test instrumentation for recording and transmitting data from up to 371 sensor points.

A less successful role involved work on a flying research laboratory designated the Tu-95LAL to measure the radiation environment of a nuclear propulsion system and its impact on equipment and instrumentation. The airframe selected for this purpose was Tu-95M No. 408 with the complete restructuring of the fuselage during 1961, 34 missions being flown with the reactor installed between May and August that year. The crew was isolated in the pressurised forward fuselage with multiple radiation sensors at numerous locations around the aircraft. The shielding provided worked very well and a considerable amount of information was learned from the tests but the programme to build a nuclear-powered bomber succumbed to the same logical arguments that caused the cancellation of similar plans in the United States.

A Tu-142MZ with new chin fairings and advanced upgrades to its avionics and radar systems on approach to Vladivostok. (Russian MOD)

CHAPTER 7

A SUPERSONIC FORCE

By the end of the 1960s, the only supersonic bomber fielded by the Russian Air Force was the Tu-22 Blinder. There was much wrong with this aircraft and a lot about it that the crews strongly disliked. Compared to the subsonic Tu-16, which it was originally intended to replace, and which had a far more distinctive and successful career, it was a disappointment. It was below the anticipated speed and short on range, it suffered several malfunctions and was prone to defects which rendered it unserviceable on many occasions from the time it entered service in 1962.

The Tu-22 was uncomfortable to fly, its crew forced to contend with a poor cockpit design and low performance. The KP variant shown here was equipped for electronic warfare. (Author's collection)

The cockpit had arguably the worst ergonomic layout of any combat aircraft deployed by an air force anywhere. It was configured with controls and switches the crew were unable to reach without telescoping pointers to reach and push switches and chords to pull others; strangely, this was an accepted standard for contemporary Russian spacecraft and exists to this day with the Soyuz vehicle, where pointers are used for reclining cosmonauts to activate controls they are unable to reach. And despite an autopilot, the controls were heavy, demanding extreme physical exertions by the pilots.

Some of the problems were associated with the amount of work the pilot had to perform. That brought difficulties to crews who were used to having a co-pilot do most of the flying. When commanders came from the two-pilot Tu-16 and transitioned to the Tu-22, the absence of a second pilot placed an unfamiliar burden on experienced men who had

become accustomed to delegating flight deck tasks. Unexpectedly, there were a high number of dropouts from the conversion training, the most successful pilots transitioning from the Sukhoi Su-17, Russia's first variable-sweep combat aircraft.

Balancing high cruise speed and its optimised wing with the need for a low-speed take-off and landing performance on a single design was impossible, irrespective of the number of high-lift devices used. Variable (swing-wing) geometry was the only single solution to satisfy both objectives, achieving a low aspect-ratio for supersonic flight and converting to a high aspect-ratio wing for manoeuvrability and agility at subsonic speeds. The landing speed of the Tu-22B was 100km/h (62mph) faster than preceding bombers in the inventory and handling was negatively affected by the wing, which had been optimised for high speed. There were difficulties holding station on a tanker due to a lack of sensitivity in the controls and

A new generation of US combat aircraft including the variable-geometry F-14A Tomcat, seen here demonstrating its swing-wing profiles, increased the vulnerability of Soviet bombers. (USN)

The US Hound Dog stand-off missile prompted the Russian Ministry of Defence to invest in a new generation of cruise weapons and repurposed delivery platforms in its own bomber force. (Author's collection)

the stalling speed of 290km/h (180mph) brought its own difficulties.

Other issues included access for ground crew who were unable to reach many of the aircraft systems, including the high-mounted engines, without access platforms and ladders. And loading weapons brought its own hazards as the Kh-22 needed liquid propellants which were highly toxic and required heavy protective garments, hot to wear and restricting movement. The downward-firing ejection seat was almost certainly fatal at low altitude and the high attrition rate of the aircraft – 22% of the 313 built – had its own effect on crew morale. Overall, the aircraft was never the feared intruder the West had assumed it to be and its vulnerability to a new generation of US interceptors, especially the Phoenix-armed F-14, rendered it all but useless.

The origin of what would become the worthy successor to the Tu-22 began with dissatisfaction over the fixed-wing supersonic bomber and the bold decision at Tupolev to adopt variable geometry (VG) for better performance all round. There were many

aspects of the Blinder's design that both manufacturer and customer knew could be improved. But there were also disagreements over what form those improvements should take and how to implement them. The Sukhoi T-4 had been a potential successor to the Blinder but that had been far too ambitious to gain approval.

US Navy F-14s escort a Tu-95 over the North Atlantic in September 1985. (DoD)

An RAF Eurofighter Typhoon F.Mk 2 keeps formation on a Tu-95. (RAF)

North American's mighty XB-70 experienced the same fate as that suffered by the Sukhoi T-4 – cancellation. (NAA)

What the Soviet Air Force wanted was a multi-mission aircraft, still capable of supersonic speed but with a wide range of mission types requiring low-speed, low-altitude operation and with the flexibility to carry iron bombs, nuclear bombs or dual-capable cruise missiles. It also wanted rough-field operational capabilities, a guiding prerequisite for many Soviet-era combat aircraft. The only solution was to base the design

The inner fixed wing sections supported the pivot for Blackjack's variable geometry outer wing sections. (Author's collection)

The overall design of the fuselage underbody is clearly visible here: nose gear, weapons bay and main landing leg doors, together with trailing edge flight control surfaces. (Author's collection)

around VG wings with a generalised configuration capable of supporting all those very different roles.

The VG wings allowed an increase in lift/drag at modest sweepback which also increased subsonic range, while maximum sweepback allowed better acceleration through the transonic and with lower stress imposed on the vertical and horizontal tail surfaces. The price for this came in a predicted increase in weight of 4% as the design incorporated pivot and actuating mechanisms and the effect that these had on load-bearing ribs. Lightweight materials would be essential, together with effective lubricants while stability and efficient handling and control support would require the pivots to be placed in wide gloves forming the inner wing sections.

The technology was extensively researched at TsAGI and within the Tupolev OKB. The VG concept had been chosen several years earlier by General Dynamics for the F-111 and the general engineering design of

that aircraft was available to the Russians through commercial journals and magazines published in America. The same concept would also be applied to the Rockwell International B-1A and B-1B.

Tupolev's initial Aircraft 145 design evolution was less dependent on changes and refinements to the configuration as it was on the results of tests and technology studies. The bureau put its own funds into the concept, which was initially designated as a development of the Tu-22K but which was clearly going to be a completely different aircraft with a much wider operational envelope. It was, however, essential to get the support of TsAGI, of the manufacturing ministry, the Air Force, the bomber fraternity and the political elites who would make the ultimate decision on concept development.

After nearly three years of work, at the end of 1967 Tupolev received official permission to proceed and the 145 became the Tu-22M but the evolution had

The Tu-145 design was a breakaway project from Aircraft 106 and would mark beginning of the programme leading to the Tu-22M swing-wing, supersonic bomber. (Yefim Gordon via Tony Buttler)

already seen several configuration changes. When work began in 1965, Aircraft 145 had used the 106B concept as a starting point – which had high-set wings capable of VG at specific sweep angles with the pivots within fixed inner sections and a leading edge sweep of 65 degrees. The outer wing panels would be set at 20 degrees for take-off and landing as well as achieving the best possible range in subsonic flight; the maximum 72-degree sweep would achieve optimum transonic flight at low altitude; the 65-degree position was optimum for long range at supersonic speeds.

When compared with the fixed-wing 106B, empty weight had increased by 5% and a projected 7% for take-off weight. However, with the VG options, rough-field performance was better than it would have been for the 106B with a maximum take-off run some 25-30% shorter. Also welcome was the theoretical ability of Aircraft 145 to fly down as low as 50m (164ft) at 1,100km/h (683mph), where the 106B was unable to fly anywhere near that level. At 2,200km/h (1,367mph) in supersonic cruise, compared with 1,800km/h (1,118mph), the 145 also had a range of 4,000km (2,485 miles), which was the most optimistic value for the 106B.

Swing Wing Tu-22M

Tupolev had based the Aircraft 145 design around a strike mission with medium or high altitude over

the target across a wide range of speeds, or it could fly at very low level as a penetrator or cruise missile platform. With a wide range of mission capabilities available, Tupolev designated the strike version as the 145K, a reconnaissance variant as the 145R and an ECM variant as the 145P. These were plausible, given the projected carrying capacity and internal volume of the aircraft, its broad range of flight characteristics and its advanced electrical power supply system together with electronic warfare suite.

In this initial design the engines were located above the fuselage as they were on the Blinder. Tupolev had wanted to retain that arrangement but TsAGI had misgivings and believed the data they had obtained showed engines in that location would reduce pressure recovery at a speed range of Mach 1.35-1.45. Tupolev concurred and relocated the two engines to a position in the rear fuselage, making it necessary to lower the wings to a mid-fuselage position with intake boxes located either side of the forward fuselage. Perhaps not surprisingly, TsAGI conducted a detailed analysis of similar intake boxes on the McDonnell Douglas F-4 Phantom II and agreed that this was the optimum location. In fact, when it appeared the initial Tu-22M had an intake shape that was almost a direct copy of the Phantom II's.

Changes too were made when the required range was extended, adding a co-pilot, changing the layout of the cabin and placing the pilots side by side. This affected the shape of the fixed inboard wing section, which was now given a fixed leading edge sweep of 56 degrees, the outer panels now moving between 20-degree, 30-degree, 50-degree or 60-degree positions or at intermediate stops by either manual or automatic control. This dispensed with ailerons for spoilers and provided hydraulically-actuated screwjacks at the pivot points.

This transition to the definitive configuration, designated the Tu-22KM, was approved by the Council of Ministers on 28 November 1967 with the first flight anticipated within 16 months. Several changes were made to the optimum mission profile which added requirements and increased technical challenges. To get the prototypes flying, the Air Force

Located at the Zulhany air museum in the Ukraine, this Tu-22M0, of which only nine were built, features an early air intake design. This would be modified for the M2 variant and refined with the M3 into the familiar box-shape. (Aeroprints.com)

wanted to divide the programme into two phases. The first would fly powered by NK-144-22 engines delivering a thrust of 196,157N (44,100lb) with basic systems of the type fitted to the Blinder. The second phase would fly aircraft powered by an improved NK-144 with a thrust of 220,676N (49,612lb), equipped with the advanced systems originally detailed and with automatic flight control electronics. They would also carry a tail gun position, newly specified, and be

configured for the Kh-22 cruise missile. In fact, two aircraft would be prepared; one with a tail gun and one with an ECM pod.

Following a mock-up review in October and November 1967, the initial series of aircraft were to be built with the interim engine and the basic equipment

Preceded as a swing-wing aircraft in Russian service by the Su-17, the Tu-22M was a completely different aircraft to the Tu-22. (Author's collection)

The Kuznetsov NK-144 powered the initial version of the Tu-22M but it was inefficient and unreliable and was replaced by the NK-25. (Author's collection)

The definitive engine for the Tu-22M, the Kuznetsov NK-25; two power each Backfire bomber. (Romashov German Viktorovich)

A Kh-22 on the inner, fixed wing section of a Tu-22M. (Kobel)

from the Blinder and designated Tu-22M0, with initial prototype construction at the Kazan factory to save time. Chief engineer Markov was in charge of the programme with I. A. Starikov as the chief engineer. Both men were highly experienced with a long history at Tupolev, Starikov since the Tu-2. Slightly delayed and equipped with the NK-144-22 engines the first prototype was finished in mid-1969 with rollout the following month, a prestigious event attended by Minister of Aircraft Production Pyotr V. Dementyev along with key dignitaries.

Piloted by Tupolev test pilots V. R. Borisov and Boris I. Veremey, along with navigator L. S. Sikachov and weapon systems operator K. A. Shcherbakov, the first Tu-22M0 prototype flew on 30 August 1969. The start of the flight test programme soon revealed some deficiencies that required further work to remedy. By the end of 1972, a further nine aircraft had been produced of which five were sent to the combat and conversion training centre at Ryazan for an intensive round of crew and ground technician training.

The results of the initial flight tests in 1970 showed a take-off weight of 121,000kg (255,805lb) carrying

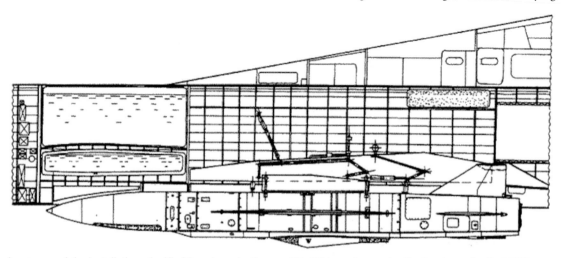

A cutaway of the installation of a Kh-22 cruise missile on a BD-45F launcher under the fuselage of a Tu-22M3. (Author's collection)

Escorted by a US Navy F-14A Tomcat, a Tu-22M1 Backfire B transits cloud cover. (USN)

Carrying the Soviet Union to a new place on the world stage, deployment of the Backfire bomber brought pressure for reciprocal deployment of the US Gryphon Ground Launched Cruise Missile (GLCM). (Author's collection)

With a Kh-22 under the starboard wing, a TU-22M3 lifts off. (Author's collection)

a single Kh-22, a subsonic range of 4,140km (2,572 miles), a maximum speed of 1,530km/h (951mph) and a take-off roll of 2,600m (8,530ft). Although powered by the NK-144-22, this was far below expectations and updates would convert it into the Tu-22M1 during 1970. Some parts of the airframe were strengthened, weight was reduced, aerodynamics were improved and the engine intakes were redesigned to give the frontal area a more rectangular shape. Boundary layer splitter plates were lengthened and auxiliary blow-in doors were changed in configuration and location. The wingspan was increased by 1.5m (4.9ft) and the leading-edge slats were modified, with the fairing on the fixed inner wing sections reduced in size and shape. It was also an opportunity to install the ABSU-145 automatic flight control system.

A Tu-22M3 carrying the FAB-500 M-54 general-purpose bomb inboard, up to nine on each pylon. (Alex Beltyokov/RuSpotters Team)

Parachute-retarded bombs released from the fuselage bomb bay of a Tu-22M3. (Author's collection)

The cockpit of an early production Tu-22M3 displays the transition from analogue to digital subsystems. (Author's collection)

A revealing view of the underside of this Tu-22M3 taking off from Ryazan Dyagilevo shows the location and size of the fuselage bomb bay. (Author's collection)

Evocative shot of a Backfire touching down. (Author's collection)

The first Tu-22M1 (retrospectively codenamed Backfire-A), still equipped with the same engines, made its initial flight at Kazan on 28 July 1971 piloted by B. I. Veremey and confidence increased as the test programme ran forward, the decision to place the type in production having been made before the end of the year. Nine M1 variants had been completed by the end of 1972 and five went to the combat and conversion training centre. But this version was still underperforming. Range was still a low 5,000km (3,107 miles) and maximum speed obtained was little better than the M0.

The decision was taken to place a developed variant, the Tu-22M2 (Backfire-B) into production

Detail on the refuelling probe for a Tu-22M1, a point of contention in arms limitation talks. (Tom Erik Gundersen)

Ukrainian Tu-22M3 at Bratislava, Slovakia. (KGyST)

and no M1 aircraft entered service. The more powerful engines were installed and some analyses were made as to the suitability of the Kuznetsov NK-25 engine with a thrust of 244,640N (55,000lb) and a higher specific fuel consumption. Development of this three-spool, low-bypass engine began in earnest during 1972 and it remains today one of the most powerful turbofan engines in service anywhere for a supersonic aircraft. It has three compressor stages (three low pressure; five intermediate pressure; and seven high pressure), annular combustors and a four-stage axial turbine. Most notable, the M2 had distinctive intake ramps reminiscent of the MiG-29.

The M2 variant offered further weight reductions, improved aerodynamics, a NK-45 navigation suite, the ABSU-145M auto-flight control system, the PRS-4KM gun with ranging radar and TP-1 KM TV sight and a specially developed ECM system. Special attention had been paid to providing an integrated set of support and electronic systems for enhanced

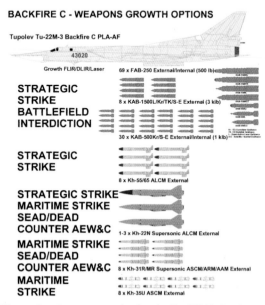

BACKFIRE C - WEAPONS GROWTH OPTIONS

Tupolev Tu-22M-3 Backfire C PLA-AF

43020

Growth FLIR/DLIR/Laser   69 x FAB-250 External/Internal (500 lb)

**STRATEGIC
STRIKE
BATTLEFIELD
INTERDICTION**
8 x KAB-1500L/Kr/TK/S-E External (3 klb)

30 x KAB-500Kr/S-E External/Internal (1 klb)

**STRATEGIC
STRIKE**
8 x Kh-55/65 ALCM External

**STRATEGIC STRIKE
MARITIME STRIKE
SEAD/DEAD
COUNTER AEW&C**
1-3 x Kh-22N Supersonic ALCM External

**MARITIME STRIKE
SEAD/DEAD
COUNTER AEW&C**
8 x Kh-31R/MR Supersonic ASCM/ARM/AAM External

**MARITIME
STRIKE**
8 x Kh-35U ASCM External

The optional weapons suite for the Tu-22M3 displays a wide range of gravity bombs, mines, stand-off weapons and sea-mines. (Author's collection)

The remotely controlled Gsh-23 defensive tail gun on a Tu-22M3. (Clemens Vasters)

compatibility, much needed in Russian bombers of this period. The M2 could carry up to three Kh-22M missiles and conventional or nuclear bombs or mines to a maximum capacity of 24,000kg (52,920lb). Carrying a single Kh-22 under the fuselage, range was now a maximum of 5,600km (3,480 miles) subsonic or 1,900km (1,180 miles) supersonic. The first off the line made its initial flight on 7 May 1973.

Defined as the K-22M2 weapon system, with the Kh-22 integrated into the aircraft as a dedicated strike package, 211 of this variant would be produced with the last in 1983. Its operational debut in 1976 brought a better response from air and ground crew than the Tu-22B before it. Work assignments on the flight deck were now shared with the side-by-side seating for the two pilots and the addition of a third and fourth crewmember helped with mission operations. Access to the crew compartment was via a roll-up platform with separate doors directly beneath the fuselage centreline. Whereas the Tu-22B had altitude limitations on the use of its ejection seats, all four crewmembers now had upward-firing seats with a much higher level of confidence in their survivability.

For reasons discussed later, when the Tu-22M appeared, and was keenly reported on by the trade and defence press of the West during the early 1970s. Fears were voiced concerning its intercontinental potential. NATO gave it the code name Backfire and it created quite a stir not only in defence but also political and public circles. The aircraft was not the game-changer it was claimed to be but it did come at the time of the START-1 treaty and was a worrying impediment to confidence in Russian compliance with limitations on strategic weapons. Previously installed with a flight refuelling probe, withdrawn to ensure compliance with limits on the number of strategic bombers, the Americans accepted this as excluding the Tu-22M from the agreed criteria for categories defined by the agreement.

As operated, the Tu-22M2 had a range of only 5,100km (3,168 miles) and a maximum speed of 1,800km/h (1,118mph) but the requirement

demanded better and the decision was taken in December 1974 to proceed with the Tu-22M3 powered by the Kuznetsov NK-25 engines producing an additional 20% thrust and a much better specific fuel consumption for improved range. Other changes included a new, two-dimensional air inlet with flow control ramps, an increase in the maximum pivot angle from 60 degrees to 65 degrees, an enclosed housing for the wing pivots, a nose extended by 0.8m (2.6ft) with a flight refuelling probe reinstalled and replacement of the twin-cannon rear turret with a single Gsh-23 cannon in an aerodynamic UKU-9A-502M barbette.

A vigorous weight-reduction programme identified specific areas with the object of cutting up to 2,700kg (5,953lb), including a modified tailplane with a shorter rudder and a lighter structure, a single-piece inner wing section, titanium firewalls, new and better thermal insulation, improved electrical wiring looms with better heat protection and improvements to the environmental control system. Most significant was the removal of the cumbersome, single-phase AC converters and their replacement with hydro-mechanical, constant-speed AC generators in the electrical system. The use of contactless DC generators were new to the M3 variant.

Improvements were also made to the navigation system and the ECM equipment countered the latest developments from US and NATO jammers and electronic targeting. These were a significant improvement over the systems carried on the Blinder and included the PN-A bombing system in the underside of the nose with the radar connected to the auto-control system which allowed low-level flight, albeit nowhere near the levels provided by true terrain-following radar operated by aircraft such as the F-111A and other contemporary NATO combat aircraft. Defensive countermeasures included the Sirena-3 warning receiver with its fairing at top of the vertical tail and radio frequency jammers in addition to those in the gun barbette.

The first M3 (NATO name Backfire-C) made its initial flight on 20 June 1977 and entered parallel production the following year, replacing the M2 on the line from 1984, a total of 268 being built at the Kazan facility. Encouragingly, initial tests with the M3 indicated a greatly improved performance over the M2, with a 15% increase in the operating radius, proportional to bombload and speed, and a maximum speed of up to 2,300km/h (1,429mph) with the NK-25 engines. Several state trials took place toward the end of the decade and the type was cleared for full service introduction in 1981 but the weapons system took much longer to clear its development cycle and that was not operational with the aircraft before March 1989.

Long before that, the Backfire was tried and tested for the wide variety of roles it had been designed to perform. The ongoing almost pathological obsession with defeating the US carrier task forces meant an anti-shipping role was evaluated with the M3 carrying the Kh-15, a short-range weapon, with up to six carried on ejector racks on the fuselage and wings. The Raduga-designed missile was powered by a solid propellant rocket motor producing a maximum speed of Mach 5 and a range of 300km (186 miles) carrying a 300KT nuclear warhead. It would be compatible with the Tu-95MS and also with the Tu-160 and could be used variously as a defence suppression weapon clearing the path for following aircraft. To replace the Tu-22 in its reconnaissance role, the Tu-22M3R carried a wide range of optional photographic and ELINT equipment and this variant made its first flight on 6 December 1985 but crashed on a subsequent test flight. It never went into production.

Several concepts failed to make it to production, including a replacement for the ECM variant of the Tu-22 due to protracted development of new equipment. Neither did a prototype get the NK-32 engines that had been planned, although a Tu-22M3-LL test bed was prepared from the first M3 prototype for evaluating laminar-flow aerofoils. Further proposals came from Tupolev, including a further development airframe with NK-25 engines and carrying a pair of Kh-45 missiles. There was also a proposed long-range interceptor for hitting enemy strike aircraft long before they reached their

targets and identified as the Tu-22DP. Several other developments, each identified by a rolling number suffix to the Tu-22M designation, proposed changes to the wing planform, some with fixed-wing, double-delta planform and with more advanced armament.

Type ratings and familiarisation with the Backfire took place at Dyagilevo air base where crews passed out in just 120 days. Service introduction began in 1974 with the 185th Guards Heavy Bomber Air Regiment at Poltava. The M3 replaced the Tu-16, with other units continuing to fly the Tu-22B. It was with this unit that the initial tranche of launch tests with the Kh-22 took place. To begin with there were frustrating problems, not least with the new NK-25 engines, which had a service life of just 50 hours. And there were problems too with the hydraulics and the new generation of avionics and electromagnetic compatibility issues plagued the early years, where a lot of the flying was for test and modification purposes.

These issues would gradually be addressed as production aircraft were delivered. When the Soviet Union collapsed, an estimated 370 Tu-22M variants were still in service of which 210 were with long-range aviation units and 160 were with naval aviation.

Tu-160 – A Bigger Swing-Wing

The search for a multi-role, long-range supersonic bomber went on even as the Backfire was in development. A requirement was outlined in a directive signed on 28 November 1967. The specified performance bordered on the fantastic: a maximum speed of up to 3,500km/h (2,175mph) at 18,000m (59,000ft) and a range of 13,000km (8,078 miles); a subsonic range of up to 18,000km (11,185 miles) and a maximum bomb load of 45,000kg (100,000lb). With capacity for carrying cruise missiles, nuclear or conventional weapons, it was envisaged as an intercontinental strategic bomber with the performance to threaten all of the continental United States.

Its conceptual origin was a product of purging Khrushchev's followers who had been fixated on ballistic missiles of all classes – paid for by starving piloted combat aircraft of the resources required to

Seeking to further exploit the basic T-4 technology, between 1967 and 1969 the company came up with the swing-wing T-4M, as displayed in this model. (Yefim Gordon via Tony Buttler)

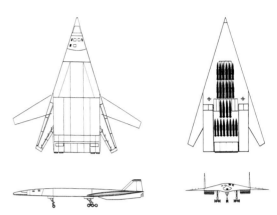

The T-4MS-200 with a projected range of 7,000km (4,350 miles), a speed of Mach 3.5 and a bomb load of 24 Kh-15 cruise missiles. (Yefim Gordon via Tony Buttler)

keep up with expanding US capabilities. Khrushchev lost his political position in October 1964, largely as a result of reformist policies and the Cuban Missile Crisis of October 1962. His successor, Leonid Brezhnev, was less centrist in his views and veered away from détente toward increased resources for expanding the army and the air forces. It was partly due to this hardening in the approach to international relations that the Ministry of Defence was given approval to broaden the diversity of a technological revolution which would see the Soviet Union surge past the point of parity in weapons quality and quantity to a burgeoning superiority during the 1970s.

The directive of November 1967 resulted in advanced designs from Sukhoi, picking up on research from its T-4 (Project 100, see Chapter 4) and using that data as a starting point to conceptualise a swing-wing, four-engine design designated the T-4M. Retaining the canard but replacing the large delta wing with a VG design. By 1970 the type model had transitioned into the T-4MS (Project 200). But this was a very different aircraft and featured a tailless, blended wing/body shape with completely different aerodynamic qualities and, as specified, a distinctly multi-role capability.

In 1970 Sukhoi won a design competition for a Mach 3, long-range strike system with delta-wing planform incorporating variable geometry outer sections, designated T-4MS. (Yefim Gordon via Tony Buttler)

Bearing a strong resemblance to the North American Rockwell B-1A, the swing-wing Myasishchev M-18 was a response to the 1967 requirement that produced the Sukhoi T-4. (Yefim Gordon via Tony Buttler)

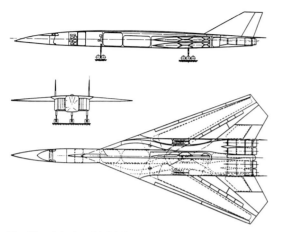

The Myasishchev M-20-2 was one of many different designs under this designation, a swing-wing bomber with four engines and chin intakes. (Yefim Gordon via Tony Buttler)

Back in play as a working design OKB, Myasishchev focused on two possible configurations, each with VG wings. The M-18 would have a conventional

tail whereas at least one concept from the prolific M-20 series would be tailless but each was capable of high altitude reconnaissance or maritime support operations, especially anti-submarine warfare.

Two years after the initial requirement, greater emphasis was placed on multi-role capability at the expense of absolute speed and very high bomb capacity. Because it had its workload full with the development of the Tu-22M, the Tu-142, the Tu-144 supersonic airliner, not to mention tests with the Tu-154 narrow-body airliner, Tupolev had remained distant from the new requirement. With the more focused approach, and with some similarities to the Tu-22M specification now evident, that changed. The Tu-144 was instrumental in providing valuable data for development of what would become the Blackjack.

Work at Tupolev began at Section K where Aleksey Tupolev quickly approved its project designation Tu-160. Starting with a clean sheet, the work was kept confidential and the design team allowed a free hand

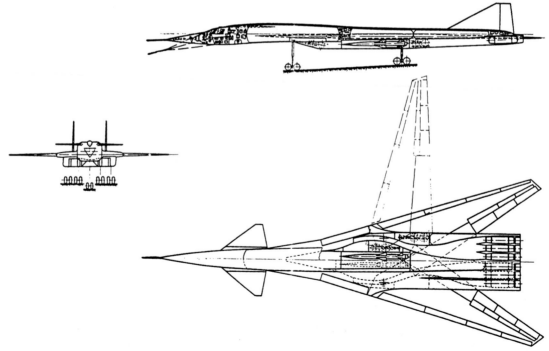

Another variant, the M-20-18 had six rear-mounted engines, twin fins, a droop nose and capacity for two internal cruise missiles. (Yefim Gordon via Tony Buttler)

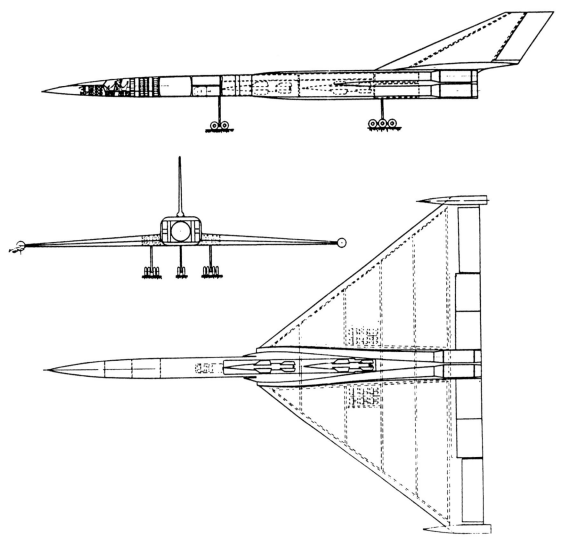

Almost the last of the series, the M-20-24 was a tailless variant with delta wing and provision for two internal Kh-45 cruise weapons in tandem. (Yefim Gordon via Tony Buttler)

in defining an appropriate configuration for the 1967 requirement. Not much progress had been made with the Sukhoi and Myasishchev concepts, and Tupolev recognised that their proposals, still evolving, went far down the road of a dedicated strategic bomber rather than a combat aircraft capable of performing multiple roles.

At Section K, data from the second-generation supersonic transport, designated Tu-244, was producing good results applicable to the new project.

Much of this work helped shape the initial design, adopting the aircraft's tailless configuration with a calculated L/D of 7.9:1 at supersonic speed and 15:1 subsonic. But because the potential high speed would come at the price of extensive and protracted research and development work on new, high-temperature materials, it was decided to limit the speed to Mach 2.3. In seeking Mach 3 as originally envisaged, titanium alloys would be essential, increasing cost by an estimated 15-20% in addition to the greater

Its hands full with development of the Tu-22M and the Tu-144 SST seen here, Tupolev only latterly became involved in competing in the 1967 requirement for a long-range supersonic bomber. (Author's collection)

demands on the structural integrity of the airframe. The VG wings were bought at the cost of complexity and weight, but if anyone was in a position to apply VG to a large aircraft it was Tupolev. Calculations showed a distinct advantage in a swept-wing configuration, allowing subsonic cruise prior to entering hostile airspace for a supersonic dash to the target. VG wings would improve aerodynamic efficiency by 20-50% over fixed wings. A wide range of supporting design possibilities were examined, a preference for hybrid engines being expressed which required a composite propulsion system providing turbofan capability for

The Tu-160 was refined into a single-fin concept with drooping wing tips and engines mounted under the fuselage. (Yefim Gordon via Tony Buttler)

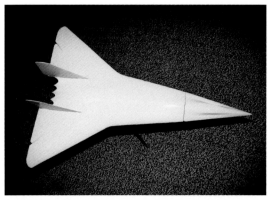

An early design iteration of the Tu-160 concept with twin fins and adjacent engines in the delta-wing fuselage bridge. (Yefim Gordon via Tony Buttler)

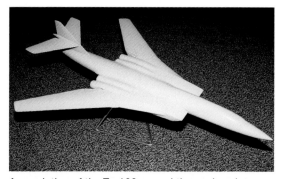

An evolution of the Tu-160 moved the engines into the fixed portion of a swing-wing design with wedge-shaped intakes and variable ramps reminiscent of the Tu-22M3. (Yefim Gordon via Tony Buttler)

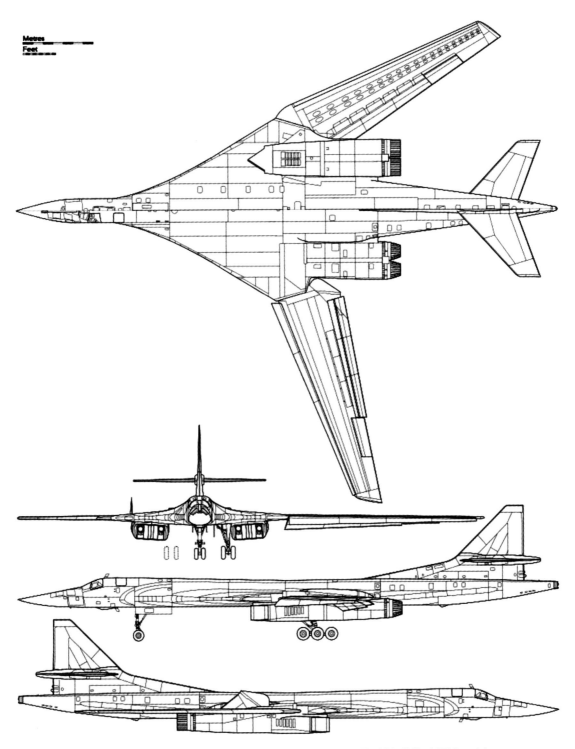

Metres

Feet

A four-view general-arrangement drawing of the definitive layout for the Tu-160. (Mike1979Russia)

The Russians made great efforts to obtain as much information as possible about the B-1A when it began flight trials, seeking to acquire technical details of the wing pivot mechanism. (USAF)

subsonic speeds and a turbojet cycle for supersonic dash.

Examining a range of design iterations, Tupolev chose initially a tailless configuration and it was this that was submitted, along with proposals from Sukhoi and Myasishchev to the Ministry of Aircraft Production through a competition in 1972. Not surprisingly, a detailed comparison was made with the Rockwell International B-1 and the M-18 was selected as the preferable contender. The Sukhoi OKB was fully committed in design and production with a range of combat types, including the T-10, or Su-27, which the Air Force was determined should not be threatened.

However, it was quickly found that the newly reconstituted Myasishchev OKB was unable to put together a big enough team of skilled engineers and designers to begin making the M-18 a reality. As such, the Tupolev concept was chosen in its stead.

The Tupolev Tu-160 has been variously identified as Article 70 or Aircraft K, from the design bureau of that name under the leadership of Valentin I. Bliznuk.

Much work was put into determining the best layout for the multi-mission bomber role – including the positioning of electronics, defensive armament and weapons load.

A lot of the aircraft's performance as well as its operating flexibility depended on the engines, where they were mounted and what type of inlet arrangement was provided. The NK-25s fitted to the Tu-22M3 had the performance but not the fuel efficiency to satisfy the full potential of the airframe. Kuznetsov had developed a more efficient version, the NK-32, with the same maximum thrust of 244,640N (55,000lb) but a specific fuel consumption lower by 20% and a 5% improvement in thrust/weight ratio. These improvements and the fact that it came from a developed engine helped decide in its favour.

The intake design for the Tu-160 took account of work conducted by Myasishchev and was applied to the widest possible range of paired engine configurations from vertical to horizontal placement above or beneath the fuselage and below the wings close in to the fuselage sides. The bomb bay was set along the underside of the fuselage centre-section so as to keep it as close as possible to the centre of gravity. But the engine configuration of the Rockwell B-1A was looked at and a similar inboard placement selected. The intake took a lot of inspiration from previous work on the Tu-144 as this carried results from accumulated test hours. With consideration of the location of the bomb bay, the paired engines were to be located on the outer extremities of the fixed wing section.

The target maximum speed of Mach 2.3 required 24% of the structural weight to comprise titanium, with aluminium a further 58%, high-strength steels about 15% and composites 3%. With this established, the detailed design would be set around fixed parameters, not least of which was the quadruplex fly-by-wire (FBW) control system, making this the first bomber without any mechanical connections between the cockpit and the control surfaces except for back-up emergency use.

With the Tu-160 there was an opportunity to design the vehicle with electronically-controlled stability and to put greater emphasis on cockpit ergonomics than had been applied to the Backfire. It represented a leap forward in cockpit and crew support arrangements and was a considerable improvement over earlier Russian bombers. Seated on Zvezda K-36LM zero/zero ejection seats, pilots would benefit from having a sidestick controller replacing the central control column with wheel or yoke. This created a more intuitive approach to flying and manoeuvrability, common in fighter cockpits for some time. The four-person crew would access the pressurised compartment through an extending ladder in the nose wheel bay and they now had rest facilities with a stove for cooking, toilet and a folding bunk.

To a greater extent than had been possible with the Tu-22M, and infinitely more so than with previous Russian bombers, Tupolev worked with weapons manufacturers to ensure that the bomb bay could carry the widest range of munitions for the present inventory and for future types still in development. Unlike its US contemporary the B-1, from the outset the Tu-160 was designed as a cruise missile carrier with multi-role bomber capability rather than the other way around. This brought it into contention with regard to an intercontinental strategic strike category under arms control limits specified by US-Soviet agreements. Nevertheless, it remained an ideal weapons carrier for a wide range of roles.

Munitions would be carried in two bays, fore and aft with more than twice the volume of the Tu-95MS, for a total capacity for 44,000kg (97,020lb). The principal weapon requirements were stipulated in December 1975 which had been from the outset the hypersonic Kh-45, one carried in each weapons bay. It was also to be capable of carrying 24 short-range Kh-15 missiles, with six on each of four MKU-6-1 rotary launchers, or 12 Kh-15M missiles and up to 12 Kh-55 subsonic cruise missiles. Or a mix of these different weapons.

Although it never entered service, with a length of 10.8m (35.5ft) and a height of 1.92m (6.25ft) with folded fins, the Kh-45 determined the size of each bomb bay. The Kh-45 was projected to have a weight of 4,500kg (9,922lb) with a range of up to 1,000km (621 miles) and a maximum speed variously quoted at up to 9,000km/h (5,590mph). Future-proofing the aircraft, the weapons system was to have been capable of supporting terrain-following, subsonic cruise missiles only then in the conceptual phase but approximately the equivalent of the General Dynamics Air-Launched Cruise Missile (ALCM).

Capabilities and Structure

A debate emerged between the Air Force and Tupolev over the inclusion of a tail barbette. The Air Force

The first new production Tu-160M prior to rollout in 2021. (Tupolev)

wanted the GSh-6-30, six-barrel 30mm cannon but Tupolev preferred to use the weight and the volume to incorporate advanced ECM systems. Moreover, Tupolev proposed a Tu-160PP variant exclusively equipped to deliver a protective cover over large bomber formations. Eventually, the notion of a barbette was dropped.

As design development evolved, radar signatures became important and Tupolev applied several techniques to reduce the radar cross-section (RCS) of the completed aircraft. But these were secondary and did little to significantly suppress the visibility of the aircraft to radar. The weapons suite and avionics, however, were key to mission success and an avionics integration test and simulation rig was assembled specifically for evaluating them. Availability of this rig did a lot to hasten operational readiness of the Tu-160, aided further by the construction in 1981 of a simulation chamber for high-altitude conditions. Measuring 40 x 18 x 9.8m (131.2 x 59 x 32.2ft), this allowed evaluation of the avionics under all anticipated conditions.

Research into the rapidly expanding science of electronic air defence systems and countermeasures occupied much of the conversation over manned penetrating bombers in the 1970s and 1980s. Russian scientists and engineers expanded their research in this area due to the debate over stealthy characteristics of individual aircraft and the need to shrink the effective radius of air defence radar sites encountered by an intruder. This in itself stimulated development in Russia of specialised centres of research, development and testing focused on countermeasures. By the mid-1980s this work had produced many new defensive avionics systems in the rush for systems to counter known developments in US technology.

The final blended design evolved through a wide range of aerodynamic shapes and configurations examined in wind tunnels and initial conclusions were that the aircraft would have an empty weight of 103,000kg (227,070lb) and a take-off weight of 260,000kg (573,190lb) with a fuel load of 148,000kg (326,280lb). The blended wing/body

Another view of the newly built Tu-160M. (Tupolev)

The prototype Tu-160 during runway and taxi trials in November 1981. (Yefim Gordon via Tony Buttler)

The fine lines of the Tu-160 closely resemble those of the B-1A which, at the time of its development had been cancelled by the Carter administration. (Tupolev)

layout supported VG outer wing sections with sweep angles of 20 degrees, 35 degrees and 65 degrees and a cruciform tail with high-set horizontal stabiliser and an all-moving upper section to the fin instead of a rudder.

Hinged inboard sections to the triple-section helped increase the lift/drag ratio while double slotted flaps capable of folding upward to form

The Tu-160 has evolved engine intake boxes refined from experience with the Tu-22M3. (Tupolev)

fences improved aerodynamic performance close to the juxtaposition of the fixed and moveable wing sections. Tunnel tests showed that with these the maximum lift/drag was 19:1 for subsonic speed and more than 6:1 in supersonic flight. The flaps carried movable curtains to close up the gap between the rear spar and the front flap segment.

A further innovation was the formation of a boundary-layer fence at maximum sweep angle by upward rotation of the inner sections of the outer wing trailing edges together with the triangular sections of the inboard flap segments. This reduced the air flow around the fixed and variable wing sections to prevent the need for a seal as would otherwise be necessary if the fully swept trailing edge slipped inside a slot on the fixed section of the wing; a feature which was difficult to design for minimal drag. The outer section of each wing also carried spoilers, lift dumpers and flaperons in six sections.

While superficially appearing similar to the VG wing on the B-1B, the wing on the Tu-160 has a

As seen on this Ukrainian Tu-160, the blended wing-body form lends itself to some degree of reduced radar cross-section but continued attempts to give the aircraft a more stealthy profile have failed expectations. (Oleg V. Belyakov/AirTeam Images)

4.7% greater pivoting surface area of 189.83m² (2041.18ft²) versus 181m² (1,950ft²) but with a span of 57.7m (189.25ft) compared with 45m (146ft) for the Rockwell/Boeing bomber. The swept span of the Tu-160 was 35.8m (116.75ft) compared with 24m (79ft) for the B-1B. The aspect ratio for the three swept positions was 6.78 for the 20-degree setting, 5.64 at 35 degrees and 2.85 at 65 degrees. Overall the wing is designed for higher flight loads than the B-1B and this is reflected through the operating envelope.

The all-moving trapezoidal horizontal stabilisers are carried on a centre-section to form a single unit. Dynamic problems encountered early in the flight test programme required a reduction in span to 13.26m (43.5ft) with an aspect ratio of 3.16 but retaining the leading edge sweep of 44 degrees and a surface area of 55.6m² (597.85ft²). Fabricated in two sections, the

fin incorporated the fixed lower section which flowed across into the upper fuselage fillet and supported the dielectric panels, while the trailing edge had ECM antennas. The moving upper section had the all-flying section for directional control. The total fin assembly had a height of 6.95m (22.75ft) and a leading edge sweep of 47 degrees with an aspect ratio of 1.15.

For manufacturing, the fuselage structure was divided into three sections, each of semi-monocoque, stressed-skin construction. Designated as the No 1 forward fuselage, the first of these incorporated the nose section, the pressurised flight deck, the nosewheel assembly with a fully retractable refuelling probe in the upper half and a radar and avionics bay below which also included a dielectric radome. The crew compartment had two forward seats for the commander and co-pilot and two aft seats for the navigator and the weapons systems operator. The windscreen consisted of two optically-flat Triplex centre panes and two curved panels, with four smaller side windows. Each aft crewmember also had a small side window.

The No. 2 forward fuselage section was integral for manufacture with the fixed, inner wing section and its leading edge root extensions carried fuel tanks and the forward weapons bay. This was also the component which incorporated the pivot boxes on the carry-through structure to the pivoting outer wing sections. This was one of the most complex of the four sections and carried the cabling and conduits from the weapons bays into the electronic control systems operated by the weapons systems operator on the flight deck.

The centre fuselage section carried the engine nacelles, the avionic bays and the APUs, together with the main wheel bays and the front of the aft weapons bay. The aft fuselage section provided the structural interface for the rear of the aft weapons bay together with three integral fuel tanks and associated plumbing and various equipment boxes. It also supported the tail fin attachment points, the braking parachute containers and the ESM system box in lieu of the originally proposed tail gun barbette. The fixed lower tail fin portion provided attachment for the horizontal stabiliser.

The fairly conventional hydraulically retracted landing gear was a typical Russian configuration equipped with all-weather damage mitigation guards and fences to prevent mud, ice and water throwing up obstacles into the wheel-bays and against the undersurface of the aircraft. The nose leg was steerable and retracted to the rear with an electrohydraulic actuator controlled by the rudder pedals. The twin-wheel nose assembly had the aforementioned debris guards to protect the engine intakes.

The main landing gear units provided six-wheel bogies with telescopic struts supporting three in tandem. The assemblies retracted aft into the centre fuselage and rotated through 180 degrees to sit inverted in the wells. They each had double transverse hinges positioning the units inwards as they shortened

on retraction to reduce the track by 1.2m (4ft). The landing gear was one area set aside for improvement during later development on the production line. Nose and main legs incorporated oleo/pneumatic shock attenuators with the nose well closed off by two doors, with the main legs also having two doors and an auxiliary closeout panel.

The NK-21 engine chosen for the Tu-160 was big. With a length of 7.45m (24.5ft), a diameter of 1.7m (5.5ft) and with a dry weight of 3,650kg (8,046lb) it had a bypass ratio of 1.36, an engine pressure ratio of 28.2 and a turbine temperature of 1,356.85C (2,474.3F). The engines were housed in pairs in nacelles attached to the underside of the outer casing of the fixed wing structure by struts attached to three internal mounting rings. The bifurcated supersonic intakes had multi-section vertical flow control ramps with the upper lip of the intake serving as a boundary layer splitter plate, the duct gradually transitioning from a rectangular to a circular cross-section at the compressor face. Six auxiliary blowout doors were located on the outer and inner faces of the nacelle to admit additional air at high rpm levels.

The TA-12 auxiliary power unit provided a supply of compressed air for engine starts and for air conditioning in the pressurised crew compartment. It could also be used for AC/DC power supply to ground equipment and for use in emergencies. The APU was situated in an unpressurised bay in the centre fuselage.

Each of the four individual hydraulic systems had its own pump driven by a specific engine's accessory gearbox with an auxiliary turbopump for providing power when on the ground or in an emergency. The hydraulic systems powered actuators for the control surfaces, the air intake ramps, the high-lift devices, wing sweep mechanism and the landing gear. They also operated the moving function of the rotary launchers in the weapons bays. The electrical system provided AC power by separate generators on each engine and a fifth was driven directly by the APU. Ground power was provided through a receptor on the fuselage underside.

To assist with reducing landing roll distance, three main braking parachutes were provided in a container on the underside of the aft fuselage and deployed electro-pneumatically. Each main parachute was 35m² (376.34ft²) in area and the three were deployed by two 1m² (10.75ft²) drogue parachutes.

The aircraft's control system was unique in Russian aircraft at the time in having a triple-redundant FBW control with an emergency mechanical back-up in the extreme case of all four channels failing simultaneously. Considerable development work went into the configuration of the flight and operations control systems, which represented a considerable change in traditional designs for large Russian aircraft. The entire suite was an integration of mechanical, hydromechanical, electrohydraulic and electromechanical electronic subsystems and equipment.

It was designed around three operational requirements: actuation of the flying control surfaces; the autopilot and automatic approach and landing system; and the wing sweep control mechanism and its operation. The latter effectively controlled the optimum configuration of moving segments (including the outer wing sweep angle, the position of the flying control surfaces and the high lift/fence devices) for specific flight modes operated in either manual or automatic mode. Flight instrumentation for controlling and monitoring these functions closely resembled that on the Tu-22M3 with several multi-functional displays.

A big step forward was also planned for the Tu-160's avionics and weapons control systems with a greater emphasis on digitisation through more than 100 separate computers throughout the aircraft. The duplex K-042K inertial navigation system, the star-navigation system and the satellite navigation equipment operated in conjunction with the Sopka terrain-avoidance radar located in the nose to provide for optional nap-of-the-earth flying for the first time in such a large Russian aircraft. Communications between crewmembers was provided by a standard intercom system with blade antennas for air-to-ground links above and below the flight deck. The SRO-1P IFF transponder was supported by antennas below the nose and on top of the tail cone.

Located in the nose radome, the Obzor-K navigation and attack radar was capable of engaging targets on the surface or at sea at long range to give target information to the semi-active homing radar on the air-to-surface missiles. Bomb aiming in daytime or at low light levels was provided by the OPB-15T sight located in a teardrop fairing over an optically flat window beneath the flight deck. A laser designator would serve laser-guided bombs. There was also provision for supporting laser-guided missiles such as the Kh-55SM.

As noted earlier, the Tu-160 relied on ECM for passive and active defence and had no armament against threats from the ground or the air. Electronic support equipment included the radar homing and warning system which provided 360-degree coverage through antennas on the forward and aft fuselage sections and on the wingtips. Additionally, active equipment and associated antennas were located on the leading-edge extensions and on the fairings over the trailing edge of the lower, fixed fin section. Active defences included an infrared missile warning system protecting the rear hemisphere of the aircraft with passive defence comprising APP-60 chaff bundles and 50mm (1.96in) magnesium flare dispensers, integral and flush with the underside of the aft fuselage.

First Flights and Production

As the design details were completed and the drawings passed to the machine shops and assembly facility, work began on the first three aircraft in 1977. The first would be for manufacturer's tests, the second for static tests and the third would represent the pre-production configuration. In mid-1980 the first prototype (70-01) was moved to the flight test facility at Zhukovsky and extensive checks began on 22 October prior to taxi tests starting on 14 November 1981 with test pilot Boris Veremey.

The first of the three prototypes, 70-01 was flown for the first time from Zhukovsky on 18 December

1981, with Veremey at the controls. The second prototype (70-02) was finished to a production standard and first flew on 7 October 1984. The first prototype would not exceed Mach 1 until February 1985. The first pre-production aircraft flew on 10 October 1984 with the second following on 16 March 1985 and the third on 25 December 1985. With the test programme accelerating in pace, the fourth production aircraft flew on 15 August 1986 and the type was cleared for introduction to the prestigious 184th Guards Heavy Bomber Regiment then based at Pryluky air base in Ukraine, to which the first production aircraft were delivered on 17 April 1987 accompanied by a small celebration complete with brass band. The elite unit had established its reputation during the Second World War and had been the first to get the Tu-16 after the Tu-4 and then the Tu-22M3 in 1984.

The second full production aircraft had crashed during take-off in March 1987 but the 12th aircraft off the line had the distinction of hosting US Secretary of Defense Frank Carlucci at Kubinka air base on 12 August 1988. The Americans were not a little fazed by its debut, NATO naming it Blackjack. And for a while they were uncertain as to its true potential, seeing it as a parallel deep-strike penetrator, when in fact it was a cruise missile carrier and only under some operational-specific roles was it intended to strike the continental United States with overland flights during missions involving large gravity bombs.

The Tu-160's performance was such that it was officially credited with 44 world records by the end of the Cold War. In attaining these, the Russian aircraft industry gained much publicity and the Air Force a great deal of attention from domestic and foreign media. It also reinforced a not altogether justified image of an aircraft capable of threatening the United States with its ability to penetrate air defences and attack strategic targets. It did not really have to; the prioritisation of its role as a cruise missile carrier ensured that it could remain distant from air and ground defences while unleashing its potential.

The Tu-160 was first displayed to the Russian people on 20 August 1989 when a development aircraft from Zhukovsky made a low pass over the annual Tushino air show. Two years later on 18 August 1991, the day before the coup by communist ideologues seeking to overthrow the demise of the USSR, crowds gathered outside the perimeter fence at Zhukhovsky to witness a full pre-flight preparation, take-off and flypast of a prototype Blackjack.

On 13 February 1992, a Tu-160 at Machoolischchi air base near Minsk in Belarus was put through its paces by the 184th to an invited audience of top-ranking military officials from the new federation of former Soviet states. In further display, a development aircraft was present in the static park at the Moscow air show of 11-16 August 1992. For several successive years this same development aircraft was made available for air shows and static displays.

Meanwhile, the flight test programme was pushed along in parallel to service familiarisation with the 184th Regiment at Pryluky. The aircraft was bigger and heavier than anything stationed there before it and the runway had to be extended to 3,000m (9,840ft) and reinforced. But the convention was circumvented when, instead of conducting training and conversion at the Air Force 43rd Combat and Conversion Training Centre at Dyagilevo air base near Razan, those duties took place at the Kazan factory with the engineering technicians doing their study tasks at Kuibyshev.

A priority task was for the Tupolev test pilots to train qualified instructors who would then disperse to the Tu-160 units and train the operational pilots. A Tu-134UBL was used as a pilot combat trainer, a variant of the Tu-134B specially built for the task. Neither the Tu-22M nor the Tu-160 had trainer variants and to save time and fuel on the operational aircraft, the Tu-134UBL was an efficient and cost-effective method. Crews actually found the Tu-160 easier to fly than the Tu-22M. Extraordinary procedures were adopted to get the air crews passed on the type; successive trainee crews used the same aircraft still on the runway where it was refuelled for an immediate return to flight. But the pilots liked it,

To save time and money, conversion training for pilots graduating to the Tu-160 begins on the Tu-134UBL which is configured with displays duplicating the Blackjack. (Vitaly Kuzmin)

the other two crewmembers appreciating the better ergonomics of the crew spaces with rest and food and a toilet.

But, for all that it was liked and admired by its flight crews, ground crew knew that the aircraft bore all the hallmarks of an aircraft rushed into service long before its time. Problems, usually with the troublesome avionics, were frequent on almost every flight and although a great deal of time and money was spent on fast-tracking service introduction, this was largely for propaganda purposes; it was several years before it became a truly operational aircraft. Losses were prevented in most cases by the high levels of redundancy in the avionics and electronics but the engines too had serious deficiencies during the early years of testing and service introduction.

Engines failed intermittently and on occasion only the enormous power available from the NK-32 kept

it flying sufficiently far to get down to the ground and prevent a catastrophe. The air intakes proved to be a serious problem, vibrations popping rivets and causing some acoustic damage. Redesign of the entire forward section of the inlet box eventually solved those problems.

The landing gear was found to be in need of a significant redesign, before which pilots were told to keep the wheels down during familiarisation flights throughout 1988, until changes to both the retraction assembly and the hydraulics were completed. Structural problems were encountered when panels began to vibrate loose and fly off and on a few occasions sections of the tail would dismantle themselves in flight. Interfaces between different materials was also a problem, including the bonding of composites to adjacent metal sections. It was this that brought about redesign and a reduction in the span of the horizontal stabilisers, as related earlier.

One problem was of a sort shared with the Boeing/ Rockwell B-1B. With the wings in the fully swept position on the ground, the aircraft had a tendency to tip back on its tail. Only with great difficulty could it be set down on its nose leg again. The standard procedure was to keep the wings fully forward at the 20-degree point, which, due to its great span, brought its own problems with parked locations on the apron and movement to the runway. Other factors produced landing problems. If the tail 'chute was deployed a little too late the extended rollout could send it off the end of the runway. The mass of the aircraft and resultant inertia could overload the brakes and on some occasions the brakes locked on take-off.

The seats fitted had originally come from short-duration combat aircraft. When placed in the more comfortable positions intended for the Tu-160 crew on very long flights they were unusable for ejection purposes. Other aspects of the Tu-160 brought high praise however, especially from ground crews used to working on the Bison and Backfire bombers where access was painfully difficult.

Ease of maintenance had been a key design goal for the Blackjack and hydraulic, electrical and pneumatic panels were located on the walls of the weapons bays and the wheel wells. Access to the engines was also good, as it was to the avionics panels and related equipment on the flight deck and the appropriate fuselage bays. The sheer size and complexity of the aircraft brought its own challenges for support crews, each flight hour requiring 64 man-hours of maintenance and up to 20 support vehicles. A few vehicles had to be adapted or modified from existing trucks.

Other aspects balanced exceptional pride and satisfaction in an aircraft marking a great step forward both in engineering design and performance, especially compared to the Tu-22M3. But there was a widely held view that Tupolev had become too complacent. Lacking any industry competition for this class of aircraft, the accessories and ancillary industries supporting the programme had fallen short of expectations, leaving crew without appropriate handling gear. This was particularly the case with the highly corrosive 7-50S-3 hydraulic fluid instead of the standard oil-based product, which did not require special clothing and protective gloves and helmets. Neither was there mitigation from the acoustic effects, the powerful and very loud engines running up sound levels of 139db imposed on adjacent ground crew, far above safety levels.

There were other issues too, brought about by a schedule agenda based on a development cycle the Americans call 'concurrency', where final development flows in parallel with service familiarisation, introduction and training. That brought its own price. Manuals and training lessons had to be adjusted as sequential improvements and upgrades evidenced by actual performance results in the air were required to keep crew current. And there was the political desire to brandish the Tu-160 as the new 'pride of the nation' as its crew referred to it. The concurrency approach was driven by the desire to get the aircraft operational but the Tu-160 was far from ready for front-line service.

CHAPTER 8

ON ACTIVE SERVICE

On paper at least, the 184th declared operational readiness in April 1987, just eight months after receiving its first Tu-160. Missions of up to 12 hours were flown and over time the unit achieved 100 flight hours a year but a great amount of work was required to accomplish that, starting off with a pre-flight preparation time of 38 hours. Support was provided in the form of up to 300 technical staff from the Ministry of Aircraft Production assigned to Pryluky air base. Just as before, the NK-32 engine proved particularly troublesome but over time the life of each unit increased from 250 to 750 hours.

A Tu-95 of the 184th Guards Heavy Bomber Aviation Regiment, based at Engels-2 providing long range and stand-off capabilities. (DOD)

The Tu-160 is operated by the 121st Guards Heavy Bomber Aviation Regiment also based at Engels-2 in the Saratov Oblast. (Russian MOD)

The avionics equipment came in for an early upgrade, the long-range navigation system getting an integral celestial corrector which would calculate the aircraft's position by angular measurements using the Sun or the stars. A new PA-3 moving-map display was also integrated at the navigator's station but perhaps the most important improvement was the addition of the Glonass satellite navigation system during the 1980s, which achieved full coverage by 2010 with a position error of 10-20m (32-64ft).

Its main payload was the Kh-55 cruise missile, with dual capability for either a conventional or nuclear warhead. Using the Kh-55 meant potentially entering hostile airspace and as such some limited measures were taken to reduce the Tu-160's radar signature – the engine inlets and ducts being painted with a black radar-absorbent material.

A specially developed organic paint was used to coat the forward fuselage and areas around the engine were covered with a mesh screen to reduce electromagnetic pulse radiation. This mesh was also incorporated into the cockpit windows, with the added advantage of screening the crew from radiation emitted by a nuclear blast.

The aircraft was put through a range of operational flight profiles, venturing across the North Pole to within a short distance of the Canadian coast, attracting various 'escorting' NATO interceptors on the way. Some of these flights lasted almost 13 hours and the first direct encounter with a NATO fighter occurred in May 1991 when a Royal Norwegian Air Force F-16A from Bodo air base intercepted a Tu-160 over the Norwegian Sea. It was at Bodo where U-2 spy-plane pilot Francis Gary Powers had been intending to land when he was shot down over Sverdlovsk in the

USSR, having taken off from Peshawar, Pakistan, on 1 May 1960.

Tu-160s were escorted on several flights by Sukhoi Su-27P Flanker-B fighters, providing reassuring radio relay capability should the crew be forced to eject over the frozen wastes of the Siberian wastelands or the Bering Sea. As the Kh-55SM became the sole cruise missile for the Blackjack, the workload of the weapon systems operator was greatly reduced by the highly automated targeting and navigation system. Much of

The Glonass navigation satellite is integrated with the bomber units, providing accurate position data and targeting information to within 3m (10ft). (Author's collection)

the launch sequence too was automated, the prime function of the operator being to bring the aircraft to a correct launch heading and to the correct geographic location and activate the simple mechanical release. As the missile fell away, deployed its wings and started its engine, the rotary launcher turned to the correct position for deploying the next one. Practice runs and

The badge of the 22nd Guards Aviation Heavy Bomber Division, re-formed in 2015/2016 and responsible for the strategic bomber force of Bear and Blackjack aircraft. (Author's collection)

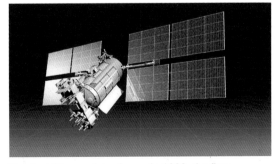

The first Glonass launch was in 1982, the first improved Glonass-M going up in 2003, all operating from a height of 19,100km (11,870 miles). (Author's collection)

Compatibility with the Glonass navigation system extends to the Bear for refined mission objectives involving its use as a cruise-missile launch platform. (Author's collection)

test launches all took place in Kazakhstan and during one flight a total of 14 missiles were launched.

The 184th's transition to the Tu-160 was slow, requiring the regiment to retain its Tu-16 and Tu-22M3 aircraft so as to maintain full operational capability while the Blackjack was going through its service introduction. Over time, some of the older bombers taken away while others were scrapped on site. The Conventional Forces in Europe (CFC) agreement signed on 18 November 1990 imposed limitations on the number of non-strategic bombers in the Soviet inventory but this aircraft also fell into

Escorted here by an RAF Typhoon, a Su-27 of the type frequently used to escort the Blackjack bombers. (UK MOD)

the category of strategic nuclear delivery systems and those limitations are covered later in this chapter.

Over time a range of derivatives and variants were proposed, none of which were approved for development. One of the more intriguing was the Tu-160SK which arose after an approach from the German government in 1994 for a partnership with OHB System to adapt the aircraft into a satellite launcher. First displayed at the Asian Aerospace exhibition in 1995, it would have carried a small space vehicle named Burlak on the underside of the fuselage where it would have been released at altitude for a flight into space.

The idea was not new and various American projects, notably the cancelled North American

In the mid-1990s the Tu-160 was proposed as a satellite-launcher using the Burlak two-stage rocket capable of placing small payloads in Earth orbit. It was too expensive for a cash-strapped Russia to support. (Author's collection)

XB-70A Valkyrie, had proposed the large aircraft as a supersonic launch platform for satellite vehicles. The Burlak concept involved a two-stage, solid propellant rocket which was capable of placing 600-800kg (1,323-1,764lb) payloads into orbits between 200km (124 miles) and 1,000km (621 miles) above the Earth. The development and test of such a system would have been expensive at a time when Russia had little spare cash for such a nuanced idea. There were conventional satellite launch systems that could do the same job.

Another proposal was to re-engine the aircraft with the Kuznetsov NK-74 engine, delivering a thrust of 270,000N (60,700lb) and promising a greatly extended range through improved specific fuel consumption over the existing engines. The engine was tailored to an evolved version of the Blackjack, rather than the original design, and its installation could only be justified in conjunction with a major evolution of the aircraft for a still-cleaner profile and a more slippery fuselage/wing-body shape which had been briefly examined by Tupolev but remained unfunded.

In other potential applications, the Tu-160P would have been a very long range interceptor, the Tu-160PP would have provided ECM jamming and electronic warfare while the Tu-160R would have had a dedicated reconnaissance capability. The prospect of taking Tu-160 engineering and technology and crafting from that a dedicated intercontinental strike aircraft was discussed and sources refer to this as the Tu-161. But it got nowhere. There was one speculative idea with highly unlikely prospects: a Tu-160V which would have been powered by liquid hydrogen for extended endurance and great range.

Some of that work was applied to the Tu-230 (or Tu-260) hypersonic aircraft but that led directly to an evolution from a small team headed by V. A. Andreyev studying conceptual designs using liquid natural gas or hydrogen to power a hypersonic strike aircraft with a required range of 15,000km (9,321 miles). It would have had a maximum speed of Mach 6 carrying a weapons load of 10,000kg (22,050lb). It was similar to the 230 but would have been powered by six combined cycle, turbojet/ramjet engines with which Andreyev believed it could achieve a range of 8,000km (4,971 miles) at Mach 6. Constrained to a more realistic concept, the Tu-22M3 formed the basis for a Tu-245 long-range strike system, which also got nowhere.

The Tu-245 design was developed from the Tu-22M3 as a proposed long-range strike aircraft but it went no further than drawings and models. (Yefim Gordon via Tony Buttler)

Operational headquarters for the strategic bomber force, Engels-2 as observed by Maxar data from a surveillance satellite. (MAXAR)

At the end of the Cold War the 184th Regiment had 21 Tu-160s in two squadrons but with much of the training still carried out in the Tu-134UBL, a modified variant with a Tu-160 nose section. Discussion about future deployment of the Blackjack ran headlong into a major debate between the United States and Russia

Nuclear weapons are kept at specified centres across Russia but the facility at Engels-2 has its own storage bunkers and arming shops. (Digital Globe/Google Earth)

The museum at Engels-2 includes an example of the original Tu-22 Blinder to remind visitors (usually service personnel) of the modern bomber's heritage. (Author's collection)

regarding possible cancellation of the Northrop Grumman B-2 in return for cancellation of further production of the Tu-160. That was not accepted by the US but it did result in a major dilemma: the only main operating base for the Blackjack was in Ukraine, at Pryluky. The first president of the newly formed Russian Federation, Boris Yeltsin, signed a decree in February 1992 cancelling further production of the Tu-95MS. This move had been linked to the request to halt B-2 production.

Now, with Ukraine outside Russia, it was necessary to equip a new unit, the 1096th Guards Heavy Bomber Regiment, with the Tu-160 at Engels-2. The 1096th had previously been equipped with the Myasishchev M-4/3MD Bison. A great deal of negotiation resulted in Ukraine keeping the 19 Tu-160s that had been on its territory when the Soviet Union collapsed – these then being operated by the new Ukrainian Air Force. About 750 Soviet personnel from the Ukraine moved to Russia to join the Russian armed services.

Open days at Engels-2 attract a wide range of personnel and serve to familiarise visitors with past and present bombers, including this Tu-95MS. (Author's collection)

Open engine panels on a Tu-160 at Engels-2 show ready access to the low-slung engine nacelles. (Russian MOD)

The ubiquitous Bear takes off from Engels-2, home base and operating station for attacks on foreign targets in Syria and the Ukraine. (Russian MOD)

The 1096th got its first Blackjack on 14 February 1992 but a lot of equipment including simulators remained behind in the Ukraine and Engels-2 had to build new infrastructure. The first flight with the new unit occurred on 29 July and the first launch of a Kh-55SM took place on 22 October 1992. The period of transition was hard and great efforts were made to maintain a strategic viability for the heavy bomber force but for crews it was impossible to log more than an average of only seven hours a month. Shortages of fuel and supplies prevented any increase in that and circumstances remained difficult for some time but they were worse in Ukraine, which itself lacked much of the support infrastructure necessary to keep the advanced aircraft serviceable.

Former Soviet military personnel in Ukraine were required to swear an oath of allegiance to the new administration and the aircraft had the red star removed, painted over by the Ukrainian insignia or left unmarked. Only about a quarter of flight personnel and just over half the ground crew took the oath. By the summer of 1992 most former Soviet aircraft on Ukrainian territory had been impounded including virtually all the Il-78 fleet belonging to the former USSR. In 1994 the 1096th was renamed as the 121st Heavy Bomber Aviation Regiment. Co-located there were the 20 Tu-95s of the 184th Guards Heavy Bomber Regiment and the few remaining Tu-22M3s of the 6950th Aviation Base.

Controls and Constraints

Over the decades, various arms control agreements had sought to constrain the rate of increase in strategic weapons including ICBMs, SLBMs and heavy (strategic) bombers. The Strategic Arms Limitation I (SALT-I) agreement signed on 26 May 1972, imposed limits under which strategic missile inventories would grow. The purpose had been to constrain the expansion of respective ICBM and SLBM strategic forces. When the SALT-II agreement was signed on 18 June 1979, it included restrictions on the range of nuclear-tipped cruise missiles carried by strategic bombers to no more than 600km (373 miles). On that date it was agreed that the US had 574 heavy bombers while the Russians had 156.

Before the Soviet Union collapsed, the Strategic Arms Reductions Talks I (START-I) agreement was signed on 31 July 1991. For the first time it set targets for the reduction in strategic nuclear weapons where previous agreements had only reduced the rate of increase. START-I set limits on the total number of ICBMs, SLBMs and, for the first time, heavy bomber delivery systems in respective inventories within seven years to no more than 1,600 in total. A further limit of 6,000 warheads across all delivery systems was imposed. But there were complex sub-limits which significantly favoured manned nuclear bombers, discriminating between limits on the number of nuclear-tipped cruise missiles on each aircraft but not conventional missiles.

Significant issues were raised about the Tu-22M, especially the M3 variant which had initially carried a flight refuelling probe. Gross misinterpretation of the limited data available about this aircraft when it first began to appear in numbers during the early 1970s fed into fears that the type was an intercontinental threat to the US and considerable negotiating time was spent discussing it. The Russians had no interest in downplaying the type, their first successful long-range heavy bomber, and the US negotiators were inclined to accept the Russians' word that it was not an intercontinental threat. As said, the key move was when Russia agreed to remove the refuelling probe and not to build more than 30 a year – which was, in any event, beyond the capacity of the production line.

But the Backfire would remain the poster-boy of Soviet expansion as interpreted through the pages of the classic report Soviet Military Power, an open document distributed each year by the US Department of Defense purporting to show the real threat posed by Soviet Russia. Perhaps surprising to many, the importance of the Backfire in this regard is arguably greater than any other Russian aircraft of the post-war period. Concern over the threat it posed to any adversary across the continent of Europe and the UK was consolidated by the deployment of the RSD-10 Pioneer (SS-20 in NATO parlance), an intermediate-range ballistic missile (IRBM) deployed in Eastern Europe in 1976.

Backfire and the SS-20 represented to NATO a threat it had not seen coming and prompted the deployment of the Gryphon Ground Launched Cruise Missile (GLCM) and Pershing II ballistic missiles in Europe. This in turn led to the agreement to reduce intermediate nuclear force (INF) levels across Europe and by the end of the 1980s this class of weapons had been eliminated. But the Backfire remained and the INF treaty, signed on 8 December 1987 and which eliminated 2,619 missiles, passed into oblivion in February 2019 when President Trump withdrew the US from its protocols. The bomber that started an escalation in European arms deployments outlived the intentions to constrain its use. But there were other aircraft in the mix.

The START-II treaty signed on 31 July 1991 allowed some Bear variants to be excluded from the gross total of strategic delivery systems, specifically the 37 Tu-95RTs or the Tu-95U training aircraft. Moreover, the three Myasishchev M-4/3M types were considered to be training aircraft and were not included in that total. However, when the United States tore up its anti-ballistic-missile (ABM) agreement the Russians withdrew. It was replaced with the Strategic Offensive Reductions Treaty (SORT) signed on 24 May 2002 under which total nuclear warheads would not exceed 1,700-2,200 by the end of 2012.

During the years following the Soviet collapse, the fate of aircraft located on the newly independent states ran a tortuous course. The Russians began a series of negotiations to get some of their bombers back. In October 1994 they refused to pay for the Tu-160s on Ukrainian territory, citing a lack of money after the Ukrainians asked for $8 billion in exchange. During this time, when arms reduction talks were underway with the Russians, the Ukrainians approached the

Decommissioning of Russian equipment left in the Ukraine after the collapse of the Soviet Union included the 60 Tu-22M2/3 types and 423 Kh-22 cruise missiles to prevent them falling back into Russian hands. (Author's collection)

Ukraine decommissioned 11 Tu-160s but returned the remaining eight of its 19 Blackjacks to Russia. (Author's collection)

forces. During 1998, with the agreement unfulfilled, the United States agreed to fund the destruction of all but two of these bombers in Ukraine at a cost of $8 million to the US government. One Tu-95 would be presented to a museum. Included in the arrangement was the destruction of more than 1,000 cruise missiles.

However, in 1999 an agreement was reached to 'sell' eight Tu-160s and three Tu-95MSs to Russia in addition to 144 Kh-55 cruise missiles. The agreement was signed by Ukrainian Prime Minister Valeriy Pustovoytenko and his Russian equivalent on 2 November. There would be no actual payment though, since the $285 million deal was set against money Ukraine owed Russia for gas supplies. Eleven Tu-160s and 18 Tu-95MSs were destroyed in order to comply with the START-I arms reduction agreement. In October 2002 the Americans reported that after the compliance over the Tu-160s and Tu-95s, Ukraine had agreed to eliminate 30 Blinder and Backfire bombers together with 230 Kh-22 missiles, which they did.

Americans about a national security deal under which they would eventually become a NATO member. The Americans wanted that but some countries in Europe, particularly Germany, objected in the belief that it would provoke Russia and sour relations.

By the end of the following year, a new arrangement had been reached whereby 19 Blackjack and 25 Bear bombers would be handed over to the Russians in exchange for spare parts for other Soviet-era equipment in the possession of Ukraine's armed

During these protracted exchanges, American resolve to denuclearise all the former Soviet republics stiffened and Washington brought pressure to bear on

The largest strategic bomber flying in any air force, the Tu-160 Blackjack has a maximum weapons load of 45,000kg (99,225lb). (Russian MOD)

Kyiv, capital of Ukraine, to dismantle its bombers. Although politically willing to accept this, Ukraine was muscled into compliance faster than it had planned and strong pressure was brought upon Moscow to remain within the constraints of START-2. Part of this agreement provided written assurances of US military support for Ukraine in the event that it was invaded. This went a long way in emboldening the newly independent country to engage more fully with the West and begin a process where it would one day join NATO and the European Union.

The importance of this historical narrative to the story of Russian bombers is evidenced by the leverage which possession of so much Russian aviation equipment on its territory provided to Ukraine as a bargaining chip when it came to military alliances with the West. When the first Tu-160 from Ukraine arrived at Engels on 6 November 1999, the Ukrainian insignia was hastily removed and the red star reapplied. There were even celebrations at the base and giant Russian flags were draped over its wings.

As the aircraft were returned, exercises over the North Pole resumed and practice launches of the Kh-55SM took place. Combined exercises saw two Tu-95MSs and two Tu-160s involved in a coordinated operation in late June 1999 for a night flight to a prefixed location in the Polar Sea, separating as they approached the long Norwegian coastline. A single aircraft was diverted to fly to a test range in southern Russia where a Kh-55SM was fired, one of the Blackjacks remaining aloft for 12 hours without refuelling.

In an important display of coordinated operations, indicative of a shift in the tactical use of cruise weapons, Backfires dropped gravity bombs while Bears and Blackjacks launched cruise missiles in a week-long period of activity in April 2000 supported by Beriev A-50 Mainstay AWACS aircraft. The significance lay in the use of precision-guided cruise weapons with conventional, rather than nuclear, warheads. This was a new application for Russia and it followed intensive studies at the Ministry of Defence into tactics pursued by the US-led coalition

The reopened production line for the restoration of Tu-160 line deliveries and the M-series modifications and upgrade packages. (Russian MOD)

during the eviction of Iraqi troops from Kuwait in the early weeks of 1991. The Russians also studied how the USAF used cruise missiles during the Bosnian War, the Americans having launched more than 13 Tomahawks in one night during September 1995.

A New Air Force

In the post-Cold War period significant changes were made to the structure of the Russian Air Force and to the way the long-range aviation units were formed and how they operated, not least in the way operational strategy evolved. By the turn of the century the Long-Range Aviation units were combined under the 37th Air Army which had been created in 1998. In doing this, three of the five heavy bomber divisions were scrapped leaving the 22nd and the 73rd Heavy Bomber Aviation Divisions. The 22nd operated a single regiment equipped with the Tu-160 and the Tu-95MS, two with the Tu-22M3 and one with Il-78 tankers. The 73rd was equipped only with the Tu-95MS.

Only Engels and Ukrainka were still operational heavy bomber bases by 2000, Mozdoc having closed in 1998 with the transfer of its aircraft to Engels and the 37th came under the Supreme High Command. Several organisational plans were put forward for dispersing the bombers to other command structures and military districts.

By the end of the 1990s a change in political leadership had brought Vladimir Putin to a position

Political support for the revitalised bomber units and for further development of the Tu-160 attracts photo-shoots with leading government officials including Vladimir Putin (signing). (Russian MOD)

where he could direct the way the Russian military was structured and equipped – and how prepared it was to go to war. Doctrinally, Russia has always accepted the integration of conventional and nuclear forces, the selection of particular systems and equipment being dependent on war aims and likely conditions on the battlefield, in theatre or geopolitically. At its core is maintenance of the capability to mount an effective response if Russian territory is invaded, or national survival appears to be threatened. This has been enshrined in Russian military doctrine since the early 1950s and it has never changed.

Putin dons pilot-gear and pretends to be a Tu-160 commander for a photo-shoot during August 2005. (Russian MOD)

A Tu-160 Blackjack leaving Engels-2 air base. (Russian MOS)

A Tu-160M incorporates advanced electronics, avionics, defensive countermeasures plus open architecture for new and emerging weapon systems. (Tupolev)

With production having ended in 1995, Russia began making preparations to modernise its aging Tu-160 fleet in 2002. The process was planned to include the installation of the new K-042K-1 navigation system and ABSU-200-1 autopilot, as well as new NK-32-02 engines, improved communications and anti-jamming equipment and a digital glass cockpit together with the Novella NV1 70 radar.

It was decided that 16 aircraft should be upgraded in several phases. The first aircraft brought up to Tu-160M1 standard, the first phase including the K-042K-1 and ABSU-200-1, made its flight debut in November 2014 and was delivered to the Russian military the following month.

The cockpit of the early Tu-160 lacked state-of-the-art displays and controls as shown here but they have since been upgraded with improved glass panels. (Alex Beltyukov/airliners.net)

Throughout the build-up toward a modern strategic bomber force, Russia continued to use retired or cancelled programmes to supply heavy-lift capability as with this Myasishchev M-4 derivative, the VM-7 used for conveying large loads. (Author's collection)

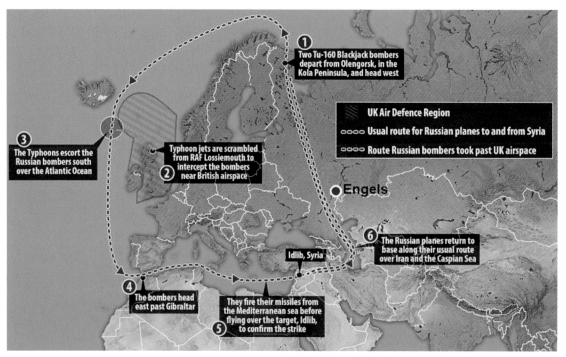

Circuitous routes can require lengthy flight times, as here during an attack on targets in Syria in 2016, and several mid-refuelling operations prior to damage assessment by the same aircraft during overflight on the return leg. (Author's collection)

The first Tu-160M2, fitted with NK-32-02 engines, was delivered to Tupolev for flight testing by the United Aircraft Corporation (UAC), Russia's state-owned defence conglomerate, in March 2021. A second airframe modified to this specification began ground tests at Kazan in December 2020 and made

The Tu-22M3 cockpit was a template for the Tu-160 but with scaled improvements and a shift from analogue to digital displays. (Yefim Gordon via Tony Buttler)

its first flight in January 2022. It is said to incorporate the communications suite from the Su-57 fifth generation fighter.

Putin decided to restart the Tu-160 production line in 2015 and the first new-build Tu-160M made its flight debut in December 2022. The plan is to acquire up to 50 new aircraft, with two new Tu-160Ms scheduled for delivery every year between 2023 and 2027 for an initial batch of ten.

The latest modernisation plan for Russia's remaining Tu-95MSs commenced in December 2009. This involves existing airframes being fitted with new Novella NV1.021 radar, new cockpit displays, upgraded NK-12MPM engines with new AV-60T propellers and the upgraded Meteor-NM2 defence system. They are also given the ability to launch Kh-101 and Kh-102 cruise missiles.

The first Tu-95MSM, named 'Dubna' after a town outside Moscow, was reportedly redelivered to the

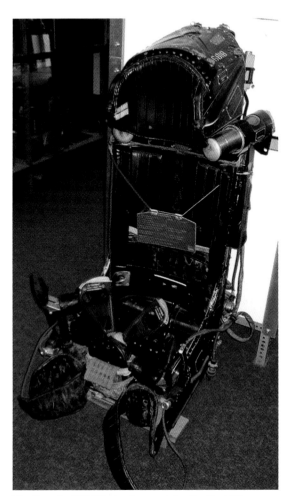

The Zvezda K36KM ejection seat for the Tu-160 is a considerable improvement in comfort and performance over that employed in the Tu-22. (Author's collection)

Russian Air Force in November 2015 and made its combat debut in Syria in November 2016, according to the Russian Defence Ministry. However, it was subsequently reported, by UAC on August 23, 2020, that the first flight of a Tu-95MSM had taken place the day before. Another press release from UAC dated January 16, 2023 – nearly two and a half years later – stated that the Tu-95MSM had conducted "another flight".

It is unclear whether the November 2015 Tu-95MSM represented little more than an upgrade to fire Kh-101s and Kh-102s or whether it had further MSM features. It may be that the August 2020/January 2023 Tu-95MSM represents the first complete package of upgrades. Either way, rollout of the Tu-95MSM programme appears to have been grindingly slow.

At the time of writing, it appeared that the MSM upgrades will allow the Tu-95 to continue in service up to 2040 but this plan may have changed considerably given the economic pressures resulting from the war in Ukraine.

Starting in the early 1980s, plans had been drawn up to replace the Tu-22M3 fleet with a new supersonic intermediate range bomber – the Sukhoi T-60 aka T-60S. Very little reliable information has surfaced about this development but it would appear to have been cancelled during the 1990s. As a result, the remaining Tu-22M3s have been left to continue in service. Russia had 150 of them in 1992 but by the mid-2010s fewer than 50 are said to have been airworthy. Nevertheless, plans had already been laid to upgrade 30 of them to Tu-22M3M standard and the first of these was rolled out in 2018 and made its first flight during the same year. The second made its first flight in 2020.

Fitted with the same NK-32-02 engines as the Tu-160M and Tu-160M2, and the same avionics, the Tu-22M3M is thought to have a range of 7,000km (4,350 miles) with a single in-flight refuelling – which it can now manage thanks to probe which appears as a distinctive hump on its nose. The Tu-22M3M also lacks the double-barrel 23mm tail cannon of the original.

Meanwhile, the Russian Air Force's commitment to cruise missiles grew in size and scope during the early 2000s, with the dual nuclear/conventional warhead-capable Kh-555, the dual-capable Kh-102 with a newly configured nuclear warhead and a range of 5,000km (3,107 miles), and the stealthy Kh-101 with a range of 4,500km (2,796 miles). The Kh-101 is arguably the most flexible and accurate cruise missile in the Russian inventory and in 2019 a Tu-160 launched 12 at the same time.

The potential weapons load for a Tu-95MS includes the Kh-101 cruise missile, eight of which can be carried on underwing pylons. (Russian MOD)

In addition to these long-range and stealthy assets, the Tu-95MS retained the Kh-55 long-range missile and the Kh-15 short-range attack weapon which now has dual conventional/nuclear capability. The Kh-55 has proven to be a mainstay of the Tu-95 long-range deployment plan and significant modifications to the aircraft now allow it to carry eight Kh-101s, or Kh-102s, in underwing positions with six in the rotary launcher in the bomb bay, raising the total number to 14, which is two more than can be carried by the Tu-160. It can also support 14 Kh-555s.

A specific requirement was that all launch platforms must be capable of switching between conventional and nuclear capability with integral attachment points, loading hoists and dedicated control systems for supporting their launch, and that applied to gravity bombs as well so that sortie roles could switch between requirements without equipment changes. The in-theatre selection of conventional or nuclear strike is a significant improvement to the Russian capability for keeping a hostile country uncertain as to its intentions, which is one of the prime purposes of this evolution. It is an application of the Russian maskirovka principle: the art of reconstructing perceived truth in war and geopolitical conflict utilising information (truth), misinformation (lies) and disinformation (hybrid extrapolations of both).

Some of that improvement came with the introduction of the latest generation of cruise missiles, which continue to underpin Russia's long-range tactical and strategic delivery systems. The hypersonic Kinzhal Kh-47M2 aeroballistic missile is now carried by the Tu-160 as well as by the Tu-22M3M. With a solid propellant rocket motor it has a speed of up to Mach 12 and a range of almost 3,000km (1,864 miles). It was introduced in 2017 and has since been seen on the MiG-31K and the Su-57. It was first used operationally against targets in Ukraine during the

Escorted by a Su-34, a Tu-160 releases a Kh-55 cruise missile during an attack on a target in Syria. (Russian MOD)

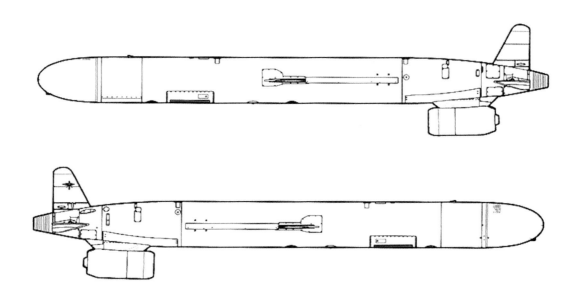

Considered now to be dated, the Kh-55 was introduced in the early 1980s, with a pop-down turbofan engine. (Author's collection)

early weeks of the Russian invasion which commenced on 24 February 2022.

The first verified report of a first use in anger had, however, occurred in June 2021 against a target in Syria. The first use against Ukrainian targets occurred on 18 March 2022 when a Kh-47 struck an underground weapons bunker and again the following day when one hit a a fuel dump. On each occasion the missile was probably launched by a MiG-31K originally based at Soltsky Air Base and moved up to Chernyakhovsk Navy Air Base in the Kaliningrad area. The development of the Kh-47 originated in a requirement for a hypersonic missile to strike ships and maritime infrastructure as well as defence systems. With inertial guidance, satellite trajectory correction and optical terminal targeting, its conventional warhead is accurate to within 1m (3.28ft).

The development of hypersonic missile systems presents tough problems for the air defence of vital assets such as aircraft carriers, central munitions and logistical dispersal nodes as well as ports and harbours. But hypersonic cruise weapons are more vulnerable

to defensive systems than popularly imagined and those are being given additional priority due to the proliferation of Russian and Chinese weapons of this type.

Hypersonic glide vehicles (HGVs), also known as boost-glide vehicles, are unpowered when they enter

Introduced during the Syrian war, the much refined Kh-101 has been used in quantity during the war with Ukraine but has proven vulnerable to Ukrainian air defensives as here on 26 January 2023 in Vinnytsia Oblast. (Ukrainian Armed Forces)

A Kh-32 anti-ship missile on the fuselage centreline of a Tu-22M3M, presenting the same exterior case profile as the Kh-22. It entered service in 2016. (Author's collection)

the atmosphere following a rocket-boost which leaves them as unpowered re-entry bodies. Hypersonic cruise missiles (HCMs) use air-breathing, supersonic-combustion ramjet or scramjet propulsion and remain within the atmosphere achieving speeds in excess of Mach 5.

HGVs are inherently more vulnerable to interception because their terminal velocity to the target is less than the critical velocity at stage shutdown and they travel more slowly as they encounter increasingly dense layers in the atmosphere. Many existing anti-missile defences are tuned to that flight spectrum. HCMs retain their speed to the target and are less vulnerable to defensive measures. Moreover, HCMs which fly at lower levels are therefore much harder to detect and present much less time to ground and air-based radar acquisition. The most vulnerable component of the system is the launch aircraft – which explains why very long range, air-launched systems are preferable. It also helps explain why Tu-160s have made very long flights around countries of the European Union to launch cruise weapons against targets in Syria.

Further improvements have been made to the Tu-22M3 with dual-capable Kh-555 or Kh-101 missiles and the nuclear-tipped Kh-32M with a 1,000km (621 miles) range. Visually identical to the Kh-22, the Kh-32M carries a 500kg (1,102lb) warhead, half that of the Kh-22 traded for greater range. It uses inertial guidance with active radar homing for the terminal phase from a distance of up to 300km (186 miles)

With flaps down, a Tu-22M3 about to land displays the arrangement of landing lights and the completely revised intake box for this and subsequent variants. (Author's collection)

This shot of a Tu-22M3 shows the subtle lines and contours for of its large air intakes. (Author's collection)

and to date it has exclusively equipped the Backfire. The Tu-22M3 is also equipped to carry the hypersonic Kh-47M2 missile.

Since the collapse of the USSR, Russian compliance with the START and New START limitations and even the definition of categories has been challenged and frequently reinterpreted for 'political' and force-deployment reasons. The flexibility of the agreements has resulted in considerable difference of opinion as to which particular aircraft fall under which band of restrictions.

Under the counting rules in the New START accord, a single heavy bomber only counted as carrying one nuclear weapon. But in reality, the then complement of 77 listed heavy bombers could have carried a total of more than 850 warheads. This was before the declaration from Moscow that it planned an increase of 50 Tu-160M2 bombers, albeit a statement unsubstantiated and unrealistic.

Although Tu-22M3s can now carry Kh-47M2s, this aircraft is still excluded under the limits of New

START, a protocol which classified a 'heavy bomber' as one which carries a cruise missile with a range exceeding 600km (373 miles), which the new Backfire clearly does. In addition the specific protocol defines a 'heavy bomber' as one with a range in excess of 8,000km (4,971 miles). The Russians have accepted that the present range of this aircraft is 7,000km (4,350 miles) but have proudly announced that it will be upgraded with NK-32-02 turbojet engines, also being fitted to the Tu-160. Russian sales literature boasts that these engines are expected to extend the range of that aircraft by 1,000km (621 miles).

Going to War

Whatever their originally stated purpose, such as 'tactical bomber' or 'strategic bomber', modern combat aircraft tend to be capable of fulfilling an ever-increasing number of roles as time goes on and they receive further upgrades. In war, tactical and strategic targets merge according to the way the conflict is fought – whether on the battlefield or through attrition, decapitation of military or political

Libya used Tu-22s in its conflict with African states as here where an F-4N Phantom II of VF-51 from the USS *Franklin D Roosevelt* keeps watch on the bomber. (USN)

Libyan Tu-22s are 'escorted' by F-4N Phantom IIs from VF-111, also from the USS *Franklin D Roosevelt* and shortly before transitioning to the F-14 Tomcat. (USN)

leadership or erosion of national industrial capacity.

Direct involvement by Russian bombers in proxy wars or in support of military campaigns against foreign powers was limited and spotty before the invasion of Ukraine in 2022. In 1977, two Tu-95s were operated out of Luanda while Russia backed a Cuban intervention on the African continent from a base in Angola. The following year, Russia sent Tu-16, Tu-95 and Tu-142 bombers on probing flights against Japanese-occupied Sakhalin Island and the southern Kinles chain as it reasserted its claim to those places.

After the 1969 coup in Libya, the Libyan Air Force received equipment from the US, the UK, France and Russia, included in which were 14 Tu-22 Blinders from the USSR. The only other export customer of the Tu-22 was Iraq, which received 12 aircraft. During the 1978-1979 war between Uganda and Tanzania, Libya sent 3,000 troops to help Uganda's Idi Amin and the Libyan Air Force flew a few Tu-22 against Tanzanian forces. Operating from the airfield at Nakasomngola, on 29 March 1979 one Tu-22B targeted Mwanza but hit a nearby game reserve in error.

The Libyan Air Force operated the Tu-22 on bombing raids into Chad during the conflict with its neighbour and western Sudan. The first Tu-22B bombing mission took place on 9 October 1980, an attack on military forces. Following this, intermittent

Tu-22 raids on targets in Chad and Sudan continued up to the ceasefire in November 1981, a short-lived hiatus before the conflict flared up again 20 months later and further Tu-22 raids were made until another ceasefire was put in place.

In response to a raid by France on the Quadi Doum air base in northern Chad, one Tu-22 successfully attacked the airport at N'Djamena on 17 February 1986, taking out a taxiway, damaging the runway and temporarily closing operations. Having conducted a low-level flight for 1,100km (683 miles) to reach N'Djamena, on its return to the Libyan base at Aouzou at the extreme northern end of Chad the Tu-22 crashed, due either to either a technical defect or rocket fire from the airport. The event, and a call for help from the crew, was monitored by a USAF reconnaissance/surveillance aircraft.

A further raid against the same target was conducted two days later with no recorded result but on 9 August a Tu-22 was shot down, ironically by a Soviet SA-6 SAM battery at Aouzou abandoned by the Libyans. One of two Tu-22s sent against N'Djamena on 7 September 1987 was shot down, bringing to an end the story of the Tu-22 in the Libya-Chad conflict. When Chad forces took Quadi Doum in 1987, two Tu-22s were captured or destroyed along with several other Libyan aircraft. The final flight made by a Tu-22 of the Libyan Air Force occurred on

7 September 1992. Lacking spare parts, they were left unserviceable.

When the leadership of the 1978-79 Iranian revolution threatened to export their own Islamic sect to surrounding areas and disrupt the balance of power in the Middle East, on 22 September 1980 Iraq launched an attack. Tu-22s from the H3 air base hit Mehrabad International Airport serving Tehran but these and further raids with the Blinder were only moderately successful; three aircraft having been shot down in October, one of which was brought down by an AIM-54 Phoenix missile fired by an Iranian F-14. By the end of September, fearing their loss as Iran reciprocated in force, 10 Tu-22s were flown to Riyadh, Iraq having secured the friendship of Saudi Arabia, Kuwait and Jordan. Iran recruited support from Syria, Libya and North Korea.

The so-called 'war of the cities' that began during February 1984 was repeated in March 1985, from January to April in 1987 and February to April in 1988. Iraqi Tu-22s conducted major raids against Iranian city and suburban targets throughout this period, escorted by fighters and some fighter-bombers in a concerted sequence of strategic bombing raids. The Iraqi Air Force had grown under a series of deals with foreign countries and both Tu-16s and Tu-22s were used in these attacks against civilian and military targets. Russian crew are known to have flown these aircraft but the mismanagement of the air war by both sides and by Russians wearing Iraqi uniforms took its toll.

While the bombers flew against Tehran, Isfahan and Shiraz, Iranian resolve stiffened and the indiscriminate use of air power merely added to the high proportion of civilian casualties. Both sides conducted brute-force warfare, the Iraqis being particularly fond of the 9,000kg (19,845lb) FAB-9000 bomb, which had its origin in the 1950s. Pilots were able to achieve surprisingly good results with this device, using a toss-bombing technique with the weapon dropped at supersonic speed. So prolific was its use that the Iraqis ran out of supplies and then started manufacturing their own variant of it, the Nassir-9 bomb.

The war escalated due to a reluctance on the part of Iraq to conduct an all-out conflict, while Iran saw it as a crusade and was intent on destroying its enemy. Initially, Iraq restricted its attacks to targets just inside Iran, so as not to expose its aircraft to air defences and to any further attrition. When Iran began invading Iraq the stakes were raised and Iraq turned to destroying the Iranian infrastructure. As the war was drawing to a close, the Tu-22 was used in attacks on Iranian oil tankers in the Gulf near Kharg Island, four aircraft escorted by Mirage F1 fighters sinking one super-tanker and damaging another. But a return sortie by two Tu-22s later that day ended with both aircraft being shot down. This was the last operation for Iraq's Blinders during the war, a total of seven having been lost and most of the remainder severely damaged. These were destroyed during the Gulf War of 1991.

The only active use of the Blinder in Soviet service was the somewhat inglorious role of covering the retreat of Russian forces from Afghanistan in 1988, using the Tu-22P for electronic countermeasures and the Tu-22PD for radar jamming while the Tu-22M3 Backfire flew operations from an airfield in Turkmenistan. Support was also needed as the Backfire unit conducted offensive operations, since they were threatened by Pakistani F-16s. The PD variant also conducted bomb-damage assessment. For military operations, the Backfire replaced the Blinder towards and beyond the collapse of the USSR.

The Tu-22M had already been used for a series of strike simulations against real targets earlier in the 1980s, beginning with a Warsaw Pact exercise conducted in 1980 to mine a part of the Baltic Sea in support of a simulated amphibious landing. Then four Backfire bombers were intercepted by the Royal Norwegian Air Force during a run up the North Sea in June 1981. A more concerted demonstration of potential intent occurred on 30 September 1981 when eight Tu-22Ms locked radars on the carriers *Enterprise* and *Midway* in the North Pacific. They flew within 200km (125 miles) of the carriers and turned away but the US Navy was relaxed about sending warnings so as to map the tactics and radar frequencies the Soviets would employ during a real-world attack.

As observed previously, the Russians pitched tactical and strategic bombers against unfriendly naval forces to observe and record key features and to collect and map acquisition radar frequencies. As noted earlier, warships have always been high on Russia's target list and NATO carrier groups in particular have received frequent fly-bys and overflights. Before stringent restrictions on proximity approaches by unfriendly aircraft, on 25 May 1968 a Tu-16RM-2 carrying sophisticated ELINT equipment conducted several very low and slow fly-bys of the USS *Essex* in the North Sea off Norway. Piloted by Col. Andrey Pliyev, on its final pass the aircraft stalled and crashed into the sea, killing all the crew and sending smoke from burning fuel high into the sky.

The 1980s proved a depressing time for Soviet military aviation as depleted resources drained spares, wore out maintenance equipment and reduced readiness levels, sometimes with the Tu-22Ms reduced to below 35% availability. Low grade equipment had an effect on the engine manufacturing base, causing failures and depriving pilots of flight time, some estimates indicating that three pilots were available for each operational Backfire. Throughout this period there was pressure on the Soviet military due to the political and military involvement in Afghanistan. Pledged to support the Amin government, in April 1979 the USSR began to move weapons and aircraft in to buttress Afghan forces against US-leaning Pakistan and to help them defeat the Mujahideen.

Supported by the US, the UK, Egypt and China, the Mujahideen were encouraged by Western intelligence agencies to attack Soviet forces while the CIA supplied arms to the terrorist groups so that they could harry the occupying Russians. And thus began a bitter struggle, one of the last of the Cold War proxy conflicts. Afghan and Soviet air assets were used to attack Mujahideen camps in Pakistan. The Backfire went to war in Afghanistan during 1984, the M2s of the 1225th Heavy Bomber Air Regiment operating

from Maryy-2 air base and conducting support raids with the 40th Army against Mujahideen units. The Backfire bombers were protected from Pakistani air defences by Tu-22PD types, with the Tu-22M3s dropping 9,000kg (19,845lb) bombs.

In attempts to break the enduring siege of Khost, Backfires flew raids against the Mujahideen in 1987. Further operations in 1988 supported the withdrawal of the 40th from the country, including Tu-22M3s from the 185th, followed by the 402nd and then by the 840th. All Backfire bombers had been returned to their bases by February 1989 but were used to cover operations in the Salang Pass as their swansong in the Afghan War. A few were used against Chechnyan rebels in the 1990s and on 9 August 2008 a Tu-22MR was shot down in South Ossetia during the conflict with Georgia.

Operations with the Backfire continued to evolve and to form a significant part of the air war against targets in Syria, their first appearance in that conflict being on 17 November 2015 when 12 Tu-22M3 were used, along with Tu-95s and Tu-160s making their debut in anger. During 22-31 January 2016 the Backfire conducted a total 42 sorties against anti-government targets around Deir ez-Zor and on 12 July six aircraft struck targets east of Palmyra where Daesh units were located.

On through the rest of the year several massive strikes were carried out against terrorist organisations including ISIS but from 16 August 2016 Iran allowed Russian Backfire bombers to operate from its Hamedan air base. This was the first time since the 1979 revolution that Iran had allowed its national military facilities to be used by a foreign power.

Further strikes were made against jihadist soldiers around Deir ez-Zor from early 2017 and were repeated later in the year. On 25 May 2021 three Tu-22M3 aircraft touched down at Syria's Khmeymin air base from where they conducted training exercises with other Russian naval and air units, with familiarisation flights over the eastern Mediterranean.

Tu-95MS/MSM Bear H bombers were active in the initial attacks by Russia on targets in Ukraine on 24

Downgraded from its original role, the Tu-22M3 operates out of the Dyagilevo air base, now conducting anti-shipping and theatre attack roles. (Author's collection)

The Dyagilevo air base in the Ryazan oblast hosts a wide range of operating units, equipped with bombers and support aircraft. (Alex Beltyukov)

February 2022. In sustained activity, Tu-95MSs and Tu-160s were in action again on 6 March, launching a total of eight Kh-101 cruise missiles against the Havryshivka Vinnytsia International Airport on the Black Sea. These types, this time from Astrakhan, were again involved launching Kh-101s at Kyiv from over the Caspian Sea with limited military success.

The Tu-22M3 was also deployed during the early stages of the invasion of Ukraine during the spring of 2022, its first sorties on 14 April involved dropping iron bombs on the Azovstal plant in Mariupol. Tu-95Ms and Tu-160s were also used to launch Kh-55 cruise weapons against Lviv, Vinnytsia, Dnipropetrovsk, Donetsk and Zaphorizhia oblasts in the Ukraine after the bombing of the Kerch Bridge on 10 October 2022. But the Russian air bases on national territory were not immune. On 5 December 2022, Tu-22M RF-341110 and a Tu-95MS were damaged during a long range drone attack against Dyagilevo and Engels-2 air bases. The aircraft were parked close together, nose to tail and wingtip to wingtip.

At around 2.30am on May 1, 2023, a force of nine Tu-95s and two Tu-160s fired a total of 18 Kh-101/ Kh-555 cruise missiles at targets in Ukraine, with the Ukrainian military claiming that 15 of them had been shot down before reaching their intended targets.

Air-launched cruise missile attacks would continue throughout May, with 30 missiles being launched

between 9pm on May 17 and 5.30am on May 18 – with Ukraine claiming to have destroyed 29 of them with anti-missile defence systems. Twenty-two of the missiles were launched by a fleet of seven Tu-95s and one Tu-160 based at Olenya air base on the Kola Peninsula and another two Tu-95s from Engels.

The Next Generation

The Sukhoi T-60 bomber may have been cancelled in the 1990s but rumours about the development of a Russian equivalent to the Northrop Grumman B-2 stealth bomber, known as the PAK DA, have been around for almost 15 years. Former defence minister Aleksey Krivoruchko has been quoted in the past as saying that the new aircraft would be in service by 2027 but that seems doubtful. By January 2020 three prototypes were said to be in production to a specification calling for a stealthy subsonic airframe with an operational range of 12,000km (7,457 miles), carrying a bomb load of 30,000kg (66,150lb) and with a sustained flight duration of up to 30 hours.

The programme was launched officially in 2007 when Tupolev, Sukhoi and Myasishchev were asked to submit proposals for what had been a slow and ponderous investigation of different concepts. It attracted significant criticism along the way – not everyone was convinced about the stealthy, flying-wing approach on what was designated Project 80.

Tupolev began formal work on the type in 2008 under a three-year study contract to examine a wide range of design concepts and different configurations. The sluggish Russian economy kept the programme at a low-key level, an announcement on the definitive configuration being made public in 2012, probably to counter severe criticism of the concept and its languid development. A progressive series of announcements ensued with the KAPO plant in Kazan being chosen for production and several Russian companies declaring work contracts for advanced electronics and communications equipment.

The defence ministry agreed the final design in 2013 but after Russia's annexation of the Crimea in 2014 the programme was reduced in scope while plans were laid to upgrade the Tu-160 as a cost-saving measure after Western sanctions began to take hold on the economy. In Russia, the price of oil fell and revenues were downgraded, putting additional strain on maintaining the same level of financial commitment. The decision to switch to an apparently cheaper way of upgrading the long-range bomber force was only one of a series of hits taken by Russia's military.

Nevertheless, on 1 March 2015, Russian news agencies reported that several mock-ups had been created using various composite materials for comparison tests. There was also a full-scale mock-up in wood of a subsonic, flying-wing design which would use radar-absorbent materials and advanced electronic warfare suites on the production aircraft. There was even a quote from defence minister Borisov that it may be publicly unveiled in 2018. That date has long gone without any such appearance. The following year it was announced that construction of the first prototype had begun and in August 2021 a new cruise missile designated Kh-95 was in development and would be carried in the PAK DA's bomb bay.

By the end of 2017, Tupolev had received a contract for development of the PAK DA and another from the Ministry for Industry and Trade approving technology development for the airframe and engine

and a definitive plan for the first production lot. Surprisingly for a Russian development project, information about the PAK DA has been far easier to come by than for the Northrop Grumman B-2 at this stage of its evolution. For the last 10 years, senior Air Force commanders in long-range aviation units have asserted that it will have a take-off weight of about 145,000kg (319,725lb), placing it between the Tu-22M3 and the Tu-95MS, around half the weight of the Tu-160.

Some design features appear similar to those of the B-2, arguably because there is only one optimum solution to a given problem. In early 2022, a patent design for a new type of shrouded inlet was published in Russia, which appears to show a novel feature for controlling the stability of air flow into the engines at various angles of attack. It is believed that propulsion will be provided by two improved NK-32-02 engines with TSA18-200-80 auxiliary power units. Some references allude to a supplementary, solid propellant RATO system for take-off and indicators point to the airframe being capable of carrying different turbofan engines.

Financial pressures appear to have pushed the programme toward maximising commonality of parts and systems, some remarks from officials at the Russian Air Force pointing to the upgrades financed for the Tu-160M being applied to the PAK DA. A number of systems and subsystems, as well as weapons, are expected to be common to both. But Ramenskoye RPKB is designing a new avionics suite integrated with a radar from Tikhomirov NIIP, breaking tradition with the former supplier TsNPO Leninets, which has provided equipment for previous Tupolev bombers.

The PAK DA is likely to have a crew of four – the same basic complement as for the Tu-95M, Tu-160 and the Tu-22M3 – with an integrated KSU-80 flight control system and NO-80 navigation equipment. NPP Zvezda is providing KSL-80 ejection seats for all crewmembers. Electronic defence will consist of jammers, focused infrared countermeasures and active defences such as chaff and towed decoys. There appears to be some interchange between Russia and China, which is preparing its subsonic Xian H-20, a stealthy flying-wing bomber similar to the B-2 but probably smaller. Limited exchange of non-critical technologies has been rumoured at trade exhibitions.

Russia has a chequered history when it comes to dual development of both a new bomber and a new missile; witness the case of the failed Kh-45 for which the bomb bay of the Tu-160 was designed and which is now considered too large for the weapons carried. Stealthy cruise missiles are in a minority of one and they are not holding up too well in combat, which is why the Air Force wants a new and greatly improved stealth weapon largely referred to as the Kh-BD. But word about that has been around for a long time and there appears to have been little progress.

The existing, purportedly stealthy, Kh-101, has reportedly not fared well in Ukraine and contains a considerable amount of US electronic equipment, including Cypress semiconductors, Intel processors and components from Micron Technologies. Equivalent components are not made in Russia and with trade embargos firmly in place it remains to be seen just how far Russian industry will be able to continue making this weapon – let alone manufacturing an improved version or even a modern replacement.

The first prototype PAK DA was reportedly in the final assembly stage by the end of 2021 and on 13 May 2022 the production plan displayed at the Voronezh Aircraft Production Association facility indicated that six aircraft were in various stages of assembly. It also appeared to indicate that a further run of prototypes would be completed by 2026. Based on Russian projections and industry sources, the first flight is now scheduled for 2025 with operational debut around 2028. On present and historic performance, however, that is much more likely to be 10 years on from the time of writing, if at all.

Just as the US Air Force sees a continuing need for a manned penetrator with heavy-bomber credentials, so too do the Russians believe in that mission role with the PAK DA. In open-source references,

the former director of the Sarov nuclear weapons laboratory has disclosed limited details of a weapon which would fit well with the types of mission the PAK DA could be called upon to conduct. He refers to a low-yield warhead in an especially hardened case capable of penetrating up to 40m (131ft) into hard rock and detonating. This fits well with current strategy for using very low-yield thermonuclear devices for destroying pin-point targets through a reliable manned penetrator.

The Sarov facility was set up in 1946 as the first Soviet atomic and thermonuclear weapons development centre. Located some 450km (280 miles) from Moscow, Sarov is still a closed city and was known as Arzamas-16 from 1966 but not publicly declared on maps before 1994. The research facility itself is situated 75km (46.6 miles) from the town and was the home of KB-11 which was responsible for the first Russian atomic bomb tested in 1949. The only other Russian facility developing nuclear weapons is located near Snezhinsk, previously known as Chelyabinsk-70.

Operational Readiness

A long-range bomber force is well suited to Russia's war-fighting doctrine and the reduction in ballistic missile numbers brought on by arms reductions talks over the last 50 years has increased both its value and it flexibility. But the effectiveness of that force depends on operational readiness and evidence suggests that since the end of the Cold War operational readiness has been low.

In one example, in 1998, only 36% of the Tu-22M3 inventory was available. For much of the 1990s, combat-readiness levels in the Russian Air Force were affected by the need to obtain spares from Ukraine, historically the highest proportionate geographic contributor to former Soviet military aviation. Twenty years after the collapse of the USSR and the Ukraine gained independence, the long-range aviation units had only 70% of the spares they had traditionally relied upon, the deficit being due entirely to the breakup of the Soviet Union. In other areas

Vinnytsia International airport in Ukraine, home to the 456th Transport Brigade with An-24s, An-26s, Mi-8s and Mi-9s, was targeted by Tu-95 and Tu-160 bombers firing Kh-101 missiles. (Author's collection)

too, fuel deficiencies prevented training programmes maintaining their proficiency levels. In 1998, long-range aviation units got only 20% of the fuel they needed to maintain pilot and aircrew currency.

By the end of the 1990s the situation had degraded such that flying hours were reduced from 20 hours in 1998 to an average 15 hours of the following year. To maintain proficiency, bomber crews at the 37th Air Army were switched to Tu-134s and Antonov An-26 types as a means of saving fuel consumed/hour of training. In 2000, the 37th was able to conduct only 11 launchings of training-standard cruise missiles. The seasoned instructors and training staff at the long-range aviation units recommend flights of at least 10 hours duration over Arctic seas or open oceans with multiple in-flight refuelling engagements and missile launches.

During the first decade of the 21st century, training flights rarely lasted more than three hours and while exercises in the Soviet era frequently involved entire air regiments, more recently these rarely involved more than four or five aircraft. More experienced pilots and crewmembers have retired out of service and been replaced by new entrants lacking the training opportunities or the sustained flight hours to grow their confidence and expertise.

Flexibility of operation, radius of effective mission and sortie planning is facilitated through aerial refuelling and that has become a major issue as the ratio of tankers to aircraft has declined. By 2010, the Russian bomber/tanker ratio was 3:1 compared with 1:2 in the US Air Force. This also eroded proficiency levels as few new crews experienced an in-flight refuelling operation, instead relying on simulators and computer displays on the ground to familiarise themselves with the techniques.

In the last decade, long-range aviation has undergone a gradual shift toward a new generation of integrated weapon systems including theatre and battlefield equipment designed to integrate across delivery platforms from rockets to cruise missiles to manned aircraft and, eventually with the PAK DA, to manned penetrators loitering in hostile air space. Russia's political structure has changed considerably and the more assertive approach taken by the Kremlin is demonstrated by establishment of leased naval facilities on the coast of Syria, the long-range flights with the Tu-160 to attack inland targets in Syria and the use of heavy bombers to launch cruise missiles against targets in Ukraine.

New generations of cruise weapons are also adding to a greater dependency on the manned bomber, which now supplements the rocket-launched, ground-based missiles and diverts attention to airfields and operational facilities from which they operate. An example of this was the Ukrainian attack on an airfield in the Crimea on 1 October 2022 to destroy infrastructure supporting Russian aircraft deployed with cruise missiles. The transition from defending against crewed intruders to attacking the places from which they operate has brought the air war full circle to threats against the very airfields on which they are dependent for their effectiveness. The development of advanced cruise weapons and guided bombs has raised the effectiveness and the operational value of shorter range fighter-bombers or strike aircraft as a supplementary adjunct to the long-range bomber.

Nuclear Arsenal

Russia's strategic bomber force now makes a very small contribution to its overall nuclear stockpile and delivery options. Of the approximate 4,477 nuclear warheads in the stockpile, only about 1,588 strategic warheads are deployed, of which 812 are on land-based missiles, 576 are in submarines and 200

are at the heavy bomber bases. Around 977 strategic warheads are in storage together with 1,912 tactical warheads for use in-theatre or on the battlefield. In addition, Russia has around 1,509 warheads awaiting dismantling but still intact, for a total of about 5,977. The enormous nuclear weapons backlog of the Cold War years is being run down in accordance with international agreements, many of which have now expired or are abrogated.

The 55 operational Tu-95MSs and 13 Tu-160s available in 2022 can carry a maximum total of 580 nuclear warheads on air-launched cruise missiles or in gravity bombs. However, it is believed that only 50 bombers are available for immediate use under the conditions of New START and that only 200 nuclear devices are situated at the bases of those aircraft. Both types can carry both the Kh-55 and the improved variants of the Kh-102 nuclear missiles; the Tu-95MS6 with six carried internally and the Tu-95MS16 with 16 missiles across both internal rotary launchers and underwing pylons, commonality being a major factor here. As part of the modernisation programme, the Tu-95 is being outfitted to carry eight Kh-102s externally for 14 per bomber. The Tu-160 is also being upgraded to carry 12 Kh-102s internally.

The precise distribution of conventional and nuclear devices on each bomber is unknown to the public domain but the secondary role as a gravity bomber and the use of the Tu-95MS in that role would almost certainly subject its crew to a suicide mission. Much more likely is the use of the Tu-160 in that role. Training continues to be a strong part of the long-range bomber squadrons' schedule, Russia's Defence Minister Sergei Shoigu confirming that bomber crews conduct weekly flights along pre-set flight paths. This again suggesting that they have pre-planned objectives and, probably, defined targets to which their software systems are pre-loaded.

The poor reliability and accuracy of the Kh-101 has resulted in an improvement and development programme. During the first operational use of the missile in support for the Syrian campaign during 2015, one crashed in Iran by mistake close to

More than 70 years on from its first flight, the Tu-95 is still a credible stand-off bomber for continental and maritime service. (Russian MOD)

Shush, which is 750km (466 miles) from the Syrian border. This version has a range of about 4,000km (2,485 miles) but a later salvo-launch of 12 missiles in November 2018 may have been associated with modifications announced by the parent company of Raduga which produces the Kh-101.

This capability would allow the 121st Heavy Bomber Aviation Regimen's bombers to simply fly a circuit above their base at Engels and theoretically still hit targets as far away as Spain. Remaining so close to base also allows rapid reload and launch and that appears to be a favoured deployment standard for any European war which might call for a mass air attack by cruise missiles against multiple countries across Western Europe. For other targeted areas, the aircraft redeploy to international air space.

Air-launched Kh-101s have been used against targets across Ukraine, starting in the spring of 2022, with varying degrees of success.

The Here and Now

So where does the Russian bomber force sit today and how does it fit within the warfighting mix of conventional and nuclear weapons? A slow process of modernisation is ongoing for all three bomber types in the form of the Tu-160M, Tu-95MSM and Tu-22M3M.

Before the war against the Ukraine, Russia was actively modernising its stockpile of nearly 2,000 non-strategic nuclear weapons across all forms of offensive weaponry on land, at sea and in the air. However, there has been considerable activity associated with new buildings at bomber bases, indicative of a greater switch to conventional warheads for cruise missiles, increasing their application to a non-nuclear mission.

Russia's nuclear weapons are stored at 40 locations around the country but the strategic intercontinental missiles are armed at all times, as would any deterrent have to be to remain effective. The value in conventional cruise missiles was demonstrated during intensive operations in support of Assad's government in Syria, indicative of a slight shift against the doctrinal policies of theatre and battlefield use of nuclear weapons which had prevailed since the 1950s.

Their value as a weapon against the Armed Forces of Ukraine remains to be seen – numerous strikes have occurred but their success or failure remained shrouded in secrecy at the time of writing.

Whether Russia can continue to pursue its ambitious programme of rearming and modernising its bomber fleet in the face of stringent international economic sanctions and against the backdrop of resources being drained by the war in Ukraine similarly remains to be seen.

Some 40 years after it began its test flights, the Tu-160 Blackjack has several more decades ahead of it with significant upgrades and capabilities coming on line. (Russian MOD)

The longer the war goes on, the greater will be the depletion of Russia's capability to sustain the conflict and to counter NATO responses to any further aggression. With attrition of Russian ground forces at a very high level, increasing reliance on its bomber forces operating from Russian airspace could be greater than it ever has been before.

Late in the day, Russia is developing a stealthy penetrating bomber imagined through speculative concept drawings from many sources, including this flying wing which may only approximate the real aircraft. It could be operational by the 2030s. (Author's collection)

Index of People and Aircraft

Note: NATO reporting names have been included for Russian/Soviet aircraft, despite these never having been used officially by the Russians themselves.

WIN £100 WORTH OF BOOKS!

Tempest Books offers a wide range of publications covering military aviation from the First World War right up to the present day. To learn more about our other titles and to be in with a chance of winning £100 worth of books, simply scan the QR code on this page.

TEMPEST
BOOKS